Praise for *Child X*

"As someone who's deeply studied psychological indoctrination, *Child X* is a staggering triumph over the unimaginable. A profoundly moving and important book, at once haunting and beautiful."

—Holt McCallany, lead actor in David Fincher's *Mindhunter* (Netflix)

"*Child X* is a vivid, deeply harrowing memoir of a childhood shadowed by hardship and illiteracy in a dark movement, ultimately of personal redemption and triumphant artistic self-expression. Its message is essential: trauma need not define who we become."

—Gabor Maté, MD, *New York Times* bestselling author of *The Myth of Normal*

"A moving story about overcoming the impossible."

—Hilary Bevan Jones, film and television producer and first female chairman of BAFTA

"A riveting trek through history and the resilience of humanity, *Child X* unpacks the legacy and unyielding resilience of a young boy just trying to survive. A book you can't put down."

—Jelani Memory, vice president and publisher at DK Books/Penguin Random House and winner of the Eleanor Roosevelt Award for Bravery in Literature

"*Child X* is brave and deeply moving. Profound and powerful, this work is a cinematic, literary masterpiece."

—**Laura Hearn, former BBC news
and current affairs journalist and producer**

"As someone who's seen war, Jamie's story is an astonishing childhood of the brutality of a different kind of combat. A harrowing and deeply inspiring journey of what a human being can overcome and endure. If blood runs through your veins, read this book."

—**Lt. Colonel Paul Toolan, Ranger and Commander of the 3rd Battalion,
5th Special Forces Group (ret.)**

"*Child X* reveals that resilience and vulnerability are a superpower. Together they are the deafening whisper that says, I will not let my past dictate my future. I was blown away by the power of this story and how it can serve all of us."

—**Jimmy Akingbola, lead actor in *In the Long Run* (HBO)**

"An exploration of the human experience that is at once tragic and soul-stirring. An exhilarating true story of what is possible for a human being to overcome—a vivid road map of the human experience."

—**John Faber, MD, forensic trauma doctor and
former national medical director of behavioral health at Humana**

"A stirring story of a boy born at the darkest edges of humanity and his road back. Raised by wolves, a lost child can find themselves. Emotional and profound."

—**Frank Ochberg, MD, founding board member of
the International Society for Trauma Stress Studies
who clinically defined Stockholm Syndrome for the FBI in 1975**

CHILD
X

Also by Jamie Mustard

The Iconist: The Art and Science of Standing Out

Hybred

Coauthor of:
*The Invisible Machine: The Startling Truth About Trauma
and the Scientific Breakthrough That Can Transform Your Life*

CHILD X

A Memoir of Slavery, Poverty, Celebrity, and Scientology

JAMIE MUSTARD

BenBella Books, Inc.
Dallas, TX

Disclaimer: This book is based on the author's memories and recollections of events, which may differ from the memories of others. Some names, identifying details, and characteristics have been changed to protect the privacy of individuals. Any resemblance to actual persons, living or deceased, events, or locales not explicitly stated to be real is purely coincidental.

Child X copyright © 2025 by Jamie Mustard
"War Cry of Babalon" (page xiii) and "The Bad Men" (page 117) by Jamie Mustard
Photographs on page 287 by Corey Drayton. All other photographs courtesy of Jamie Mustard.

All rights reserved. Except in the case of brief quotations embodied in critical articles or reviews, no part of this book may be used or reproduced, stored, transmitted, or used in any manner whatsoever, including for training artificial intelligence (AI) technologies or for automated text and data mining, without prior written permission from the publisher.

BenBella Books, Inc.
8080 N. Central Expressway
Suite 1700
Dallas, TX 75206
benbellabooks.com
Send feedback to feedback@benbellabooks.com

BenBella is a federally registered trademark.

Printed in the United States of America
10 9 8 7 6 5 4 3 2 1

Library of Congress Control Number: 2025002899
ISBN 9781637747087 (hardcover)
ISBN 9781637747094 (electronic)

Editing by Gregory Newton Brown
Historical consulting by Corey Drayton
Editorial Support by Claire Schulz, Executive Editor
Editorial Support by Rick Chillot, Senior Editor
Copyediting by James Fraleigh
Proofreading by Michael Fedison
Text design and composition by Jordan Koluch
Cover design by Sarah Avinger
Printed by Versa Press

**Special discounts for bulk sales are available.
Please contact bulkorders@benbellabooks.com.**

for Stevie

and the kids from The Red Brick Building

Special Acknowledgment

 profound thank you to artist Corey Drayton for his contribution to this book as a historian, and friend.

Author's Note

The movement that Lafayette Ronald Hubbard left behind when he died holds its face behind an invented language and the constructs he created. I've changed the name of these terms and these constructs in this book to reflect what they actually are, as one can experience it within the movement, rather than forwarding language that can obscure what something is. Saying what things are, rather than using the movement's vernacular, is intended to make my story comprehensible and accessible.

There's a lot of reference to the burning heat of Los Angeles in this book. It was written before the LA fires. It is the city that made me. My heart goes out to the lives lost, and everyone affected by this tragedy. Los Angeles is my hometown and is a city for which I have deep affection and love.

Contents

Prologue: Mexico   xv

PART ONE: MOTHERSHIP

1.	The Baby Factory	3
2.	Nightmare Dive Bombers	13
3.	Greenwich Village	19
4.	Phoenix Rising	29
5.	Angels	37
6.	The Invasion	49
7.	Black Fighters	57
8.	The Belly of Two Beasts	65
9.	Archives of Zanzibar	81
10.	Starboys	87
11.	Children of the Revolution	105

PART TWO: CHRYSALIS

12.	Oregon	119
13.	Return to the Jungle	133
14.	The Crumbling	155
15.	Asylum	163
16.	Fortress	177
17.	West Sussex	189
18.	The Escape	205

PART THREE: AUTUMN

19.	New York	223
20.	Georgetown	237
21.	London	243
22.	Vallauris	271

With Appreciation   283

The road was thick with bone,
blood, skin, arms, and severed feet
loose heads
that had been cut high above the throat
suckling at the bosom of our leviathan's carotid
we all marched on

                                             we had a war to fight

                                      —WAR CRY OF BABALON

Prologue

Mexico

The South burned as the wet sun beat down on the dry plains of the Edwards Plateau in West Texas. Far south, resting on the north bank of the Rio Grande, the city of Laredo was a bustling town of eighteenth-century Spanish haciendas and rust brick buildings. Its name may have come from the Basque for "beautiful pastures," yet the streets were all Texas heat as a young couple rolled through town in a heavy Ford.

Cottonwood seeds and pollen drifted through the air. There were no towers or skyscrapers. The downtown storefronts stretched lazily toward an endless horizon, by night bathed in the glow of neon signs. The haciendas had gripped this defiant desert since the late 1700s, now a banal setting for the two newlyweds in the car, Roy and Dorothy Gilmer, exhilarated to begin their lives together.

It was August 4, 1940, and they were headed for the crowd of people waiting to cross into Mexico. Soon, the couple imagined, they would be in a place they'd never been, exotic Mexico. Their excitement was innocent and palpable, but far, far away, war was brewing in the South Pacific. Even though the United States would not officially join the wars in Asia or Europe for another year, unease swelled through the line of travelers waiting to cross into Chihuahua.

Roy and Dorothy, idling in their car and waiting to present their papers to the Mexican border guards, had just married on July 26, in Jackson, Mississippi. Dorothy, inspired at the prospect of honeymooning in Mexico, had spent the long drive to Texas sipping water from Roy's thermos and taking in the scenery to distract herself from the heat. For this Black couple, traveling through the segregated South in 1940 was very different than it is today. What few towns, service stations, and public toilets existed on the road were often not open to use by "coloreds."

Watching oak groves fly past in the wet heat, Dorothy remembered a drive from Tennessee to Mississippi as a girl in 1926. Her father, James Benjamin Dillard Jr., the town doctor in the small rural community of Henning, Tennessee, had been offered a position at a historically Black university in Mississippi. The entire family—James; his wife, Bettie; Dorothy, the oldest child at nine; and her younger brother and sisters, Jimmy, Lucy, and Maude—piled with all their belongings into their Model T Ford and squished next to each other on one bench seat.

"We were fashioned like sardines in a can," she would say many years later, "but we had fun."

The family journeyed 125 miles across Northern Mississippi, along narrow, rustic roads. Dr. Dillard eventually grew hungry, but there were fewer amenities in 1926 than in 1940 and no restaurants on the dusty route, the innovation of roadside diners still a decade away. The family had to find the nearest small town on a map, then park some distance away, out of sight. It was then Dorothy's job to find a restaurant in town and, using her father's cash, order food to go. Dorothy had this role because her complexion and eyes allowed her to pass as White.

Her new husband, Roy Jones Gilmer, was a tall Black man with tan, biscuit-toned skin. His deep-set hazel-brown eyes contrasted against high cheekbones and a thin Cary Grant mustache. His neat-cut hair glistened in the South Texas heat. Tucked under an arm was a wide-brim Panama hat, impractical on this one-hundred-degree day, but the anchor of a dignified and respectable man's wardrobe in the tropics. He wore tailored wool slacks the color of corn, twice darted at the front and hemmed meticulously above

MEXICO

xvii

shined wingtips. Beneath a linen collared shirt, unbuttoned at the neck, was the lean frame of an active, potent man. He was no linebacker, but his wasn't the skinny frame of an accountant. Roy was just right; matter-of-fact solid, akin to the strong Craftsman homes being erected throughout the South as the Depression era ended and war loomed.

Once at the border, Dorothy and Roy parked, entered the customs lobby, and approached the Mexican officer. Even though the man was smiling through his bushy salt-and-pepper mustache as they produced their identification papers, Dorothy knew something was wrong.

"Good morning," he said in a friendly Mexican drawl through his beaming smile. The officer hadn't even looked up at them closely and seemed barely interested in examining the documents. He offered Roy a brief exchange about baseball. Willard Hershberger, Cincinnati Reds catcher, had just taken his own life hours before a double-header against Boston, and it was all over the newspapers.

Glancing past the officer's khaki shoulders, Dorothy could almost smell Mexico through the press of humanity crowded into the meager lobby. A lonely steel fan creaked in the corner. Young Dorothy turned to the customs officer's face just in time to see the happy grin on his stubbled square jaw recede and turn dark.

"Your papers is good." He paused. "However, I can't let you into Mexico."

Dorothy felt a black chill drip down her spine. She had never traveled outside of the South, let alone the country. This was an uncomfortable turn, as she felt her stomach twist up in knots.

"See, it say here," the officer continued in rough English, "on your papers it lists you as 'Negro,' yes?"

He pronounced the word "Negro" in Spanish, voice thick with discouragement. Dorothy suddenly realized that the jovial man, who was the same hue and color as them, had at first thought that they were Hispanic.

"I must take a fee bond," he said. "One thousand US dollars. We'll return to you when you come back to the US." There were different rules for Whites and Blacks at that time in the segregated American South.

The customs officer's eyes rolled up toward Dorothy. "I'm sorry," he said. Dorothy shifted her exotic green eyes to Roy, who had turned absolutely cold.

After a beat, Roy said, "Wait here, Dorothy," and squeezed her arm reassuringly. Then he turned and passed through the thick line of anxious travelers stacked behind them.

Dorothy waited patiently. About thirty minutes later, Roy reappeared and placed $1,000 in cash into the officer's hands. Roy's calm expression never wavered; there was no sign of triumph, indignation, or concern. This gesture was as simple as passing the salt at dinner. For the first time, Dorothy—herself the daughter of a prosperous Black physician—became aware that her new husband, a Black man from the South, had more than she understood.

In 1940, $1,000 was an enormous sum, equal to $21,976.50 today. Back then, gasoline cost eighteen cents per gallon; not much more than a pack of cigarettes. Dorothy's heart jumped; her world grew foggy. She was becoming all too aware of how little she knew about the world.

It was time to grow up.

X

One hundred twenty years before the border incident, Samuel Meharry, a young Irish-immigrant salt trader roving the frontier of 1820s Tennessee and Kentucky, found himself desperately in need of help. Incessant rains had swelled the already vast Mississippi River, turning the dirt roads into a muddy soup. Samuel's covered Conestoga wagon, heavy with sacks of salt, had become stuck. Forced to abandon the wagon and his horses, the sixteen-year-old Sam set out into savage rains as the faded sun kissed the horizon on its way into night.

Trying to get ahead of the oncoming darkness, Sam, who was a White boy, came upon a small cabin. He didn't know it as he approached but in it lived a Black family recently freed from slavery. The family became

MEXICO

xix

alarmed at the site of a desperate, rain-soaked White teen breathing heavily at their door. Even with their deep fear of slave hunters, who often didn't distinguish freedmen from runaways, the wary family welcomed Sam in for a meal, then, in talking with him, offered him shelter from the storm and bedding on the floor for the night.

At dawn, the Black father and his sons set off with Sam, hoping the wagon and the horses had survived the torrential night. In the Kentucky wilderness of their day, every step the family took risked discovery and capture by freebooting bands of slave hunters out for bounty despite them being free.

Before the sun was very high, they found the nervous horses still attached to the undisturbed wagon. The Black father and his sons worked with the horses to haul the wagon from the mud. Due to this uneasy act of kindness, Sam was able to deliver salt vital for surviving in the wilderness, but not before he promised this Black family that someday, when he was able, he would "repay their act of kindness by doing something to help their race."

It took the young Irish immigrant more than fifty years to make good on that promise. In 1876, Samuel Meharry, along with his four brothers, took $30,000 in cash—$863,000 today—to start the first medical college for Negroes in the South.

Today, Meharry Medical School stands between Meharry and Albion Streets on the south side of a soft bend in the Cumberland River just outside Nashville. Its red brick buildings tower above an otherwise flat landscape rich with oak, ash, and elm trees. Laid out in clean, monolithic lines, the imposing school was meant to stand for all time. It became one of the most prominent Black medical schools in the world. It has never been segregated.

Dorothy had first met Roy while he was attending Meharry in the late 1930s. A mysterious orphan, Roy chose to work as a porter at the train station alongside the other medical students. He didn't want them to know that he, a Black medical student, the son of a doctor and a musician and teacher, had a large trust fund—not only from his grandfather, but from his aunt, a successful Black businesswoman who took Roy in when his parents had died.

Roy was a millionaire in 1940s money, but he didn't really think about it too much because it wasn't money he'd earned. This orphaned Black Prince had come from a common yet unseen world on the East Coast of America—that of the accomplished, successful Black families of judges, doctors, and businessmen. It is an American legacy then unknown, and still now unsung.

It should have been my legacy.

X

After Roy and Dorothy crossed the bridge spanning the Rio Grande, the car swerved back onto the baking asphalt in Chihuahua, Mexico.

Dorothy's heart still sprinting in her chest, she now felt a sweet chill spreading from head to toe, her oatmeal skin alive with sensation. She didn't ask Roy about the money, how he came to have it, how he didn't seem concerned to hand it over to the customs officer—who, for all she knew, might use it for drink and women on her husband's dime.

At the far end of the bridge, with Texas in their rearview, the couple parked their car beside the road. They cranked down the windows and sat in silence, letting the air cooled by the Rio Grande wash over them.

Then Roy eased the car into a gentle left turn. He looked over at his wife, beaming with love. With the hot sun diminishing, my grandparents' steel chariot raced into Mexico and dematerialized into the amber sun.

MOTHERSHIP

Chapter 1

THE BABY FACTORY

Scientists argue about whether we can remember anything before we are two years old. For me, I have very clear memories of being just a few months old that come to me in vivid flashes. Caretakers I have spoken to have confirmed these early memories, and now I have a difficult time discerning between what I remember and what was told to me.

A baby born in 1970s Los Angeles, I was whisked at birth from a medical facility on the wealthy West Side to a machine, a decaying tenement on the border of a dilapidated Mexican slum at the edge of Downtown Los Angeles. My mother handed me off to a man and woman dressed in naval uniforms. They gently laid me on a blanket and covered me in the back seat of a bone-white Pontiac GTO, then raced across Los Angeles drenched in oranged sodium-vapor light.

All of us babies were housed in an industrial room on Beacon Street, just behind the Original Tommy's Burgers, its enormous blue and yellow and neon sign bleached by the sun. Muscle cars grumbled constantly rolling by, vibrating The Baby Factory with the bass of their engines. The expansive nursery was ripe with smells, peeling paint, and cracked linoleum floors caked in dust and slime. The crying and screaming of the other newborns in their rusted, 1970s industrial-steel cribs rang out constantly. Outside my barred windows, I remember beautiful, moon-filled nights with pungent, hot air that warmed and soothed the city. Inside, it was screaming, always screaming.

Aside from our caretakers, few parents or adults came to see us babies. One "nanny" cared for too many babies, who often left us lying for hours in bulging diapers and our own sick. I was a summer baby. In the heat of June, the rancid odor of the room—bodies, sweat, and waste—was overpowering. Our cries went unheard. There were constant illnesses, rashes and fluids—bathing was even rarer than human touch. When bathing did happen, they lined us up in a long, dark hallway in front of the utilitarian shower room. Our diapers, sometimes heavy with days of waste, were discarded. Then we were lifted up and dipped for a few scant moments into yellow bathwater where we were quickly splashed, one baby after the other. The water, odorous and stagnant, remained unchanged until our next scheduled cleaning.

Red is the only color babies can see while their eyes develop the cells to discern color. Through my chronically crusted eyes, I could see in this monochromatic glow one of the "nannies," a White woman with big, curly 1970s locks and a red top, making her way through the rows of screaming infants. I couldn't yet discern the apricot prism of the Los Angeles smog, or the exquisite blue of the California moonlight under which no one sang us to sleep. The nights were cold. There were no nannies at night.

My mother loves to tell a story of how one February morning, when I was six months old, an earthquake shook the foothills of the San Gabriel Mountains and rocked LA. The babies wailed as The Baby Factory shook. The green fluorescent lights hanging precariously above us swayed back and forth—if they fell, it could have meant death. Paint chips rattled off the putrefied tenement walls. The nannies tried desperately to open the room's only door, which had jammed shut in the sagged frame from the earthquake.

Five minutes after the quake, when the "nannies" burst in, us babies' wailing was loud. The caretakers checked the damage through the dust

THE BABY FACTORY

hanging in the air. Broken glass popped under their feet. The woman in red came straight toward me. I watched her face through the rust and worn paint on the crib's bars. She covered her mouth in a show of alarm and startled amusement as she stared into my jet-black baby eyes.

"This one's laughing," she said. No one seemed to hear her over our cries. I smiled up at the nanny.

My mother likes to say that I was the only baby in the earthquake that thought someone was merely rocking my crib.

X

At eighteen months I took my very first steps in life along the nursery's dusty linoleum floor. The building had likely been a slum for a long time since its turn-of-the-century construction. The dry oak planks were scarred with heavy use, and the adobe ceilings were covered in yellowed paint from years of desperation and cigarette smoke. I often walked through the rows of urine-soaked cribs to the mammoth window and peered out at a sun-bleached world of sky and gaseous bronze smog.

If Los Angeles is full of one thing that you can never ever fully remove, it's what 1930s LA writer John Fanté described as its dust. Because of the water piped in by the aqueduct, people forget that all of the steel and concrete was built in the middle of a desert, so Hollywood's early pioneers could shoot films all year round. I've heard stories from guilty caretakers about us never going out for months on end; when we did, we were afraid of the sun. When I wasn't quite two, we were taken out on a rare excursion to see the decommissioned *Queen Mary* ocean liner in Long Beach. I didn't understand at the time why the movement would take a group of toddlers to see a 1930s steamship. I had never been outside in an open space with so many people. The giant boat sat there like a gigantic spaceship.

When its steam whistle suddenly blew, I jumped, startled, into the arms of a seven-year-old girl assigned to watch out for me. She and her father left The Baby Factory right after this trip, but when I connected with her later, she said that I had stayed on her mind for almost a half century.

Everything beyond The Baby Factory overwhelmed my senses. I didn't know it then, but two years before my birth, my older brother, Joshua, born in England, had been smuggled onto this very same gargantuan vessel without papers and brought to America by my mother. Joshua would spend the first twenty years of his life stateless, without a country. I believe that as he grew older, the fact that he never officially existed in his country weighed on him.

There is only one baby picture of me—a Polaroid taken when my grandmother, Dorothy, visited Los Angeles. The movement didn't need pictures of me. I was secure in The Baby Factory. I have memories of the slum, so many memories, but very few memories of my feelings.

I was numb.

I was one of so many raised in a movement that saw us as property to be kept for their purposes.

X

I was around three when my mother married a Sicilian man named Paco Michel (pronounced "Michelle"), who had children from a previous marriage far away on an island called Hawaii. Back then people in the movement's private navy could be married to people not in the inner core. This is no longer the case. Even though he didn't live with us, my stepfather Paco took a strong interest in me, or perhaps he was just Sicilian. It was at this age, with this strange man, that I began to feel anything more than an ephemeral tic of warmth.

Paco was remarkably unremarkable: average height and wiry, with dark Sicilian hair that receded from a sharp widow's peak, and a long Moorish face. He was kind. When I was two years old he would carry me downstairs from The Baby Factory to the street corner and into Tommy's for a burger and fries. When I bit into the burger, it tasted like Technicolor: vibrant with flavors I couldn't describe but I knew it was good. It was juicy with kitchen grease and warmed up my tiny body. Angels.

With Paco's Sicilian roots, warmth toward children was cellular. His

THE BABY FACTORY

total acceptance of me, this Mulatto brown boy, could not have been more natural to him. Wherever Paco took me, he introduced me proudly and without hesitation as "my son, James." Whenever I would hear this, every nerve in my body would turn warm. It was a sensation that was unfamiliar and that I didn't understand. I can only describe it as burning love.

Paco liked to take long drives into the desert, often starting as early as five in the morning. When he picked me up on Sundays before dawn in his faded matte-white Chevy van, I'd sit on the engine cover between the front seats, wrapped in a Mexican blanket. The engine beneath warmed me.

"Where we go?" I would ask him.

"Where the road takes us," he answered, filling me with a sense of adventure and a hunger to see what was beyond my concrete world.

Paco would take me a half a mile away to MacArthur Park, now a crack-fueled version of what it was. The park is an eight-block swath of urban greenery surrounded by cement and steel on the edge of Downtown Los Angeles. Foaming with drug addiction and despair, in the dusty haze of the 1970s, the park was filled with heroin addicts, criminals, gangs, the homeless, and strangely, a pond where you could rent brightly colored foot-powered plastic paddle boats. As a three-year-old, all I could see was the adventure these candy-colored boats held.

In the park there was a man who gave free candy to the kids—we called him "the candyman." As a toddler, whenever I arrived at the park with the nannies and other kids, I would wander around the gang members and depleted junkies in the heavy heat, looking for the candyman. The grass was so littered with discarded burger wrappers and the glint of needles that it was hard to find a spot to shade myself from the ceaseless Los Angeles sun.

The park had a Mexican preacher shouting into a microphone amplified by his boom box. In loud Spanish, he yelled about the end of the world. In the searing summer heat, as if in an act of masochism, he wore stiff polyester suits, cheap and soaked through with sweat, with a wide diagonally striped black, brown, and white tie. His hair was always weighed down with perspiration, stuck to his forehead as it glistened in the white-hot

8 CHILD X

light. Even as a child I noticed he always positioned himself in the sun. He yelled into the microphone as if he was fighting the sun itself.

At that time, the neighborhood around MacArthur Park was a known cruising destination for gay men. While I was still a toddler in The Baby Factory, the preacher and future mass murderer Jim Jones, who had been running the Peoples Temple since 1965, was watching Clint Eastwood in *Dirty Harry* at the Westlake Movie Theater a mile away. An arrest was made. Jones was arrested for lewd conduct and hauled out of the theater by the local Rampart police.

Rampart was a couple of blocks down from the Original Tommy's Burgers. Thirty-five years later it would be revealed that Rampart was the most corrupt police precinct in US history. It was the nerve center of the murders of Biggie Smalls and Tupac Shakur with Bloods and Crips infiltrating the force. In the summer of 1973, years before some of the greatest anthems of my youth, like "Dear Mama" and "Big Papa," cops from this station were eating Tommy's Burgers by the dozen down the street from us packed into The Baby Factory. There was never a time I went to Tommy's without seeing a half-dozen cops or more eating their lunch.

They did nothing to help us.

X

When I was about three, we left The Baby Factory and were moved to a dilapidated Gothic tenement on Melrose and Gramercy, a mile southeast of Hollywood Boulevard. A quarter-mile away was Hancock Park, a wealthy neighborhood of 1920s Spanish and Craftsman mansions.

My new house was a decaying red brick building that lay three blocks down from the palatial and pearly Bronson Gate entrance of Paramount studios. Since then, it's been renovated and is now a showroom for expensive fireplaces. It is not uncommon in Los Angeles for neighborhoods with palatial homes to sit next to slums. I didn't know it at the time, but some of the most iconic films of the 1970s, like *Chinatown*, were made just down the street from The Red Brick Building where I spent my early childhood.

THE BABY FACTORY

The slum where we lived was somewhat exotic even in Los Angeles, designed in a Brutalist version of the same Romanesque style as Meharry Medical College in Nashville, Tennessee, where my grandparents met and continued their ascension to Black affluence.

X

I didn't know that more than five hundred years ago, in what is now known as Turkey, the Islamic Ottoman Empire often demanded children as tribute. The ten-year-old sons of their Christian Albanian, Greek, and Serbian subjects were handed over to the sultan, conscripted into his armies, and circumcised. Called the Janissaries, these fearsome soldiers—now the sultan's property—trained from childhood. For three hundred years they fought directly under him in wars against Hungary, Austria, and Poland.

Somewhere in the history, the Janissaries revolted. In a response to their rebellion, the current sultan set fire to their barracks, killing four thousand of them. The rest were hunted down, executed, or exiled.

The commander of our movement was a man named Lafayette Ronald Hubbard. If you were to ever leave and speak out against Hubbard's elite navy after signing his billion-year contract, even as a child, they would sever all your family ties and any relationship you ever had that was connected to his movement. Hubbard had a doctrine: anyone who ever left the movement's elite spiritual navy was a dreg of humanity, a reduced form of life among humans, scum.

I didn't know it then, but I had been born and taken away from my parents to be groomed as an asset with no name. I was being trained by the movement to be part of a machine determined for war. In the dorms, all of us kids were being kept in a holding pen until our bodies grew. I lived with a hundred other kids in makeshift barracks lined with World War II industrial bunk beds stacked three high. They could have been the taller cousins of the industrial cribs back at The Baby Factory. Because I was only three and too young to assert myself, I was always relegated to the

CHILD X

third-tier top bunk, at least twelve feet off the ground. Getting up to my bunk was like climbing a mountain.

X

Some of my earliest memories were constant dreams of falling. I would wake up on the green shag carpet floor, with the familiar stench of rotting plumbing, to strict military morning assemblies in the dorms—the movement wanted to make sure none of the kids had vanished in the middle of the night. It wasn't a dream. I was constantly falling from a third-tier bunk and somehow managed not to break my neck. There was a constant pressure: you never knew when older kids were going to beat you or take something you had.

Every morning, the large room was filled with rows of neglected children, laid out in single file lines with our names called out one by one.

"Jamie!"

"Aye, sir!" I responded in the sun-faded Red Brick Building in Hollywood. The pseudo-navy members in charge of us in their unkempt, rarely washed navy blues reeked of cigarette smoke and the odor of going unshowered. They expected us to line up single file by "division" like soldiers and be inventoried.

Because of Hubbard's doctrine, we were constantly made to clean the crumbling rooms that could never truly be cleaned. This would condition us for the constant labor that would be our futures. Once a week we had to pass an inspection with a white glove—a military exercise where an officer passes a white glove over a wall or a doorframe. We failed the inspection if they found a single speck of dust. I was a three-year-old trying to remove every fleck in a city built on a desert. If one speck was found, we would be forced to reclean everything and not be allowed to sleep until we passed the inspection. We were told that everything would need to be clean for planetary salvation, which we all wanted.

Our playground was an unused parking lot with no trees and rough concrete completely exposed to the sun. There were no smog laws in 1970s

THE BABY FACTORY

Los Angeles. I watched Chevy Chevelles, Datsun B210s, and El Caminos with their chrome trim too hot to touch lurch down the street. The growling of V8 beasts under their hoods gorged on leaded gasoline. Cars backfired constantly. It was hard to distinguish between a car acting up and distant gunfire.

Between the shimmering haze, which was so thick everything more than sixty feet in front of me seemed like a mirage, was a pastiche of screaming signs and strip malls. If you squinted just right in the searing sun, Sunset Boulevard could look like a dirty Monet. The blinding sun and the unceasing smell of burning asphalt and gasoline felt like it was inside and under your skin. The searing heat was uncomfortable, yet so familiar that I didn't notice it. I sometimes wonder if this constant discomfort inured me to the more serious pain in my life—and the dangerous circumstances that would desensitize me to the physical damage to my body—that lay ahead.

X

On an extremely hot day, when I was around the age of five, we were asked to go downstairs and stand in line. Before us stood adult Hubbard navy members with stacks of paper in front of them. I was completely unable to write, and as I got to my place in line, I was asked if I wanted to be like my mom and help save the planet. I missed her so much, so the opportunity to be anything like her meant the opportunity to maybe see her. I was excited to be connected to her, to be a part of her, like the kids before me in line, and the ones coming after me. I excitedly and slowly scratched an illegible scribble onto a contract, committing my service to the movement for the next billion years.

A private navy adult named Carl stood above the table with his wheat-brown hair and Monkees haircut. "What happens when we fix this planet?" I asked him, wide-eyed.

"We'll go on to the next planet and fix everyone there," Carl, in his quasi-navy uniform, answered.

"But how will we get there?"

"We'll take spaceships to get there."

Carl said it matter-of-factly, without ceremony.

I saw me and my mother in a big room on a spaceship on a giant bed facing a giant window. Wrapped together in a blanket, she held me and I leaned into her as we sat on the soft bed, her back leaning against the gray wall of the ship. We looked out of a looming flat-glass window built into the spaceship's alloyed hull, into radiant twin suns burning in the black of space. Before the suns was a giant blue and green planet, similar to Earth, shimmering against the stars.

My heart pounded with excitement for the adventure to come. For days I thought about being with my mom, spaceships, going to other planets, and the goals of the movement: helping people to stay rational, to not get sick, and to always be in control of their emotions.

For the first time, my isolation had a purpose.

Days later, I came out of my dorm room downstairs and heard screaming from the cadet offices at the far edge of the building. I peeked through a doorway into the main office and saw the commanding officer of the cadets, Jess, who was in his late teens, screaming at a thirteen-year-old blond kid named Bryant. They were pushing and shoving each other. Bryant wasn't listening to what Jess wanted him to do. This was a tenement. There were holes in walls and exposed sockets all over the building. In one sudden motion, Jess grabbed Bryant's hand and jammed it into an exposed electrical socket. Both of their bodies jolted. Bryant wailed and screamed, shaking his head violently while tears flew from his face. Jess appeared satisfied and content, and it was over.

Chapter 2

NIGHTMARE DIVE BOMBERS

In 1967, several years before my birth in Los Angeles, in East Grinstead, West Sussex, England, Lafayette Ronald Hubbard knew that he was becoming unappreciated by the British government. His time at his palatial 1792 manor house, which he had purchased in 1959 from the Maharajah of Jaipur—with its fifty-nine acres of pristine English fields—was running down. One fine spring day, Hubbard pulled sixteen of his most loyal adherents into a room in the manor amidst those sprawling green fields and started to talk.

"This is not the first time we have been together," he avowed, alluding to the fact that this unlikely and eclectic group had, in previous lives, worked together to accomplish astonishing acts of valor.

He went on to tell them that the only way for the movement to be victorious was to take to the high seas and be what Hubbard called "fabian"—a reference to the ancient Roman general Fabius, who was known to attack at unpredictable times from unpredictable directions and retreat invisibly into forests where he could not be found. Hubbard was establishing his own private navy that would exist on a flotilla of boats that he would first call the "sea project," and he, as a former US Navy commander, would appoint himself "Commodore"—a naval rank above captain but below admiral, termed for someone who commanded a flotilla of ships but not a full navy. The term came from a Dutch word "comandeor," for "commander," that the French stole from them as "commandeur," which the British in turn stole from them, landing on "commodore." This decision by the newly self-ordained naval officer would alter the course of my unborn life.

While Hubbard was on the high seas, my life existed under his command in this Red Brick Building, a tenement slum on the East Side of Los Angeles. It was a time of emotional fear and constant loneliness.

There was the emotional pain of having no parents; both my mother and Paco were off doing important work for the movement, saving the world and trying to make a living. There was the physical threat of abusive "nannies" and older kids. And there was the constant heat and pressure of a smoldering Los Angeles.

My childthoughts went to our quest. Every time I felt loneliness and a bubbling disdain towards my mother for abandoning me, I would focus my childmind on the mission: she was saving the planet. Once the humans were fixed, I would be able to see my mom an hour or two a day. My role was to not make trouble so my mother could focus on her unwavering desire of Earth's salvation.

The Red Brick Building was set against a long driveway that went from one end of the red façade to the other, across from the "playground." Because I was exposed to the sun all day, my skin got incredibly dark and my bright, green Mulatto eyes shined as if emanating light. Strangers would stop and stare at me if I looked them in the eyes. I used to think they thought I was blind.

There was a not-so-uncommon event where I fell on the burning cement playground behind the building, like many of us kids. I tripped on a sharp piece of concrete jutting out of the ground from the broken asphalt, and fell on my wrist the wrong way. I was bleeding. I cried out in pain. What happened next might have affected me more than the injury.

NIGHTMARE DIVE BOMBERS

A male nanny came out of nowhere. "Stop dramatizing," the nanny sniped. "Knock off the bank. I don't wanna hear any more HE & R out of you."

As a child of four or five, I was often hit with phrases and concepts I could not process. I had no idea what HE & R, Human Emotion and Reaction, meant—but he meant stop reacting, or expressing any human emotion whatsoever. From the time I was born, any expression of emotion was considered "dramatizing"—meaning you're making something look and sound worse than it is, playing it up for attention. The "bank" was another word for your "subconscious or reactionary" mind and it taking control of you. As an ancient fallen god, any nonlethal injury was insignificant, even if I was a toddler. The nanny was imposing that nothing had really occurred, and I had not been hurt. It was my reactionary mind that had been triggered from horrible events in my previous lives—*that's* why I was crying.

In the doctrine, all emotion comes from something negative in the past, and I was groomed to believe that nothing in the present could faze me. In my blind haze, I believed this completely. I felt guilt and shame any time a negative emotion washed over me. Human Emotion and Reaction is not allowed, not even from a toddler. Since I had no idea that "bank" meant your reactive subconscious mind, when I first heard the term, I thought the nanny wanted me to rob a bank.

I didn't know it then, but to the nannies and to the other adults in their makeshift navy uniforms that smelled of cigarette smoke, I was a trillion-year-old fallen god in a child's body. I'd been killed in wars. I'd slain armies. I'd commanded battleships, I'd ripped atmospheres off of planets and destroyed alien races. As I grew, I was told in the context of my lifetimes that my childhood was but a mere drip in an ocean of time and that, because I was an ancient spirit with billions of years of experience, I didn't need to be coddled or cared for—I was an indestructible spirit, and my childbody was an impediment and physical prison that hindered the power of my true identity. At some point, I'd known and done everything in the known universe and beyond, and all I needed to do was remember.

16   CHILD X

Just remember. There would be no childhood. That was stolen—a thievery
in the moonlight under a beautiful Los Angeles sky.

X

Earth's 1960s have been remembered as a utopian time of self-expression
and possibility that was needed to overturn a crushing world—and in
some ways it was. The '60s was the social noir that likely caused the physical pressure chamber that would be my childhood over a decade later.

Berlin, Germany, was sliced in two in 1961. German children reached
to touch their grandparents through barbed wire before a concrete wall
separated them completely. Nuclear missiles in Cuba brought the US and
the USSR mere seconds from a world devoured by nuclear fire.

In 1962 Marilyn Monroe died of a drug overdose in LA. Part of America's soul died with her.

In 1963, in the light of day, President John F. Kennedy had the back of
his head blown off in Dallas.

In 1964, conscription started in the United States, forcing drafted
young men to go to Vietnam where tens of thousands would die. At nineteen years old, no one wants to die.

By 1965, the shooting of a Black teenager by police sparked six days
of riots during a long hot summer in Harlem, just as American marines
arrived in South Vietnam for combat. Two air crashes over two days in
Japan killed more than three hundred people. War ravaged Africa from
Uganda to the Congo. Back in America, Civil Rights activist James Mere-
dith was shot by a sniper while churches burned in Mississippi. American
planes also bombed children in Hanoi.

By 1967, a fire during a routine test on the launch pad suffocated to
death the three-man crew of Apollo 1.

Then, in 1968, Dr. Martin Luther King Jr. was gunned down at the Lor-
raine Motel in Memphis, Tennessee. Riots in Watts, riots in Chicago. Black
neighborhoods around the nation burned, and the National Guard pa-
trolled American streets with rifles, machine guns, and grenade launchers.

NIGHTMARE DIVE BOMBERS

The Chicago mayor ordered police: "Shoot to kill arsonists; shoot to wound looters." By the summer, Robert F. Kennedy was shot to death in the kitchen of the Ambassador Hotel just down the street from my childhood playground, the beautiful but grotesque MacArthur Park. Bobby drew shallow breaths, his insides on fire, torn up by bullets, in surprise and sadness, his blurring eyes staring up into the face of the seventeen-year-old boy who cradled his head and placed a rosary in his hand.

In 1968 guerrilla attacks in Vietnam killed thousands during the Lunar New Year festival. Preceding the war, in 1963, a Buddhist monk in Vietnam set himself on fire, immolating himself on film for the world to see. This image burned Vietnam into the Western mind.

In 1969, a pregnant actress, Sharon Tate, star of *Valley of the Dolls*, along with four of her close friends, was butchered, her baby cut out of her stomach in her home at 10050 Cielo Drive in Benedict Canyon. As she bled out, she repeatedly wailed, "Mother, mother, mother." The killers—a self-proclaimed "Family" of hippie anarchists who would usher in the death of the '60s counterculture of free love, mystic experimentation, and self-discovery through drug-induced self-indulgence—used Tate's blood to write the word "pig" on the front door. All over the news, these murders mutated American self-perception, setting off thirty years of conservative watchdog-ism that would scour everything from board games to rock 'n' roll for signs of Satan.

In 1970, National Guardsmen in Ohio opened fire on protesting college students, killing four and wounding nine others at Kent State University. President Nixon then doubled down on the American presence in South Vietnam, and the war greatly intensified. Conflict in Vietnam turned into a national identity crisis that felt like a daily lashing of the mind.

The 1960s was a series of catastrophes that were unrelenting for a decade. A nation's sense of itself unraveled. No one could have gone through all this and come out whole. It makes sense that this searing psychological furnace spawned a rebellious generation starving for mental shelter and spiritual relief. The boiling point thrust kids coming of age in the early '70s into escapism, a movement of "free love" and idealism that resulted in millions of illegitimate children and the annihilation of the nuclear family. They dropped in and dived into anything that would balm their blackened minds.

Humans needed a break.

The 1970s, with its disco, heroin, and hedonism, was a reaction to the 1960s and its succession of horrors: the assassinations, the war, the unrelenting pressure.

The conflict in Vietnam finally had entered the American Zeitgeist, culminating in a front-row seat to the death in Vietnam courtesy of *LIFE* magazine—a grimacing man shot in the face, a teenage girl running naked through a rice paddy, her skin blackened by American napalm.

Every morning over breakfast cereal, the world was hit with a daily shiv of terrible events and human death which could have only resulted in global nihilism, a generation that felt that nuclear fire might be destined to consume humankind. This was real.

A generation became disenfranchised, and searching for a way out of the chaos, mentally exhausted, they joined cults and communes across the world: the Moonies, Charles Manson and his Family, the Children of God, and Jim Jones's Peoples Temple in the jungles of Guyana, where 909 people, including 300 children, were killed.

And then there was the movement, which my mother left her affluent, proud, and powerful Black upbringing in Hartford, Connecticut, to join. Later I would come to know that there were very few Black people in this mission, and it would make me feel even more strange about where I was brought.

Many Generation X babies were the children of cultists, junkies, schizophrenic veterans, and nihilists. We were the cultic children born from revolutions in movements all over the world. It's a dark irony that a generation that created so much change, like the passing of the Civil Rights Act of 1964, also created so many cults and left so many abandoned children. While it succeeded in furthering "change," it destroyed itself.

That is why I was born into a baby factory. Their change became my nightmare.

Chapter 3

GREENWICH VILLAGE

We sat in the sky. All around me was the overwhelming noise of the airplane—people talking and laughing. My older brother Joshua sat next to me, swinging his six-year-old legs back and forth. Paco nudged and whispered at him. They laughed. My mother sat quietly across the smoky aisle. She raised a lit cigarette to her lips, drew in a deep breath, and held it like treasure.

I lifted myself out of the airplane seat, gripping the rounded plastic window frame for leverage, and peered outside. It took all my strength to pull myself up and slide out of the seat belt. I was four, and this was my first time on an airplane. I could feel the growling roar of the engines pulsating every part of my body.

Across the aisle, my mother was quietly lost in a book—probably something by Robert Heinlein or Robert Ludlum. The cigarette burned down almost to nothing. The spaceship of the airplane, with its noise and gathering of people, was new and thrilling. I was so happy to be going somewhere with my family high up in the sky, away from the damp, musty smell of The Red Brick Building.

Through the cigarette haze, I looked at the other people around me. There was a man who wore a dark brown suit, hair pluming from his unbuttoned white shirt. His coal-black hair, long in back, slicked down greasily from a receding hairline. "La bomba! La bomba!" the words came from across the aisle from the man toward my mother. He had been saying strange words since the airport in Los Angeles—"La bomba! La bomba!"— and pointing to his luggage. My mother got up and came back with a stewardess and pointed to the strange, nervous man. "La bomba!" the man said again and pointed to the luggage compartment above his head. He scratched his sweaty lip and smiled; one of his front teeth was crooked. The stewardess explained to my mother that the Italian man didn't speak any English and had been rebooked on our flight because of a bomb threat on another plane.

It was a waning spring evening when we landed at JFK International Airport. The sun was different here, not screened by a heavy brown haze like I had seen—and felt—in Hollywood. This lowering sun hung in a pale-blue sky, quickly clearing away the clouds, and it felt like a gentle, crisp caress. My grandmother Dorothy, my mother's mother, had paid for all of us to fly to New York from Los Angeles and visit her in Westchester County.

In the noise of the busy street, my grandmother and her new husband, Robert, pulled up in their cinnamon 1970 Cadillac. Robert silently grabbed our luggage, and I watched him from my stroller as he placed each bag gently into the Cadillac's huge trunk. Paco stood with my mother on the curb, talking to my grandmother, then placed me in the car. It smelled of oiled leather and oranges, and I drifted to sleep.

When I woke, it was dark, and we were easing onto the sweeping gravel driveway that led to my grandmother's house at the end of a cul-de-sac on Meadowview Drive in Hartsdale, New York. Their home was backed up against a small rise that was thick with ferns and tall red pines. Lit by the headlights of Robert's Cadillac, they rustled in the breeze as if embracing us.

Paco helped me out of the back seat, and I immediately experienced how different the air was from the smog and heat of Los Angeles. The air here was wet, with different smells—the sweetness of the pine trees like

GREENWICH VILLAGE

grapefruit, the tang of dank water, and the cool dampness of the bushy ferns gathered around the house. It was like nothing I'd ever smelled in my life. I could feel it making my skin wet, making every breath moist in my throat. The sounds were different too. Wind fought through the red pine branches high above, and there was another sound that I didn't recognize or fully understand: the sound of water traveling over terrain. I felt like I had landed on another planet.

My grandmother's house was a twentieth-century wooden home with a triangle roof, built of red brick on the ground with light gray timber above on the second floor, but back then to my four-year-old eyes, coming from a heat-baked concrete slum with a habitat of one square block, it was a castle complete with its own moat—a creek rushed from the big hill behind the house and parallel to the gravel driveway of tiny white, gray, and black rocks. It was just a stream running down and in front of a modest house, but from my deprivation, it was a palace.

We entered through the back door, and the first thing that hit my senses was the scent of oranges and the smell of Robert's cigars. My grandmother was always fighting that smell, using citrus oil to smooth away the robust black-pepper and cocoa odor that attached itself to everything in the house. To this day, the smell of cigars and oranges is one of my favorites. A dignified and robust man, Robert was a Black New York State judge in the city.

If languor and deprivation had an odor, it was The Red Brick Building, with its mold, old carpet, cigarette smoke, infrequently washed bodies, and the burnt-oil stench of traffic. There was no air conditioning; with the windows open, it constantly smelled of car exhaust. At this point in my life, that one square block was the only place I had to compare my grandmother's home to.

"How about some warmed milk and honey, and cookies?" my grandmother asked. It was completely exotic to me. I was a boy who lived in a slum, who had just taken his first airplane ride. The journey across the country, the stimulation of the plane, the sights and sounds had made me exhausted.

Upstairs, in a living room awash in warm lamplight, were huge paintings. I had never seen an oil painting. I barely knew that vivid, rich bright colors like these were even possible.

My grandmother gave us warm ginger snaps fresh from the oven with heated-up milk and honey to dip the cookies in, where they would get mushy making the spicy sweetness of ginger fill my mouth. I never had anyone before care for me. The sensation was incomprehensible and overwhelming. My heart burned.

Later, in the small, marble upstairs bathroom, wearing a gentle smile, my grandmother removed my clothes and placed me into a warm bath. My stomach rumbled with milk, honey, and ginger snaps.

Very quickly, her joyful face transformed into a grimace. Her eyes bulged. "Paco!" she yelled.

Paco appeared in the bathroom doorway. My grandmother pointed to me, naked in the steaming water. She didn't explain to Paco, who had been smiling back at her dramatic expression. He turned to look at me, cringed and saddened. His face fell to his chest.

"Get the car!" screamed Dorothy.

Paco nodded with obedience and charged from the room.

That beautiful spring night, we raced to the emergency room in White Plains with a severe infection to my genitals that ran from my abdomen to my upper thighs. That entire area was bright red and tender to the touch. The doctors told my grandmother, my mother, and Paco that if this infection had gone on much longer, it was going to go septic and come close to killing me. It had been there for months, but as I lived in dorms, no one ever looked at my body. I was never taught or asked to shower or brush my teeth as I lived in brightly colored polyester or army blankets that went unwashed. I was so numb that I didn't even realize the sore was there. Discomfort was all I knew, to the point where it felt like part of me, a limb.

It would not be the last time my grandmother's accidental attention to my body would save my life.

I could not have known that a decade and a half later, in the same kids' room where I was staying, with its yellow-and-black-striped comforter,

GREENWICH VILLAGE

my grandmother would stand for an hour and fifteen minutes trying to explain to me the use of a comma.

She kept calling it "a pause in a sentence."

I would have no idea what she was talking about.

I would be nineteen years old, semi-literate, thinking I could never learn.

X

In New York, my grandmother's cousin Amy came to visit. She was married to Babatunde "Tunji" Olatunji, the famed African drummer who became a legend in the 1960s and 1970s for bringing Nigerian drumming to America. He had been a close friend of John Coltrane, and together built the Olatunji Center for African Culture in the center of Harlem—the venue of Coltrane's last-ever performance in 1967.

A week after recovering from my infection, Shade and Modupe, Tunji's two daughters—both born and raised in Lagos, Nigeria—came to Westchester and begged my grandmother to let them take me to New York City for the day. The two beautiful, black-skinned young women constantly stared at me and pinched my cheeks. I don't think I ever looked at Shade and Modupe and didn't see their round faces smiling. Astonishing in their bright, colorful, cinematic Nigerian dress, they waited on me and washed me in love.

I was a little boy who'd lived in a slum. I had never experienced this level of tenderness before. All of the warmth and human contact felt alien, but I soaked in it—I loved them.

I had no idea that their father was a giant who would someday alter the way that I would see my life. In 1969, Carlos Santana covered Tunji's song "Jin-go-lo-ba," which he would one day perform with Eric Clapton. A kinetic, fierce, emotional anthem, the song swept the nation as an instant success. Santana and Tunji would eventually join forces and record together. Tunji arranged for Nina Simone on the album *At the Village Gate*, and for years played with Miles Davis and Max Roach, eventually backing

Stevie Wonder on his soundtrack for *Jungle Fever*. Tunji was a cultural force.

As early as 1961, while the US placed nuclear missiles in Turkey within striking distance of the Soviet Union, Tunji was recording with Quincy Jones—later the producer of Michael Jackson's meteoric *Thriller*. By 1962, Khrushchev, the premier of Russia, then placed nuclear missiles in Cuba, stationing atomic death within reach of American suburbs. That same year, jazz legend John Coltrane dedicated a song to Tunji on his self-titled studio album, *Coltrane*.

Tunji set in motion a deep pride among American Blacks, giving them an ethereal sense of mythological African power. Tunji was immortalized right next to Martin Luther King in Bob Dylan's haunting song "I Shall Be Free." He had been a close friend of King's, having marched with him across the South during the Civil Rights movement. Khrushchev was present in the fall of 1962, possessed with the Cuban Missile Crisis and on the razor's edge of nuclear annihilation with the US, when Tunji was asked to perform before the United Nations. That day, at 760 United Nations Plaza in Manhattan, Tunji shook and wailed to his hypnotic beats, pounding on his wooden goatskin drum; the immovable Nikita Sergeyevich Khrushchev took off his shoes and danced.

My day with Shade and Modupe in their traditional Nigerian dress started with the Bronx Zoo. Its domed buildings, only eighty years old then, looked ancient. We strolled past a large Italian stone fountain. A group of laughing kids were throwing pennies into it. We came to a line of cages as I looked up from my stroller, Shade and Modupe beaming above me. We were in the section for large cats, and we rolled and stopped before their steel-poled black cages. I was awed by the size and power of first a tiger, and then a lion, and then I thought they looked sad.

I was transfixed by a pair of metal fox ears that were bigger than a real live fox. I put my head between them, and all of a sudden I could hear every faint sound in the zoo. I didn't know it at the time, but a small infection had started in my ears, causing hearing loss. The amplification

GREENWICH VILLAGE

of being able to hear like a fox—to be able to hear, period—raced up and down my spine, and I smiled in quiet exhilaration.

After the Bronx Zoo, Shade and Modupe drove me into the city and rolled me in my stroller through Greenwich Village. My childmind was electrified by the constant thrum of the streets as the three of us rolled through the East Village, which smelled of sewer steam and hot dog juice. On the ground level of every building was something different: shops, food, signs that spelled strange words in stranger languages.

We stopped at the corner of Thompson and Bleecker, in front of the Village Gate Jazz Club, its 1920s sign rimmed with unlit bulbs the same color as the dirty white-stone building. It looked like the circus signs I had seen in cartoons and made me feel wonder and delight. Once again this was very different from the East Hollywood Mexican, Nicaraguan, and Filipino slums I was used to. I desperately struggled to understand where I was. I looked around me, searching for the familiarity of Mexicans and poverty. There was art. There was concrete. There were coffee shops. There were unlit neon signs that promised every color in the rainbow. This busy, lively place in all its seediness and beauty ignited a burning in me. It was alive.

Walking down a side street there was a man in baggy tan chinos, a wife beater, a beautiful tweed coat, and a fedora carrying a painting. As young as I was, I understood. These were my people. This was where I was supposed to be. I didn't know it at the time, but this was what I would become.

X

Later that evening, Shade and Modupe rolled me up to the grand arcing entrance of 875 West End Avenue on the Upper West Side of Manhattan. Shade pressed a metal button on the wall, spoke a few hurried words, and there was a tangy buzzing sound. I didn't know who or what she was talking to. The glass door clicked open, and we went inside.

Shade and Modupe propelled me into a vast space that felt limitless. The sun was setting, and through the many large windows the sky had taken on deep purples and pinks beyond the brick buildings. A tall man seemed to feel us enter from far across a massive room. He turned his head from the window as we walked in. Smiling, he radiated pure joy as if it was forced into you.

Tunji's eyes gleamed, bursting with love. "Welcome, daughters! And Jamie!"

"Hi, Papa!" Shade and Modupe said, almost at the same time, their round brown faces bright with smiles as they rolled me to the center of the giant room.

I smiled toward this larger-than-life man showering all of us with his tender warmth. In The Red Brick Building on Melrose there wasn't any joy from the adults when someone—when a child—simply walked into a room.

The setting sun brought out a sea of colors all around me. Bright, expressive faces on the walls—masks—gazed, laughed, and cried at me. They were painted in reds, greens, and blues. Some of these faces were framed with long wispy African hair, elaborate feathers from large birds, or great alien crests, making them look like beings from somewhere else.

I had walked into Africa recreated in an enormous pre-war Manhattan apartment.

Everything in the home was hand carved and imported from West Africa. There were tables and stools carved out of deep chocolate woods that looked like some strange wizard had bent and shaped them—like the gnarled trees I had just seen climbing into the blue sky from the streets of Greenwich Village. I was awed by every inch: the colors, the textures, the hides of strange and wild animals, the burnt-bark-colored wooden furniture, and the masks with their expressive, otherworldly painted faces.

Alien statues, their striped faces high on top of long necks, peered out from the broad, waxy leaves of endless houseplants, big and small, creating a jungle inside this interior world. Palms burst out of large stone pots painted with zigzagging colors. There was a hint of spice in the air. For the first time I was seeing a curated interior world, Tunji's world. Tunji was the descendant of African kings, and you felt the full force of a benevolent king in his presence. He was an animating force that overwhelmed my senses.

Toward the end of that trip, my uncle Stevie came to visit. A towering, muscled Black man with a painterly mustache, goatee, and crown of African hair, he tossed me in the air of my grandmother's 1970s wood-paneled family room while I laughed. As I flew through the air, Stevie, who would eventually become a heroin addict, spoke to my mother and grandmother in strange words that I'd never heard before. The words were large, complicated, urbane, and erudite. My uncle was a god to me, and I promised myself, as I soared through the air and landed in his arms, that I would learn to use words like that one day. It was the first time I remember being aware of language and what it could do, how it could move people.

X

A year and a half after my expedition to New York City, a handsome, six-foot-one, one-hundred-and-eighty-pound, dark-black African prince showed up at the back entrance of The Red Brick Building in Los Angeles, demanding to see my brother Joshua and me. It was Tunji's son Kwame Olatunji.

The visit must have been prearranged because we were allowed to leave with this strange African man, who put us in a rental car. We went to a UCLA Bruins football game in Downtown Los Angeles, just a few miles from The Baby Factory. I had never seen a young African man, or a Black man, carry himself like Kwame. This was a foreign experience of hot dogs, Cokes, popcorn, and ice cream. Kwame, a kind, confident, caring but serious man, had the presence of a panther. He had entered Harvard at the age of sixteen and played football for them.

This was the first time I had ever been to a football game, and for those few hours the grimy strangeness of the dorms was swept away. Even though my hearing was growing fainter, the pressure of almost eighty thousand screaming people in a football stadium was something that made me unsteady. The voices piled on top of each other, like the large men on the field slamming into each other to stop the one with the ball from carrying it across to the other side. I watched the ball sail through the air, marveling at how a single man could throw something so far. I watched the people in the stands, their faces swinging from excitement to anguish in the blink of an eye.

Decades later, as a grown man, I would hear that Kwame had died on a gold-mining expedition in Sierra Leone. When I heard this, my heart broke for Kwame's mother, Amy; his warm and loving father; and his sisters. Even though I only spent a few hours with Kwame when I was five years old, I would never get his face out of my head.

I would spend my childhood not knowing where I came from, or the significance my lineage held in the world. I would be anonymous, isolated, shrouded, mentally entombed in an LA slum, far from the people who I would have to work harder than I would ever realize to find my way back to.

Chapter 4

PHOENIX RISING

[105 YEARS BEFORE THE BABY FACTORY] In my desert silo as a child, even after my visit to New York, I had no idea that my family had been freed from slavery in 1865. Their Black descendants carved a wealthy nation—built on Black fortunes—in parallel to the greater United States. There is an untold story in America that in the years that followed the end of slavery, freed slaves were buying land, building businesses, becoming leaders of vast incomprehensible wealth.

My family was not just a phoenix rising, but a phoenix exploding from slavery with a fury like a bat out of Hades. The story of what my family built immediately from the ashes of slavery culminated in my grandfather Roy's graduation from medical school just seventy-five years after abolition.

This is my lineage, what I was supposed to be: free, cultured, affluent, educated, powerful, humane.

However, it would take the dark fantasy of the 1960s, just one hundred years later, to destroy for me everything that my ancestors had built.

A grandchild destined for opportunity, I was instead born into poverty and conditioned for the control of a slavemaster. I was born into a world where I was taught to believe I was property of a White man named Hubbard, my master and commander, and pushed to fall in love with science fiction beliefs to be allowed to survive. Hubbard's belief in Earth as a prison planet would shape my mind from my birth. As the sun rose and fell over The Red Brick Building in Los Angeles, a plantation of red brick, smog, and heat was the only world I knew. I would grow up to believe in fulfilling my mission to save the planet. But I knew that something was wrong.

X

Freed slaves would produce my grandmother's mother.

My great-great-great grandfather on my mother's side, Edmund Scarborough, was born as a slave in Kosciusko, Mississippi, in the 1830s. Edmund, a half-breed like me, was named after his slavemaster father, who owned the plantation, fathering a child with his slave Edmund's enslaved mother, Rachel. When Edmund turned eighteen, his slavemaster father freed him and offered him the chance to go to medical school in the North.

Edmund felt he could only live with going to medical school if his mother, Rachel, was also freed. His father refused to part with Rachel, whom the slavemaster said he deeply loved. Edmund would not leave his mother.

Ironically, Edmund and I both remained slaves for the sake of Black mothers, yet for opposite reasons: Edmund because he wouldn't leave his mother, and me because my mother believed that I was property of Hubbard, her commander. She had decided from birth that I would spend my life dedicated to the cause.

Decades later, entombed at nineteen in my own illiteracy, having barely gone to school, I would also get a fleeting chance to pursue higher education. My Black mother would shame me and tell me I was failing her in her mission to save the world.

She said to me, "You want to go join the wogs." This was the Hubbard equivalent of a "muggle" in J. K. Rowling's fantasy world. Both worldbuilders, Rowling would build worlds that brightened the lives of children, while Hubbard would build a world that would darken their souls.

X

PHOENIX RISING

For Edmund, in Mississippi, he lived under the shroud of a war. America was at war with itself. After five bloody years of grotesque warfare—brother killing brother on the fields of Antietam and Gettysburg, where men in blue and gray grimly marched in great lines into walls of gunfire, wailing for their mothers as they were torn to pieces by showers of flying metal—the South burned.

As slavery ended in North America in 1865, Edmund married Julia. The newlywed and newly freed slaves set out for the small Black town of Pickens, Mississippi. There they opened the town's first and only general store. Edmund and Julia would have five children, all of whom would study at Rust College. Rust was a small Methodist college for Colored students, where White professors from the North administered and taught everything. My ancestors would always see education as freedom. Yet my own education would be that we are all fallen gods trapped in flesh-bodies, and only the movement could restore us to our former, radiant, glorious, all-powerful selves.

Edmund and Julia would produce my grandmother's father.

Emmanuel Sweet, also a great-great-grandfather, was a young Choctaw who escaped the Trail of Tears—the forced relocation of American Indians by the US federal government. Entire families were force-marched across harsh terrain, exposed to the elements. Many had no clothing that would help them survive the bitter, cold snows and torrential rains that rushed up from the Gulf of Mexico and drowned the prairies. I was not the only one who suffered.

As winter snows fell on the Great Plains in the Midwest of the United States, Emmanuel and his Native brothers and sisters were forced to walk in grim defeat across the land where, for ten thousand years, they had once hunted venison and buffalo, and cultivated the corn that would eventually feed the expansion of European settlers during more than two hundred years of their own genocide.

In these endless, flat expanses of beaten, storm-swept grass, many marched hungry. The Choctaw horses starved. The Choctaw children, too small to walk the thousand miles from Mississippi to Oklahoma, would fall exhausted on the trail and be left to the elements.

CHILD X

In the 1850s, it was not uncommon for freed Black slaves to live with the defiant Choctaw—the tribe had fought alongside American revolutionaries against the British.

Upon his escape from the Trail of Tears, Choctaw Emmanuel met a beautiful French Irish immigrant named Sophia Stith, and they also moved to Pickens, Mississippi. This small Black-only town in the middle of nowhere was one of the few places in the United States where they would be accepted as an interracial couple. The pair started an active fishery on the Big Black River that runs through the east side of Pickens. Of the hundreds of acres that Emmanuel and Sophia built, a seventy-acre parcel remains in my family today. It is owned by my mother, my aunt, and my cousins, and is worked by local Black farmers who now pay those with Black ancestral blood to rent the land.

X

Ninety miles from Pickens, the fabled city of Vicksburg, Mississippi, would become the last stronghold of the Confederacy, sitting high on a bluff and overlooking a slow-moving easterly bend of the Mississippi River just along the Louisiana border. In the 1880s, it lay decimated after the Union Army's three-month siege in 1863 spilled the blood of tens of thousands.

Lucy, Sophia's daughter and my grandmother Dorothy's great-grandmother—a tall, dark-skinned woman with red hair, freckles, and blue-green eyes—would eventually move 90 miles back to Vicksburg and open a boardinghouse and saloon on Levee Street. Lucy's saloon made up the cornerstone of the old railyard in the heart of the city, a handsome brick "roundhouse" commanding the area like a castle keep. Its steam-driven turntable could heft a grand locomotive, turn it around, and set it gently on steel arteries that reached as far as Texas.

Lucy's saloon served workers who were building the railroads that would force a rural South into an industrial future. Her saloon, boardinghouse, work ethic, and eye for business were so respected by these rugged men, she earned enough to purchase a home. Lucy's two-story house still stands at 700 Locust Street.

In the aftermath of a dark, brutal civil war, Lucy married my great-great-grandfather James Dillard Sr., another half-breed son of a slavemaster. James served as the personal slave to his White half-brother with the same first name, James Hardy. Toward the end of the war, James Hardy would enlist in the Confederate Army. James Dillard would not take his father's last name.

James, my great-great-uncle, the White slave master's legitimate son, would be brutally killed during the siege of Vicksburg defending the slavery of his own brother. Despite this, my great-great-grandfather was distraught at the loss of his brother. Illiterate, traumatized by the ferocious gunfire, disease, and starvation, he was now left completely alone to fend for himself after the fall of Vicksburg. Someone would eventually tell me that, no matter what you think about the evils of slavery, it was a relationship among people.

I have sometimes pondered that my great-great-grandfather and great-great-uncle lived at the end of the razor's edge of slavery, where their brotherhood forced them into an unholy, demonic, and diabolical brotherly bond. To this day I share a similar bond with my White-passing brother, Joshua. The pain of our survival, and the bondage of our childhood at the hands of a distinguished-looking private-navy commander sailing around North Africa and the Caribbean that has torn us apart.

I wonder what could be more ridiculous, my mental and physical bondage under the crush of a sci-fi navy commander, or two brothers forced into a slave and master relationship denying their brotherly love.

To this day, Joshua and I struggle to know each other. Through his doctrine, Hubbard would turn families upon families, but rather than separating them by race, he would separate brother and sister, mother and son, father and daughter if anyone dared criticize the movement.

Alone after the war, James, my mixed-race great-great-grandfather, fell into drinking. He was trying to survive in a world where he had no place, neither White nor Black. It was not unlike my life of gunfire, disease, abandonment, and illiteracy. I was a mixed-race child conditioned with strange ideas in the belly of a cult that would leave me with no place in the world. It made me a slave more than one hundred years after my ancestors were free. To be raised a chattel slave in the American South is also to fill one with strange and unholy ideas, whether owned by a slavemaster or the property of a sci-fi mothership.

X

Before opening her bustling saloon, my great-great-aunt Lucy had trained as a nurse. With the business doing well, she decided to moonlight at a Vicksburg hospital to earn even more funds to create opportunities for her son. Lucy loved the way that medical doctors were treated in her hospital, with great reverence and respect. She desperately longed for her son, my great-grandfather and namesake, James Benjamin Dillard Jr., to have a sense of value, and asked an elderly White physician who always tipped his fine hat to her and treated her kindly to mentor him in medicine.

Something that is not commonly known is that race was invented in the 1700s as a lie to ensure forced labor in the Americas. Before 1500, English-speaking Europeans using the word "race" meant a clan who usually shared a family name, or ancestral ties to a certain area of land; it didn't have anything to do with skin color, language, or culture. We have to "other" people in order to own them. Then we can do anything to them and still sleep at night.

The White doctor with the fine hat would end up laying a path for an alternate future that I would never have, as it was taken from me by Hubbard before my birth. The doctor gave my great-grandfather, James Jr., stacks of books to read on medicine, history, and philosophy. When the time came for him to become a man, James Jr. chose to formally pursue an education that should have been impossible. The now elderly White doctor urged him to consider attending one of two Black colleges: Rust College or Meharry Medical School. Eventually my great-grandfather would move his family and set up his practice in a small Tennessee town.

PHOENIX RISING

Over an era, my family would send generations of its children to Rust College as a catalyst of possibility.

In the poor Black town of Henning, Tennessee, my grandmother Dorothy, then just a child, would watch her elegant father, James, the town doctor, ride his horse with a leather medical bag swinging from the saddle as he galloped away to a house call. Heroic like Zorro, he treated people in trade for chickens, goats, other livestock, and crops.

In those days, my grandmother would walk to school with her sister, Lucy, and her schoolmate—Lucy's close friend. Years later my grandmother would marry my grandfather and, years after that, keep me from being destroyed. Lucy's schoolmate friend would go on to win a Pulitzer for *Roots* and collaborate on *The Autobiography of Malcolm X*. His name was Alex Haley. This cliché of the Black grandmother swooping in to save the poor Black grandson is one that to this day makes me sick, because I feel that it truly diminishes who this woman actually was. She was a monastic humanist with infinite compassion and empathy for all. There was a stoic rhythm and discipline to how she lived for all of her one hundred years.

My grandfather Roy was born in 1915 as World War I raged into madness in Europe. After falling in love with my grandmother at college and eventually braving the border at Laredo, the two would find themselves in Mexico City on their adventurous honeymoon.

The famous Spanish conquistador Hernán Cortés had been in these same ancient mountains nearly four hundred years earlier, seeking conquest. In 1940, Roy and Dorothy stood on the same lands having *economically* conquered the physical enslavement of their own people twenty years before the beginning of the Civil Rights movement.

In an ironic twist, only twenty-six years before Cortés was deep into the territory of Mexico, Spain had furiously wrested its own freedom from the Black Moors of North Africa. It seems as though conquering people has nothing to do with color but what humans have always done to humans despite being one biological family.

Roy and Dorothy hiked up Grasshopper Hill in Mexico City's center and then to Chapultepec Castle on top, once the home of Emperor

Maximillian of Austria. Just four hundred years before that, it was a place where Aztec kings held human sacrifices.

They had previously gone to the bullfights where majestic black bulls were sacrificed. Dorothy had seen a young matador gored by a bull. As the crowd cheered, Dorothy shivered in horror. On the hike up Grasshopper Hill, Roy told Dorothy a story of the one time where he had felt a similar horror.

Roy's mother was married to an esteemed Black doctor (another lineage that would be shrouded from me since birth). She had an expensive car and she loved to speed. One day a White cop pulled them over and was so angry at seeing two Blacks, a woman and a young boy, behind the wheel of this refined automobile that the officer remanded her key and forced her into the back of his squad car. The officer told twelve-year-old Roy not to move, then sped off with his mother, leaving Roy alone, trembling in horror.

Sitting in the car alone, those moments that passed felt like an eternity. In the height of his fear, the small boy reached over to the seat next to him, unlatched the leather case nestled under the fur coat his mother had left behind, and lifted out the one thing that meant the most to him in the world—his violin. Roy began to play. In this moment, Roy vowed that he would use every resource in his life, every cent his family had ever earned, in every opportunity he was ever given to never have this experience again.

Like the matador, when Roy entered the arena of life, he would choose to fight, and he vowed that he would never be gored like the matador. Through education, inherited wealth, his ceaseless work ethic as a physician, the power and support of his loving partner—my grandmother Dorothy—and his inexorable charisma, he would defy the human defilements of his Blackness. Roy would all but accomplish this. He would be the master and king of his own life, but this would not be enough to save his grandson that he would never see born.

I would have no idea where I came from. My past, my present, and my future would need to be deleted if I was going to be owned.

Chapter 5

ANGELS

V ery good, kids," Carl said, grinning triumphantly, like he had just swallowed a small animal. His yellowing teeth matched his shirt.

Carl promised that since it was January, and the movement should have the planet "cleared" by June—meaning every human on Earth would be freed of mental trauma through machine-based counseling—then we kids could see our parents again.

We cheered.

I didn't know what a cleared planet was. I didn't know what a mind was. Four and a half years into my cauterizing baptism of fire with little human touch, rations of detached love, and aggressive, militaristic care-takers, June sounded a million years away. My birthday was coming up in June. I would be five. I would see my parents again for my birthday. Carl was a navy-uniform-clad officer who was in charge of drilling movement doctrine into us kids.

"Structure Chart!" Carl shouted. "What is it?"

"Structure Chart!" one hundred kids shouted back in chorus. There was nothing louder than children shouting in unison. Our high-pitched voices piled on top of each other, amplified by the large room, the one where they now sell lavish fireplaces to punters on the west side of Los Angeles, and where we were drilled on the movement's massive, byzantine structure chart that explained its chain of command via "Chinese Schooling."

A form of Chinese education Hubbard had appropriated, "Chinese School" was meant to teach people how to memorize and retain things quickly through repetition. The pseudo-navy adults in their navy uniforms stood in front of the class, while a collection of abandoned children gathered every day in a room with peeling paint and sagging water-damaged ceilings, eagerly repeating concepts over and over to remember them verbatim. It was the beginning of the perfect mechanization of our childminds.

When Communist revolutionary Mao Tse-Tung led the Cultural Revolution in 1960s China, he placed his fanatic army in charge of schools. Militarized, politically zealous teachers led drills with the class answering in unison. Only what the workers needed to know to be productive was taught. History before the revolution did not exist.

This was our educational model.

I was spoken to as a fully formed adult. Like an animal, I would never be taught to bathe, shower, or brush my teeth. From three years old I was never given clean sheets or bedding—I never had any concept of sleeping on anything other than a bare mattress. It was private navy doctrine that if the dorms got too dirty, they pasted a "Pigs' Room" sign on the door. They raised us like little piggies and then labeled us little piggies.

Joshua was in a different dorm. He was two years older and seemed like he was a million miles away. He was not happy with his circumstances, and I didn't get the idea he liked me very much. He has since told me as an adult that he loves me, but he doesn't want to know me because I'm a reminder of what happened to us. The reality is, outside of the occasional trips to New York, I didn't see him much. Often he would pass me in the halls of the dorm and bump me with his shoulder or look right through me as if I wasn't there.

Every morning at 6:00 AM, kids aged five to fourteen lined up for roll call. We were in Hubbard's Junior Navy: a collection of derelict teenagers

ANGELS

and children being trained in an LA slum to be members of the movement's elite naval militia. We wanted to join the adults. Some kids joined at eight. Others stayed in the Junior Navy until fifteen. It was *Lord of the Flies* in the burning heart of Hollywood.

In front of our "class," Carl looked like some twisted outcast from the Monkees with his 1970s haircut, navy blue–black slacks, white military shirt yellowed by cigarettes and sweat, and black military tie covered in lint. He smelled of Marlboros. I wanted to please him with my performance in the class so he would notice me.

X

I wasn't a child soldier in the Congo or Sierra Leone, but none of us were socialized with structure or love. The adults were interchangeable and distracted. We didn't have the consistency of parents, or an awareness of our relation to a family like most kids. Us kids had each other, and we had the doctrine we studied, even though most of us couldn't write it.

Joshua was an apparition who lived in a separate dorm and bullied me when we were together. I was a people pleaser and tried to make the best of it. Joshua got angry and rebelled. Sometimes I think his was the more rational response. I saw him as somebody that lashed out at me to quell his anger of abandonment. I don't really know him.

We ate in the industrial "galley." The big kids would often take food away from the smaller kids, leaving us with nothing but scraps. The food was slop, and there weren't any desserts. To this day, when I see my older brother and we have dinner or lunch, sometimes he wraps one arm around his plate, protecting his food—something I saw him do every day at The Red Brick Building. Every day, meals were a form of violation, pressure, and paranoia. You just didn't know when something bad was going to happen.

There was a constant physical threat for not being invisible. Either an older kid, or an officer of the child's pseudo-navy, would threaten you, or have you engaged in endless cleaning of something that could not be cleaned. The doom that I felt from the physical threats that never came was worse than the threats themselves. I constantly felt on edge. Anything could happen. The constant heat haze of Los Angeles blurred everything, people and buildings bending and shifting like apparitions. I wondered, *What am I doing here?* I was five, then I was six, and I was flooded with the constant feeling that I had been born in the wrong place.

Once or twice a week, my mother, who was always off doing important movement work, came to visit me with rationed moments of love. She gave me treats and candy as we sat in the expanse of the room that would eventually hold luxury fireplaces. After an hour, I wouldn't want her to leave. The nannies physically restrained me from her naval skirt as she walked away, back to her vital post. I violently cried, screamed, and begged for her mercy not to leave me alone in the dorms. Tears flooded my cheeks. My throat tightened. My entire body shook. After she was gone for ten minutes, I would go numb. I felt the earth falling away under my feet as I clung to her. She was the only way to avoid tumbling back into the black.

X

The Red Brick Building remained a sweatbox.

I'd only known the odor of greasy, unwashed bodies and the lingering pungency of rank bed sheets that were never cleaned, strewn on top of the congealed, oily, sheened, urine-stained bare mattresses where all of us future leaders of the movement slept. Measles, chicken pox, and other viruses, along with hepatitis, swept through the dorms. Whenever we got sick we were sent to "sick-rooms" alone or sometimes with other kids. Each time we knew we were bad and we caused being sick to happen to ourselves. We would have to be good and not get sick if we were going to, one day, work for the movement.

Every couple of months, Paco would show up like an apparition, grab me and Joshua in his van, and drive all over the city on days when his work was light. Paco knew everybody, and everybody knew me—*his* son. Every once in a while, Paco would bring boxes of day-old donuts from a Filipino

ANGELS

donut shop to The Red Brick Building for all the young "cadets." It was an overwhelming burst of sugar that broke us out of our mental prison, if only for a few hours.

On a few of these day-releases, Paco took us to kung fu movies in downtown Los Angeles. On the giant movie screen in the decaying grandeur of a Chinatown theater that had been a palace in the 1920s, I watched movies like the Shaw Brothers' and Golden Harvest's *Master of the Flying Guillotine* and Bruce Lee's *Fists of Fury*. Riveted, I was thrilled by Lee's speed and mastery of his own body. These movies invaded me. Many were about a child suffering years of brutal training to become an extraordinary fighter. I related to them instantly. Even in Chinatown, it was hard to relax. We would always return to the machine.

We were completely unaware that we were being raised as a vessel for labor. I know of three kids there with me at this building who have committed suicide as adults. I know there are more. I can't bear to look.

THE ORGANIZATION OF CHILDREN IN LAND-BASED UNITS
CHILDREN AS ASSETS

"In the American society exists a degraded contempt for children. Adults regard them as dear little cute things . . . this attitude is not allowed [in the Hubbard Private Navy]."

CS-7 4 L. Ron Hubbard Commodore

X

In the movement, there were a few kids like me who were mixed. There was a half-Filipino, half-White kid named Casavias. He was my friend. His father, upon returning with scars from Vietnam, went straight to work on Hubbard's *Apollo* in North Africa—the original flagship in the private navy's flotilla of boats working to save the planet—as the commander's personal valet. There he was, while Casavias and I were being stored until we grew big enough to work for the commander, in the searing sun in the middle of East Hollywood.

Casavias was lean, gentle, and sweet. He looked like one of the tiny young boys training to be a kung fu master. We were completely unaware that we were the children of the *Apollo*. The movement would eventually force him, in his early twenties, to receive an adult adoption to hide him from his mother and father for more than two decades.

When Casavias's Filipino Vietnam vet father, the former valet and close friend of Hubbard, left, he attacked the movement so vehemently, it was the only way the leadership could tolerate Casavias staying—he had been left behind in the movement when his parents broke free.

There was a White kid with blue eyes named Seb—short for Sebastian. He had the most triangular head I have ever seen on a human. It was unreal—an enormous flat head tapering geometrically down to a pointed chin that looked synthetic. Atop his flat head was a tuft of black hair that made his eyes shine like jewels. He always wanted to do stuff, so I stuck to him like glue and kept him close. Like Casavias, Seb was sweet and gentle and luminous with a soft, warm kindness that I craved.

X

Later that year, when I was still five, I was sent down the street to the Gothic Van Ness Elementary School, where I was put into a class for children with learning disabilities. We never studied anything; we just learned posture and colored in books. Every afternoon at 3:00, members from the movement would come get me and walk me back to The Red Brick Building.

Toward the end of my time at Van Ness Elementary, a teacher observed that I wasn't wearing underwear. One of the workers walked me back to the dorm, telling me that I would need to have underwear if I wanted to be in school. Passing through the double doors, I rambled back to the bunk-lined room. I took a corner and nearly collided with Louise Vikkers, who was coming out of the bathroom. She was the nanny in charge of me.

"What are you doing here?" she raged.

ANGELS

43

"They sent me home because I don't have underwear," I nervously whispered with a frog in the back of my throat.

Louise was a wiry, sandy-blonde woman with skin too fair for Los Angeles, and intricate 1970s braids that fell from her armpits. She shook with anger and told me that it was my fault that I didn't have any underwear. I was five years old, and I believed her. My body shook with nerves.

"That's not okay, you losing your underwear," Louise hissed.

I don't think I ever owned any underwear.

That evening Louise told me that I would not be allowed to sleep until I found my underwear. She came back into the bunk-lined room, with its stink of childbodies, every hour until two in the morning to see if I'd found them. This was the latest I'd ever been up in my life, and the dark felt like an eternity. There was no way out.

The heavy door at the end of the dank, cavernous room would open, and Louise's profile sliced the rectangle of light created by the fluorescents burning in the hallway. Even in dark silhouette, I could see her pinched face and her hawkish eyes laser-focused on me. I hadn't found anything. Disgusted, Louise sharply receded behind the door, and I felt myself shrink. It was only a matter of time before Louise's beak appeared in the harsh fluorescence of the door and she glared at me again.

I felt that this could go on for days, so I slipped down among the bunks to the floor and crept to the next towering row of bunk beds. I went into a drawer owned by Sander, who was quietly sleeping, and stole a pair of his underwear.

An hour later, Louise poked her bird nose through the door. I showed her Sander's underwear. "Well done," she said with a smile, her eyes brightening, and the door closed again for good. I was able to go to sleep. I felt too exhausted for guilt or remorse. She never questioned how I magically found underwear at four in the morning, but events like this— strangeness, with no parents—were life in The 1920s Gothic Red Brick Building.

X

Life was also becoming, for me, an absence of sound.

One day as I was walking down a 1970s Melrose Avenue in front of The Red Brick Building, brightly chromed cars growled past in both directions. Each time a sun-bleached car rolled past, it pushed hot air and fumes over me so that I felt the heat wash over my skin. Something was missing from the habitat, though: the backfiring of the cars. It had been a constant soundtrack for almost as long as I had been alive. Now it was disappearing.

Around this time, I went with my mother and brother for another visit to my grandmother's. Back in Westchester County again, my grandmother told my mother that she didn't think I could hear.

"Dorothy, I know he's faking it," my mother argued, claiming that I could indeed hear. "I can prove it to you."

My mother quietly whispered in my grandmother's ear twenty feet away from me: "Don't tell Jamie we're all going out for ice cream and cake."

Because the infection was causing mucus to clog in my Eustachian tubes, my hearing would come and go.

"I want ice cream!" I yelled.

"You see?" my mother replied.

"I'm sure nothing's wrong, Rosalinde," my grandmother said to my mother. "But let's go see Lucille. She would love to see you anyway." My grandmother had a way of getting her way without ever making someone feel forced. She had a way of standing up for me and my body when no one else did.

These visits to Westchester were complicated, though. They were thrilling and different and I felt loved there, but the dread was constant as well. From the moment my brother and I would arrive, we would be thinking about going back to the machine. Even in these deep reprieves, we couldn't escape the roar of the machine hovering above us, suffocating us.

X

We drove to the next town over, to a small craftsman home on a quiet street in New Rochelle, New York, with 1960s additions.

ANGELS

Dr. Lucille C. Gunning, a tall, skinny, older, dark-skinned Jamaican woman, peered into my ears with a medical flashlight. It felt cold to the touch. Dr. Gunning smiled and said I was doing well. She then told my grandmother to immediately take me to the hospital an hour away in New York City. I'd known Lucille as a family friend who had worked for my grandfather just after medical school. She had also treated my mother when she was a child and developed Type 1 diabetes at twelve. I would not know until after she died that Lucille was a nationally renowned pediatrician and innovator in children's sickle-cell anemia and pediatric cancer. In 2012, she was honored along with New York state senator Suzie Oppenheimer as a Champion of Change by the Westchester Black Women's Political Caucus. I would be deaf today if not for Lucille. Angels.

The next morning, I woke after surgery. My tonsils and adenoids were gone.

"He probably won't be able to hear normally again—we just don't know," I heard the hospital doctor say as my throat and ears were sharply burning as if small daggers were being poked into the side of my head.

The doctor told me I would have to wear Silly Putty in my ears for protection, as the drainage tubes in my ears could not get wet: no showers or swimming for years—for me, a lifetime—without Silly Putty. Cartilage takes a long time to regrow. I believed with complete certainty, based on what Hubbard had said about bad things happening to people, that I had done this to myself.

X

Once we were back in Los Angeles, I rarely ever saw my mother. Eventually, she had an apartment, a single-room studio in our decaying building. At one point, to the great relief of my brother and me, she gave us a key. This tiny room, with its musty water-stained walls and thick, dirty shag carpeting permanently cloaked under a layer of crud, was a place where we could escape, be by ourselves, and even watch TV outside of the chaos of the dormitory and its angry, boiling, junior navy kids.

CBS was airing reruns of *Star Trek* in the afternoons, and we spent months watching Captain Kirk, Bones, and Spock battling Klingons and visiting strange planets. I was captivated by Spock's logic; Vulcans were superhuman, impervious to fear. They didn't react emotionally or get sick. I wanted to be a Vulcan. I would constantly look at my reflection in my mother's worn bathroom mirror for signs that my ears were growing pointed like Spock's. My ears grew pointy as I got older; I believed I willed them to change.

Every movement office in the world had a box where you could stuff a written letter to Hubbard. The same was true for the junior navy offices in The Red Brick Building on Melrose. I could barely write, so I begged my mother, in our little time we had together, to help me write him letters, so I could stuff them into the box.

One humid late-summer day, Hubbard wrote back. When I held his letter in my small hands, I felt so appreciative that he'd taken the time to write me. I understood that my life had to be hard, so Mr. Hubbard and my mom could do their work. I had written to ask him if he knew who my parents were. The great man wrote that he didn't know my mom but knew who my dad was. He told me that he knew who I was, that I was a good boy, who was "in-ethics." I burned. I was doing my part in saving the world. It was signed with his original signature, *Ron*.

My mother's diabetes had developed in 1957, when she was twelve and was told that if she did not force insulin every day for the rest of her life, she would die. In her medicine cabinet, she kept rubbing alcohol for the syringes she injected into herself every day to manage the condition. One day, my brother and I took the alcohol and our mother's matches for her cigarettes, created elaborate designs on the bathroom floor, and then lit them. They flared into beautiful sculptures of fire before disintegrating instantly as the rubbing alcohol flashed and burned out. I felt such a sense of joy and wonder watching the flames rise up, dance on the grimy floor, and vanish in the dusky light of her tiled 1920s bathroom.

Our fires were discovered. Joshua and I were ordered into public spankings. Through a written executive order for severe infractions of

ANGELS

Hubbard's naval code, parents were ordered to publicly spank their children—the children they never saw—naked on stage in front of the kids of the entire Red Brick Building on Melrose. The parents didn't want to do it, and the spanked kids writhed and protested with visceral humiliation. We were too young to process what was going on in front of us—our only recourse was laughter.

Here we were, one hundred kids laughing at the pain of another child being beaten. Wide-eyed, our swollen childfaces looked on, transfixed to the stage in our inability to comprehend what was going on in front of us. Kids roared with uncontrollable laughter, some of us with tears rolling down our cheeks. We jeered with monstrous excitement as our bloated eyes and puffed cheeks and faces morphed into cartoonish, oversized caricature. We walked in with terror before the laughter began.

I sat with my mother and brother in the office with Jess, the teen commander of the naval children, as he quietly and slowly explained to my mother in front of us that she would be performing a public spanking.

She refused.

"It isn't going to happen," she said.

It's the only time in my life I remember my mom taking a stand for me.

As I sat in a beat-up folding chair, awaiting my fate while they talked, I spotted the large ornamented wooden letterbox, out of place in its polished mahogany luster, placed neatly on a desk by itself next to a wall with a picture of a rotund Hubbard sitting at a typewriter above it, wearing a Pepsi Rolex watch, and a large bronze bust of the distinguished commander to its right. A lone cockroach emerged from the gap between the table and the wall. I thought, *That's where my letters go to the great man.* The roach scurried through the large open slot where the letters were pushed in.

The weeks that went by felt like an eternity—time moves slowly when you're five. I was terrified that they would find someone else to do the spanking or persuade my mother to change her mind. I was far more scared at what seemed like the inevitable degradation of being naked in front of one hundred other children than I was at being beaten.

A beating that never came. Angels.

Chapter 6

THE INVASION

I n my dreams, the sky burned red. Explosions tore an airfield to pieces. Men raced through plumes of fire toward death, to large industrial guns; unseen Japanese planes growled wild above the jungle canopy, spitting streams of hot metal into the night sky. The Earth rocked and the jungle split apart like flesh—

As a child I always had vivid dreams.

When I was seven, Joshua and I were moved out of The Red Brick Building to dorms across the street from the decaying, sprawling, former Cedars of Lebanon hospital. It covered two massive city blocks, surrounded by strip malls and slums.

Here, across the street from the derelict hospital painted dark bone and sepia, we had sheets that felt like soft sandpaper. It was a welcome reprieve from The Red Brick Building on Melrose with its bedsheets that went years without washing; bare mattresses; constant reek of urine; and the dank, earthy tang of mold. Elvis Presley had had emergency dental work at this old hospital in the 1950s. Now it was our new MOTHERSHIP.

Conditions weren't better—the shiny, congealed mattresses stayed the same, and there were *more* roaches—but it was a change, and change wasn't a feeling I was used to. I had been told years earlier that the planet would be clear in months. It wasn't. Now I'd long given up hope that it would be cleared any time soon so I could see my mother. In this new dormitory, we still rarely saw our parents as they ran around the decaying industrial hospital in their disheveled blue naval uniforms. This seemed completely normal to me. They might as well have been in a parallel universe, preoccupied in their mission, living in the spleen of Hollywood.

Our childworld was a twisted version of *Peanuts* where we created our own universe of comfort, war, and friendship. The adults' voices were something *other*. Since we weren't in school, I and my friends spent our days secretly breaking locks and trespassing into barricaded parts of the hospital not yet excavated of leftover medical devices, equipment, aquariums, or cages. We heard whispers of leftover cadavers in undiscovered parts of the ancient building. A small band of us broke into locked parts of The Old Industrial Hospital that would not be renovated for years. I'd never seen a place with so many identical hallways, ripped and worn from years of foot traffic. Monkeys and rats had been kept there for experiments. It was thrilling to imagine that the beasts who'd lived in those cages had escaped and were lurking deep in the depths.

Down the stairs and out the back door of the Advanced Division was the ancient pit that used to house the hospital's large apes, chimpanzees and orangutans, for experiments. It was bigger than half an Olympic swimming pool and two to three stories deep, filled with abandoned cages and baking in the LA sun. Behind the pit lay the highly secure archive files that held the machine-based-counseling folders of doctrine members with their endless detailed notes of phantasmagorical reincarnations. Just past the pit was a set of stairs that eventually led into the catacombs of tunnels running beneath the buildings.

On the other side of the street were locked industrial rooms connected by tunnels where we broke in. The rooms were often filled with massive glass jars, test tubes, flasks, and tanks holding strange pink forms of animals suspended in formaldehyde. Every lock our band of friends broke and every door we breached held the promise of an exotic 1920s carnival act, with glowing jars with an odorous sweet-and-sour tang, a

THE INVASION

half-woman, half-snake, and men that were hybrids of animals. Seduced by the strange, we peered into weirdly shaped vessels, as floating, swollen animals, distorted by curved glass, were frozen in time; animals we could recognize—pigs, frogs, even large snakes—but just a little bit bloated and deformed, like they'd evolved on another world. They had the perfect appearance of boiled chicken. This was powerful for a childmind marinating in the promise of spaceships and walking on other worlds. Across from the new mothership, I was also now an experiment.

X

In the new dormitory, I shared a room with three steel bunk beds lined up in parallel against the far wall. My bare mattress was in the closet with the foot side facing into the room, perpendicular to the other beds. I liked having a little more darkness when the searchlights came through the windows at night. Roaches scurried across the stained carpet. Even in the dimness I could see the plumbing-stained walls. My bed felt like a protective cocoon shielded by the closet so any threat could only approach me from one side, whether it was a raging kid or a hostile nanny. It made me feel safe.

Everything was shared. The shower room, which I never used, was an old 1930s bathroom. At night, the sounds of honking horns and screeching cars, with gunfire popping in the distance, rocked me to sleep like a lullaby.

Those evenings, the police helicopters of Los Angeles constantly hovered outside, invading our child dormitory with shaking bass and blasts of light. There were gang shootings just south of us, and it seemed as if the helicopters were always looking for the perp. All the outside chaos faded into something we barely noticed. This was the only world we knew; it always had been and would always be.

"Hey, kid. Kid."

A voice in the darkness of the slum dorm. I awoke to my stale bare mattress.

52

CHILD X

It was midnight. The arm of a male nanny reached into the closet where my bed was and roughly jostled me. I gasped awake, breathing in the stench of the stale steel bunk bed. "You have to get up. They're coming."

Who was coming? I was raised on descriptions of spaceships. My mother was somewhere else training for a mission. My eyes adjusted. I saw other nannies violently rustling my friend Sam Schultz and the other boys awake. They grumbled and protested but were wrenched to their feet.

I looked toward the door, at the sliver of green-tinged light that gleamed under it from the hallway. Hurried shadows stomped back and forth; there were banging and unintelligible shouts from down the hall. The shouts were growing louder. There could be aliens out there beyond that door.

Suddenly three sharp bangs crashed into our door. I jumped, electrified. I didn't notice the firm arm lifting me from the sparse mattress that made up my bed.

"Get your shoes on." My arm burned where the nanny squeezed it.

I was just finishing up lacing my high-tops when the nanny hauled me to my feet and jostled me toward the door where Sam and the others were nervously waiting.

"Stay quiet and stay together," the nanny hissed, opening the door. My seven-year-old mind couldn't process why they were marching us across the street to The Old Industrial Hospital at midnight. This had never happened before. Something was horribly wrong.

The air smelled of burnt rubber as we were herded across the street. There was dim light inside the huge structures in front of us, with flashlight beams darting around like hungry fireflies. Something was different but I didn't know what it was. They stopped us all in a large group for a moment before the Brutalist behemoth. Then we were quickly moving again, toward the front entrance of Lebanon Hall, a stream of a hundred kids under a balmy purple Los Angeles sky.

We stepped into the foyer of the Lebanon Hall entrance of The Old Industrial Hospital into men who wore suits in sober browns and grays, only differentiated by their ties. I had never seen so many adults in one place,

THE INVASION

53

not even in the galley at mealtime. They moved in groups of five and six, talking loudly in hurried coordination. In my mind I called these strange men "the suits."

Beams of flashlights darted through the side rooms, into bathrooms, into closets, into any drawer they could find; they shined into the crevices and under the uncleaned mattresses in the dormitories.

"Jesus, God," one of the suited men stammered as he came downstairs and saw us, his flashlight helping him avoid a roving cockroach or two as he hit the bottom of the stairs. "They got kids living here?" We were moved so quickly, I never saw the man's face, but I could tell from his voice and reaction that what he saw wasn't what he'd expected to see; still, the suit sounded nice.

The nannies led us into the next massive room, the galley where all the crews ate powdered eggs. We ate at rows of long plastic folding tables on one side and an array of stainless-steel food warmers and steel platforms jutting out of the side large enough to slide a food tray down. They huddled us past the food warmers to the far end of the galley next to the officers' mess.

The suits poured into the galley a hundred kids, stunned and dreary-eyed, having no idea what these men could possibly be looking for and why they were here after midnight. The nannies led us further into the bowels of The Old Industrial Hospital's main buildings, into a large stairwell that could have been the size of an apartment. They had us stop halfway up and down the stairs; we stood quietly, enjoying this strange kind of attention that we never got but craved.

The nannies stood around us silently, like statues, watching the suits enter through the foyer, a wave of gray and brown, carrying cardboard boxes, the beams of their flashlights darting over us. As I stared at these men, I wondered if they were lean, alien invaders wearing tight, fleshy man-suits.

"Harper," another suit shouted, "there's more up here. Bring your team up."

As he passed, his hand snatched something roughly square and black from inside his blazer, and I saw a stunning flash of a gold shield with a bird resting on top. The man had a badge. The nannies at the top of the stairs saw it and stepped aside, letting the suits swarm into the dormitories above. I looked back down the stairs and saw Sam staring at the men piling upstairs, his eyes wide with adventure.

More suited men were walking past the shredding machines, bringing in boxes. A man in a gray suit, chewing gum, stood nearby with his hands on his hips, pushing back his blazer. I could see the black butt of a gun poking out from under his armpit. His eyes looked into mine. He smiled.

The othering of foreign human beings is baked into our biology. A teacher and mentor would tell me years later that every tribe of humans on the planet had some way of visually identifying themselves to other members of their tribe. When the Romans landed on the isles off northwestern Europe, the ones they called Britannia, they came face-to-face with fearsome natives. They carried great spears, dressed head-to-toe in furs, and their faces painted with woad—the deep blue face paint they made from a plant that grew wild in the hills.

Humans existed for a long time in scarcity. Water, game, herbs for medicine, berries for subsistence, and shelter were hard to gain. We needed to know who we were supposed to share resources with and who not to and we grew hardwired to recognize tribal members visually. You need a bias to survive. However, on this night, these kind men with badges and guns felt familiar and good and somehow, I wanted them to stay, but I didn't know why.

We moved all night, a hundred of us kids, from grand room to grand room, from hallway to hallway, eventually laughing and chattering. Sam made faces in the slashes of moonlight that tore through the darkness of The Old Industrial Hospital. It felt novel, even exhilarating—like a game, far different from our daily languor.

After hours of this, we were moved back into the galley around daylight. We'd been constantly moving for six hours and had no idea what was going on. The suits seemed fascinated with everything inside the decaying grandeur of The Old Hospital.

THE INVASION

I had just been part of the largest FBI raid in American history. The invasion was in response to the largest domestic spying campaign ever perpetrated on the US government by our movement, carried out by my caretakers. "Operation Snow White" is what they called it. They engaged in spying, wiretapping, blackmail, and extortion.

These days I find it incredible that a man claiming to have the key to freeing the world sailed the Middle Passage, Atlantic, and Caribbean. His "playground" was the same Middle Passage where different ships once sailed toward the genocide and displacement of my ancestors.

The fifty thousand documents the FBI discovered, spurred by the religious navy captain who mostly kept his distance out at sea and called himself "Commander," seemed completely normal in my world. Even to this day, when I think of that night and so many other events, it all seems rather banal. In that twenty-one-hour raid that would uncover countless illegal activities, it was the movement's framing of a woman who survived the Holocaust as a baby, journalist Paulette Cooper, that endures. She simply wrote a book about them that they didn't appreciate.

This invasion would send eight members of the movement's secret police, ominously known as "The Guardians Office," including Mary Sue, the wife of the enigmatic commander, to prison for years. Mary Sue fell on her sword so that the elusive leader would become only an unindicted co-conspirator in his mission to save the planet.

The next day, all of us children went back to being penned so we could be grown until we were old enough to help.

The next day, it was as if nothing had ever happened.

Chapter 7

BLACK FIGHTERS

[27 YEARS BEFORE THE BABY FACTORY] Roy struck a wooden match. The end of his cigar sizzled under the flame, filling the canteen with thick gray smoke, heavy with chocolatey Indian tobacco and clove. Roy stared at his cards with a half-smile on his face and fire in his eyes.

At night my grandfather would play poker in the Burmese jungle. He sat with a mixed group of pilots and mechanics at a rickety metal card table in the airfield canteen in Chungking, Burma, the wool of his olive-green uniform itchy against his skin. One of the boys, a lean hawk-faced mechanic from Ohio called "Sticks," always brought imported Indian cigars from the street kids hawking them in Rangoon. The wartime barter system of the airfield meant that it was in the flyboys' best interests to keep the mechanics happy. Decent tobacco greased the wheels that guaranteed their planes were fixed first.

The radio was blaring Rimsky-Korsakov's "Song of India" when Tokyo Rose broke in, cooing, "This is your Japanese sister, the voice of truth, with our special program for our friends in the South Pacific. I hope you're finding your jungle stay not too bad, considering the climate and all . . . what your superiors are making you boys do, all for a tiny road in a country that none of your sweethearts have ever heard of."

58   CHILD X

"Turn her off already," Sticks groaned, pulling a stiff snort of cognac he'd paid five packs of cigarettes for. "Let's get back to the game."

In the rugged mountains beyond the base, under cover of darkness, Japanese soldiers had barricaded the road. There would be no supplies until five hundred pounds of bombs again cleared the gravel path. The war in Burma was measured in yards gained and lost—like a football match as a game of death. Roy chewed on his cigar, then asked for a card, hoping to turn his two pair into a full house. "You boys take care, now," Tokyo Rose chirped, "the jungle doesn't care who it eats."

There were only two seasons in Burma, dust and mud. Every piece of equipment and every thatch-roofed jungle hut that passed for a barracks was caked in mud-orange slime. The scent of sweat, aviation fuel, and cardamom swallowed the barracks. Cardamom was everywhere: grown in the jungle, eaten in the food, perspiring from the skin, microparticles floating in the thick, wet air. The Army had managed to carve out an 1,100-foot airstrip from an expanse of wild thicket, just east of "the Hump"—the pilots' nickname for the high peaks of the Eastern Himalayas that bordered China, India, Burma, and Tibet. The airfield afforded Roy and his brothers in arms—a cadre of American men who, in the deadly jungle of Southeast Asia, couldn't afford to be segregated—a touch of civilization.

Roy was the only Black surgeon in his unit, so even though he was part of the esteemed Tuskegee Airmen, most of his day-to-day colleagues were White. My grandfather could never see the difference. Since he made all medical decisions, the staff in the barracks honored and looked up to him with his warm charisma—seven thousand miles away from a racist America. Roy had looks, smarts, money, and means. He would never be gored.

During the heat of the day, Burmese labor gangs patched up every hole a bad landing or a Japanese mortar blasted into the airstrip. Racing above around the clock was the deep growl of P-40 Warhawks, brawny propeller-driven aircraft, heavy with bombs and six machine guns that could reduce the mostly wooden Japanese fighter planes to matchsticks. The sheer rumbling power of these airplanes, always flying in groups of

BLACK FIGHTERS

twos and fours, vibrated my grandfather's ribs as they passed overhead, ravenous for Japanese targets.

In 1937, Japan, desperate for more resources, had invaded China. Japanese armies were quickly grabbing territory all over Southeast Asia. By 1941, Americans were in Burma, a blistering-hot, mountainous jungle nation smaller than Texas, defending the Burma Road, a gravel track that ensured vital food, water, and medical supplies could get from British Burma to Chiang Kai-shek's Nationalist guerrillas in China to resist the Japanese invaders. While Nazi Germany enslaved Western Europe, the Empire of Japan continued to carve up Asia. Coal, oil, and slave labor were vital to the island nation's ability to compete with the industrial West. At the end of 1941, the Japanese had bombed the American fleet at Pearl Harbor, an offense that Americans felt could not stand. The United States immediately joined what would become World War II.

My grandfather's task was to keep the bodies of the US Army Air Corps flying and to sever the limbs of the maimed before they were sent off to Sri Lankan hospitals or home. A round from a Japanese fighter could punch a baseball-sized hole in an American pilot. But Roy mostly removed shrapnel and sewed up the wounds of the maimed. Shards of flying metal severed arteries, and my grandfather often operated on floors slick with blood.

Roy lived for years among the wails and screams of the dying, among indiscriminately broken bone and torn flesh. The brotherhood of enduring war makes skin color and even the bond of ancestral blood into a weak and watery wine. The bond of the sisterhood and brotherhood of war can become stronger than blood.

He did not notice in these moments who was White or Black.

Some of the dying were pilots who had bailed into the gnarled jungle canopy from planes on fire and spitting black oil from shot-up engines. A parachute was enough to save a man's life, but too often the dogfights happened close to the ground, without the altitude parachutes need for a gentle landing.

At night, the jungle was slithering with life. The heat of the day would subside, and the density of nature would emerge, struggling inexorably in a churn of primal survival. As the cooling of the air pressurized the jungle floor, mist rose, seeping from the ground creating a dense fog three to four feet off the ground, then dissipating and rising into the thick canopy above. There were no stars in the thick of the Burmese jungle. Few would have dared brave the wet darkness created by the ban on campfires and electric lights. Even cigars in the night air were disallowed outside of the barracks. Japanese snipers would sit alone, bivouacked in the jungle trees, waiting for unsuspecting targets.

My grandfather had never seen a banyan tree before. They dwarfed anything he'd encountered in Alabama, or Tennessee, or the deepest and darkest swamps of the South. The trees resembled gargantuan spiders fit with tentacles like some Island of Dr. Moreau mutation, digging deep into the wet earth. The gaps between the roots were big enough for a man to walk through.

A symphony of life hummed under the jungle canopy. Any rustle in the trees could be a large cat prowling, or a snub-nosed monkey on the hunt as the individual and diverse inhabitants of the jungle mirrored the war in their unceasing quest to remain alive.

Upon his return to the United States after the Allied victory, New York was thick with the same jazz clubs, swing music, and big bands that Roy had left behind several years earlier. However, something was different. The streets were buzzing with a lively excitement that could only come from the thrill of victory and the regret for those lost. In the revelry, you would hardly have known there had been a war, as amnesiac survivors unknowingly sought to regulate their nervous systems. Cigarettes, steaks, booze, and sweat were abundant, as women, down to their last pair of nylons, danced in the postwar jazz clubs with reckless abandon, swinging men who'd often returned with a thousand-yard stare. Roy was no different.

When Roy returned from the war, he would never be the same.

The Alhambra Ballroom in Harlem was so thick with cigarette smoke

BLACK FIGHTERS

that you could see pools of light caressing the coiffed hair of women and the slicked-back hair of men. As Bessie Smith sang, her voice made Roy and Dorothy forget all about the war and their time apart. The warm musical balm made them think of a forgotten Tennessee and the warmth of the Black homes of their youth.

For most of the war, prior to Roy's deployment to the jungle as a doctor and captain, his and Dorothy's social habitat was the territory between Harlem and the Commodore Hotel near Grand Central Station. They attended as many jazz clubs as existed, seeing Ella Fitzgerald, Billie Holiday, Frank Sinatra, Sara Vaughan, Cab Calloway, Nat King Cole, and Duke Ellington. This was at a time when the world's biggest stars played in densely packed small clubs, many years before Elvis and the Beatles would shepherd in the stadium that lacked the depth and intimacy of seeing lip sweat and spittle spray off the mouth of Frank Sinatra. Intimate was the beautiful, sexy world of how my grandparents consumed art before the arena. They went to opera houses, saw plays on Broadway, and yelled with victory and loss at the horse track.

After the war, Roy's cousin Amy, the young future wife of Babatunde Olatunji, started school on the East Coast, not far from New York City. Roy asked Amy about her experience in the city's jazz clubs, where her eyes flared in puzzlement.

"You've never been to Birdland?" my grandfather asked, stupefied. "We need to fix that."

Days later, the three arrived outside the club above Fifty-Second Street in Midtown to a line around the block. As they approached, the large doorman nodded at Roy and with a wide smile, said, "How many you got, Doc?"

Roy raised three fingers, and the trio floated past the velvet rope, through the doors, into the pulsating, darkened club.

Of her three sisters, my grandmother Dorothy was the lightest. A staggering beauty with movie-star good looks, pale mocha skin, and bright hazel-green eyes, she could often pass as White. Maude, with her chocolate skin, looked Black, while Lucy—the closest friend to a child Alex

Haley (who at the time was just another Black kid with a war to fight in the South)—looked completely Native American.

During the war, my great-aunt Lucy riveted ships at an industrial war plant in Alabama when she met Thomas J. Money Jr., a young lieutenant and Tuskegee Airman who, after the war, would go on to become a full colonel in the US Army Air Corps—the precursor to what is now the U.S. Air Force.

Thomas's nickname in college was "Gabe" because even though he was a Black man, his friends said he looked like Clark Gable—enough so to pass for White to get into and through Officer Training School. A proud and defiant man, Thomas, immediately upon completing OTS, went to his White commanding officers, told them he was actually Black, and demanded to be transferred to a Black unit. They obliged, and that Black unit was the famed Tuskegee Airmen.

Throughout 1943 and into 1945, the all-White US Fifteenth Air Force flew extremely dangerous bombing missions over Nazi-occupied territory. Their mission was to drop thousands of pounds of bombs on factories, oil refineries, airfields, and railyards, denying Nazi Germany the ability to supply its armies and to batter German civilians into psychological submission. Every bomb crew was expected to fly twenty-five missions before they could go home. A single mission meant there were many dangers; the air was near freezing at the high altitudes the bombers flew. Without an oxygen mask, a man would pass out and suffocate.

The Tuskegee Airmen, the "red-tails" of legend, were called that due to the bright red paint brushed onto the glistening silver tails of their P-51 Mustang fighter planes. In a hard-to-believe irony of American history, twenty years before the Civil Rights movement, Black fighters fought countless dogfights with the Nazis in the skies over Italy, defending a country in which they were not equal, made to believe and live as if they were less than human. Under the leadership of Colonel Benjamin O. Davis Jr., these Black pilots were the only airmen under relentless enemy fire to never lose a single bomber under their protection. Only Black fighters did this as White European and Americans fighter pilots in every other

BLACK FIGHTERS

63

Allied fighter group lost bombers on every run. Ironically, it was racism that would create the dread of the Black Tuskegee Airmen, who struck fear into the heart of every member of Hitler's Nazi master race. These Black fighters, with their superior skill, were known to come from nowhere, screaming out of the blinding sun as if Satan himself rode with them.

Incredibly, it was racism that drove them to develop such tremendous skill. Most Allied airmen were in the air and flying after six weeks of training, even if they'd never seen an aircraft in their life. The men of Tuskegee had to train all day, every day, for thirty-six months. And when they took to the air they flew as if every lynching, shackle, chain, and ancestral wrong propelled them through the sky with every moment in the air as an act of rage and will against the lie of White superiority.

The US military was still segregated and would never let Black pilots fly in combat; "Negroes can't see at night" was the authoritarian excuse some Army commanders used. A band of lost brothers, these Black fighters of Tuskegee never would have seen combat without a national shaming of the military and the American people, led by a defiant Eleanor Roosevelt.

Knowing they could not fight, Mrs. Roosevelt, the First Lady, visited their airbase in Tuskegee on a renegade trip to Alabama. Upon walking onto the airfield with her all-White entourage, she shocked the world by demanding to fly alone with a Black pilot, with a mischievous and innocent smile on her face, where she gently said "fuck you" to the world. The light brown man that soared with her across the Southern sky had the same light brown hue as my grandfather. She chose her moment, ensuring the press was there with cameras on her visit, shaming the US government into letting these men fight and die for a country that hated them.

The disconnect was dark.

X

In 1946, within two weeks of Roy's discharge from the Army, he and Dorothy brought their infant daughter Rosalinde, the mother who would eventually abandon me to a militaristic science-fiction movement, back home to their White Jewish Westchester County neighborhood, where they were accepted. Roy would buy a house across the street from Sidney Poitier. Rosalinde would attend the finest schools while her younger brother, Stevie, born two years later, eventually would be sent to boarding school in Switzerland.

After the war, my grandmother's brother-in-law, Thomas Money Jr., would move to Washington, DC, where he would serve for twenty years under the direct command of Benjamin O. Davis Jr., the only Black general to win the Silver Star, America's first Black four-star general, and himself the son of Benjamin O. Davis Sr., America's first Black brigadier general, and the first Black general to win the Bronze Star.

"Thomas ran that base for Benjamin," my Aunt Lucy would tell me at seven years old on a muggy, wet summer dusk as fireflies buzzed among the greenery in her front yard on a rare release to Vicksburg. "Your uncle walked silently but carried a big stick."

All I could think about, during that trip, was the dread of returning to The Mothership.

How did I, this brown boy named Jamie, end up in the internal organs of an oven-hot Los Angeles, doomed to a life of illiteracy and pain?

Chapter 8

THE BELLY OF
TWO BEASTS

My younger brother, Jono, was born just before the invasion. Upon his arrival, I was moved out of the dormitory, away from my sheltered bunk bed in the closet, and into another small, derelict one-bedroom apartment with my mother in a white brick building that sat at 4816 Fountain Avenue. It was a constant back-and-forth with ninety percent of the time, spent in the dorms. We kids nicknamed our sinister new home The Fountain. I didn't know it at seven, but this building would end up being the fountain of the pain I would carry with me for the rest of my life. It was the only tenement on the block without trees, and it caught the full force of the sun, making it dry and desolate.

Right after we moved to The Fountain, my mother seemed to vanish again. I didn't see her for almost a year. One day a pseudo-navy member came to see me in the dorm and said that he was bringing me to see my mother.

"Your mother has been granted thirty minutes to see you while she completes her rehabilitation program," he told me. In most groups, when someone is failing, they're kicked out. But Mr. Hubbard, with his deep compassion as self-proclaimed Mankind's Greatest Friend, had explained

66 CHILD X

to us that he had created a program where my mother and others like her could redeem themselves and then reenter the movement's inner core. This was Hubbard's own personal Maoist reeducation camp.

As we walked across the street to the large main compound at the abandoned Old Industrial Hospital, and walked downstairs to the industrial Deco elevator that would take us to its top floor, I wondered if I would recognize her.

The man pointed to a table that had three chairs at it and asked me to take a seat. I sat there silently just taking it all in. All the adults we were going to see wore all-black one-piece uniforms, like the coveralls a mechanic would wear, with bright armbands of golden yellow or off-white on the upper arm four inches wide. I didn't know it at the time, but these were the same armbands worn by the Jewish *kapos* that ushered the doomed into the gas chambers of Auschwitz and Birkenau.

Other adults and kids gathered around flimsy card tables, some talking to each other and hugging, all coming to visit the downtrodden, black-clad saviors who had been sentenced to years of hard labor and rehabilitation. Then they brought in my mother. As she approached me, I realized I was in a waiting room for some kind of prisoner visitation. She wore a black overall suit and black T-shirt. A faded yellow armband was wrapped around her upper right arm.

When I saw her face, it was like she had never been away, and I loved her.

"It's good to see you," she said flatly. She was there with me physically, but the rest of her was gone. I didn't feel like I was talking to anyone. It went on like this for thirty minutes. I didn't see my mother again for another year and a half.

In Hubbard's reeducation camp, anyone who was thought to have betrayed the fold was sent away, forced to wear all-black boiler suits and armbands, for anywhere from three to twelve years. Some did hard labor all day in rat-filled tunnels under The Old Industrial Hospital while water dripped on them from ragged pipes overhead. They had to run everywhere. They could only speak when spoken to. They ate slop leftovers from the galley and slept on rotting mattresses on the floor.

THE BELLY OF TWO BEASTS

One day, Sam Schultz and I rambled out of The Fountain. He pointed up at the looming tower above us in the bright sun and told me that's where the people in the reeducation camp were sleeping. I saw them in my imagination wrapped in sleeping bags on the bare rooftop, years before they put up their massive sign. I wondered where they slept when it rained. It barely rained in Los Angeles.

X

Left behind in the dorms, my older brother Joshua, who was then nine, was refusing to get up in the morning. The movement's solution to get him out of bed was to fill a container with cold water from the bathroom and pour it on him. That's when he stopped believing.

A year later, my mother had not only finished her reeducation but was gone again, training to return people to sanity with a machine, for the movement. My mother's absence felt normal. Having a mother is not part of my lexicon for my existence. Every child from The Baby Factory was unmothered. I'd grown up entirely in dorms, except for occasional times when I was pulled out here and there for a month so I could be useful.

The Fountain. The Melrose. The ATA— "Apollo Training Academy." The Annex. The Cadets. Places with pleasant names that were really warehouses to store children. They didn't exist as actual structures or organizations, even though the movement pretended they did.

Joshua and I grew up a block from our father, John Mustard, a man who lived in The Old Industrial Hospital and who we rarely saw and never really knew. Jono, my younger brother, had been living with Paco, his father, since his birth. My mother had divorced Paco because he wouldn't join the inner clergy of the movement, and one could no longer stay married to someone not part of the private inner navy. She quickly married Randall Reese, another machine-based counselor like herself.

Jono came to live in a small apartment in The Fountain with my older brother, me, and my mother when she returned later that year from her latest "mission." I thought she wanted to see me, but I quickly realized the truth of why I was moved back in with her. My mother would be a slave making me a slave.

I was eight and a half years old, and my job every day, seven days a week, was to bring my baby brother two miles to daycare at The Château Élysée Annex in the morning. Then I would have the rest of the day to do what I wanted.

The movement's Gothic hotel, affectionately called The Center for Artists, was built in 1923 and modeled after a French-Normandy château. Dropped into the middle of Hollywood, this haunting building once housed 1940s film stars, then became a retirement home, then a flophouse for transients. Inside were 1970s furnishings, couches covered in textured orange fabric, wood-paneled walls with a mix of period lighting, and cold fluorescent overhead ambient lights. The commander knew that recruiting up-and-coming actors and film stars would be a boon for larger recruitment for the movement.

Adjacent and connected to the Château was a 1960s plasticine office building built in utilitarian square and rectangle shapes—cream tan panels, plate glass windows, and plastic entryway steps, right off the assembly line. The front steps opened to the sun. The Annex, what looked like a rotting dental clinic, would become the second center of my world for the next four years.

It was a schizophrenic design; the two attached structures were engaged in architectural warfare. Mixed-up architecture that makes no sense epitomizes the excesses and extremes of Los Angeles. The Annex became the place where the children's quasi-navy of "cadets" were assigned.

In the back of the Château sat a courtyard right next to the bridge that led to The Annex. The courtyard was vast and open to the sun. Beyond it and down some stairs was a massive, rotting tennis court that had probably been left for dead in the 1950s. In the center of the Château's courtyard sat two giant, massive columnic sculptures.

The "godheads," as I always referred to them in my head, were thirty feet apart and stared each other down with blank and serene eyes. The towering heads were something out of an Isaac Asimov novel, and I thought

THE BELLY OF TWO BEASTS

they looked like living gods. In the 1990s, the bridge was torn down and the godheads removed. There's a café there now. I never stopped thinking about what became of those looming multi-ton structures—if they sat in a scrap heap or lived with a billionaire in Bel Air.

The Annex was long with linoleum and plastic hallways. The former procedural rooms were tiny and square, and every plastic chair or wood panel was bathed in green fluorescent light.

Someone was always coming and going between the Château Hotel and the monolithic Old Industrial Hospital across the street from where I lived a couple of miles away. I could walk up to anyone in the Château Hotel's crumbling asphalt parking lot and ask for a ride back to The Mothership.

A block down from The Mothership, across from Los Burritos on Sunset, were several blocks of 1940s stucco motels painted in bright and cream colors. Their neon signs faded by endless sun. In their heyday people stayed there from all over the country, hungry for stardom. Now they only housed whores.

I would walk past the dozens of prostitutes standing on the sidewalk in front of these motels; women of every shape and color, many of them beautiful. They wore bright bikinis and lingerie, illuminated by the sun—a circus of sex and costumed flesh you would never see in Hollywood today. I had no concept of sex.

On the motel balconies, the pimps stood in mink fur coats, which made no sense in a 90-degree Los Angeles drought. Some crossed muscled arms over cotton wife beaters, gold watches or chains against their dark chocolate skin. They leaned against swept-back Cadillacs or theatrical cars made to look like 1930s roadsters, with custom flourishes—white-wall tires, mirror-shined rims, and exaggerated fins. These rumbling, life-sized candied toys were shinier versions of the throbbing masterpieces that the Cholos created.

The pimps often watched me as I walked past. Now and then one of them would nod, throwing silent gestures of tribal understanding. Their primary-colored hats had peacock feathers, making the operation look like a circus. Even though it looked like a carnival, I knew in my body that it was a little bit dangerous.

By the age seven, before we all moved to The Fountain and my responsibility of shepherding my brother to daycare was put upon me, I started taking the bus by myself. I took the RTD—Rapid Transit District. In 1970s Los Angeles these buses were heavy, loud, corrugated-steel ships that coughed black smoke and seemingly could go anywhere.

Four blocks up from the ornate Château, the street would start to curve, and urban sprawl would turn into luxury homes, with giant palms and magnolias creating a canopy of shade all the way to the park. The road led to the entrance of Bronson Park with a short walk up to the Bronson Caves. I could also walk, if motivated, to the Hollywood sign, or up to the observatory where movies like *Rebel Without a Cause* and *Phantom from Space* were shot. I spent that summer after the invasion riding the bus and roaming the streets of Hollywood on my own.

Sometimes I would walk up Vermont until I crossed over the magnificent Los Feliz Boulevard, where the slums surrendered to mansions housing movie stars.

This was my radius—my childworld. It hadn't occurred to me back then that there were classes of people in Los Angeles, and you could see it in the landscape. The massive castles of the wealthy looked out from the hills onto the Mexican slums, views the rarefied elite would kill for.

Once I took over caring for my brother, if no one was paying attention to me and I wasn't being made to work, I wandered the streets of Los Angeles. I made money by passing out flyers for Peter Gillham's Vitamin Store. At five cents a flyer, if I passed them out for an hour, I would have enough for the bus and a movie. I would put them on cars and in mailboxes, but sometimes I would dump them in the trash, go play video games, and then lawlessly collect my fee. I reveled in these moments of invisibility because I knew at any time the movement could put me back to work.

Near the stairwell where we'd been kept during the raid was the entrance to a division named after the commander's English home. It was called The American St. Hill Division, where they trained people in

THE BELLY OF TWO BEASTS

machine-based counseling, a primary tool of the movement. An above-ground tunnel ran between this Division and the main building of The Old Industrial Hospital. There was a canteen that sold snacks and cigarettes for the constantly smoking members of the private navy. I would pretend to pay for something, drop fifty cents into the cash jar, and when no one was looking, take out ones and fives and tens that were already in the jar. My normal take was between $7 and as much as $30, a fortune to me.

One day, as I was leaving through the tunnel, I heard a shout. The canteen worker had caught me stealing and angrily threatened me with a report. It never came. For weeks I wondered if I would be awakened in the middle of the night and taken to the children's reeducation camp. Hubbard said physical labor brings you into present time. Navigating The Mothership and the dangerous neighborhood was like a game of chess, a game I'd never heard of.

X

Day after day, in my era of invisibility during the summer after the invasion, I would hop off of the bus between Hollywood and Argyle in front of the Pantages Theater, after passing the giant Pep Boys sign with Manny, Moe, and Jack. By the time I would reach the Vine Theater, a block later, there was almost always a Black man there, muscled arms straining his white, muted red, or sometimes ocean blue wife beater. In bright 1970s skin-tight-flared blue jeans, he stood on the block. His skin glistened with sweat in the searing sun and even through his dark sunglasses I always knew he was looking at me.

There was a day he spoke to me. "What's your name, little man?" he asked.

"My name's Jamie."

"Hi Jamie, I'm Reb."

He offered me a huge hand. When we shook, I felt the immense power and strength of his frame. I felt the gentle awareness of someone who

72 CHILD X

actually saw me, in a world where I was invisible to my parents, my care-takers, and anyone driving past; where, like any other brown boy in Los Angeles, I faded into the concrete, completely invisible.

Cars growled past, cruising slowly down the block. Reb's gaze followed them. "What are you doing?" I asked.

"I'm standing here because this is how I make my money," he said. Before I could ask how, Reb shifted the topic back to me. "What are you doing down here, little Jamie?"

"I'm gonna see a movie."

Reb asked me how I could afford to see a movie, and why I wasn't in school. I told him I hadn't even seen my mother in a year and a half, and I didn't have to go to school.

Reb reached into his pocket and pulled out a wad of cash. I heard the crisp sound of paper sliding free from his brass money clip, and he held out a worn $10 bill. This was when American money was still green, and the folded bill popped out against the burnt bronze of Reb's skin. I reached through the disbelief and took it.

"Thanks, Reb."

"Any time, Jamie. Any time. When you're on Hollywood and Vine, Reb's always got you." A bright smile exposed his shimmering white teeth against his chocolate skin and widened across his entire face.

I went to the Vine Theater and watched a sci-fi movie. The $10 was enough to buy popcorn and a hot dog. I even had enough for a Coke.

The next day was really hot. Another child navy kid named Toby woke me up and said that two Mexican kids had cut through the alley and were using the back of our building to climb down to a lower parking lot. It was a shortcut between blocks. To distract myself from the heat, I ran down there with my pocketknife and confronted them. Anything to get away from my body feeling overheated in that moment.

I came across two Mexican kids, one standing on top of a stone wall, the other climbing down it to a lower lot. The older boy was my age and stood in front of me and his brother, a few years younger, was climbing down the stone wall to the lot. I said nothing, looked him in the eyes, and

THE BELLY OF TWO BEASTS

displayed my knife. He was in my territory. Toby watched behind the back door of The Fountain through a glass window.

Then the oddest thing happened. The Mexican kid looked down to make sure his younger brother was okay, looked back up at me, and stared back intently into my eyes—his brown into my green. We were both paralyzed. After about thirty seconds, the boy pulled his T-shirt down to expose his heart, his eyes locked on my eyes. He was telling me to kill him or go away.

I wasn't going to kill anyone.

When he saw this, after a pause, he calmly turned away, went to the wall, and climbed down to join his brother.

As I watched them walk away across the baking lower lot, my heart filled. My younger brother was a toddler. He was protecting his little brother. In that moment, as he climbed down the wall to join his brother, I felt like I loved him.

X

At the time, Paco was living in an apartment in Hollywood. He came by The Fountain and took us to Chinatown to see *The 36th Chamber of Shaolin*, a Hong Kong kung fu movie where a teenage fugitive takes refuge in a Shaolin monastery and suffers a gauntlet of thirty-five deadly rooms, each with unique battle challenges, that eventually shape him into a kung fu master.

As I watched the movie in the musty theater, I thought, *I'm going through my chambers like him.* Years later, this movie would profoundly inspire Staten Island rappers Wu-Tang Clan.

There were months when I would go down to the ancient wooden basement to shut the world away. Sitting alone on the top steps, where no one could hear me, I would scream to myself, my eyes awash with tears. Whenever it got too much, I would go into the rotting stairwell below the rusty sodium vapor light and scream, pray out loud, and cry into the black.

I would crumple my face, force power from my mind, and start to pray.

I would repeat my prayer out loud as a mantra and pray to God, a God that I didn't believe in, that my parents would die in a car accident. This way my abandonment would have a reason. I could not show emotion.

I still had constant and paralyzing ear infections. When I couldn't roam the habitat, I needed to do something with my mind. Since I didn't have a father to teach me how to ride a bike, I decided to teach myself. When my ears felt like they had pins and needles in them, I clung to The Fountain. I found a small bike in the basement and dragged it up to the hallway. As I started to ride, I would fall over to one side and catch myself on the wall. If I fell to the left, I pushed off with my left hand. If I fell to the right, I pushed off with my right hand. The low-profile carpet, caked in dirt, slowed the bike and made it easier to predict when I would fall to one side. After two or three hours of this, I stopped falling over and the bike kept going.

The next day, I got up to see if I could still ride a bike. I began to ride down the hall and didn't fall over at all. Satisfied, I went outside, rode around the block, and felt free. I didn't need a father.

X

A few months later, when I was almost nine, my mother returned from her training. It had been a year and a half since I'd seen her. After completing the reeducation camp, she had been in Clearwater, Florida, learning to use the machine to restore all men and women of mankind to their supernatural state, free from their flesh bodies. In the world of the movement, this training made her special. When she returned as a highly trained benevolent sorceress, other members looked up to her in awe.

During all these years that I wasn't going to school, I would be taken to the Apollo Training Academy to learn the movement's doctrine. It was the same for a child as it was for an adult in the movement: it started very simple, helpful, and easy, then got more complicated and manipulative as you moved up. My first course was about how to look up words in a dictionary, and then I did a child's course on germs called *Goopy the Germ*.

THE BELLY OF TWO BEASTS

Goopy was a green, bloated monster with large, ragged teeth. He looked like a bad smell would if you could see it. I had grown up without sheets, showering, or a toothbrush, and now at almost nine years old they were teaching me about germs.

It was around this time when the movement asked me to report to the main building for a "very special job." The pseudo-navy needed someone with a small body to clean out the industrial air vents in The Old Industrial Hospital. Adults I'd never met wrapped me in a white, adult-size, plastic-and-rubber hazardous-materials suit. It covered my tiny body head to toe. The adults tightly duct-taped my ankles, wrists, neck, and chest to fit the oversized suit to my limbs. The private navy members explained to me that they themselves were too large for this job.

I could smell the sharp tang of industrial chemicals and that burnt smell of plastic on the suit as they put it on. The stench didn't go away until they fastened a mechanical respirator to the flame-resistant, white plastic-paper hood that covered my hair. It was hot in the suit and the plastic faceplate fogged as I learned to breathe, the strange animal hissing of my breath in the respirator covering my ears.

For months I was made to crawl into the air vents in the ceilings of The Old Industrial Hospital, lugging a plastic bucket filled with a pink substance called Naval Jelly—an industrial blend of mystery gel and phosphoric acid that the commander had used to strip rust off his original flagship, *Apollo*. I smeared Naval Jelly on the air vent walls, stripping decades of rust and dreck that had built up there while film stars were giving birth and having surgeries on the edge of Hollywood. I didn't know what claustrophobia was, or what industrial chemicals were, yet I was living with them.

I drew hard breaths through the respirator as my thin arms scrubbed away awkwardly at the steel of the vent walls. My arms burned. I felt a rush of blood pumping through my body. I was useful; this was my part of a grand quest to save the planet.

As days turned to weeks, and weeks to months, what started off as excitement at being strapped daily into a chemical-resistant superhero costume every day turned to dread as I left The Fountain. Eight hours a day in the vents was hard, and I would pray for the yelling from outside to start the forty-five minutes it would take me to back out or reach the other side and be pulled out. Some days, when fear and exhaustion overtook me, I fell asleep in the square, steel caves.

Eventually I was taken off air vent duty. For the first time—and for around six weeks—I was placed in a public school. No one told me why my routine was changing. The movement was always changing things.

Lockwood Elementary School was a run-down concrete structure surrounded by cracked, rising asphalt shaken loose by decades of earthquakes and countless aftershocks. It had been built for the mostly Hispanic and Black kids living in inner-city poverty on the East Side of Los Angeles. I got straight Fs—I didn't have kindergarten or first grade, and I didn't know any math or writing. Every day was a constant reminder of what I couldn't do.

In the six weeks before going to Lockwood, an old nanny would try to comb my hair straight with a steel brush as she called my soft afro a rat's nest. She constantly drew blood.

Part of my illiteracy was having no reference to the outside world and using words that Hubbard either invented or distorted. For example, if someone was upset or disturbed, we didn't use those words. He created the word "enturbulation" to describe making someone turbulent on the inside. Hubbard did this with hundreds of words, so I often didn't know if the words I was using were words used or understood by the wogs. Because we had special words, it was another reason to keep our distance and even look at others as less than us.

The movement referred to any non-member as a "wog." For the purpose of this book, I'm going to refer to it as "the outworld." "Wog" is what all members of the movement called non-members. It wouldn't be until I moved to London, years later, that I realized it was an old British colloquialism that some consider to be racist: "The wogs begin at Calais," which used to mean anyone who wasn't British: Asians, Africans, even other Europeans—especially the French. To us, it meant the unenlightened. Today, in England it's equivalent to "nigger."

THE BELLY OF TWO BEASTS

If you were dealing with another person in the movement, you didn't refer to them as a person. You called them a "terminal," like, "Did you talk to the terminal to find out what dormitory you're in?"

These words tended to mechanize and dehumanize human interaction. We were machines living in a machine. Being raised with a strange language of new, manufactured words exacerbated my intense feeling of being something alien, something "other."

By the time I got to Lockwood, I was completely convinced by the movement that public school had nothing to teach me. I don't know why they sent me there, but it wasn't to learn. As I walked out of school my second week, I could see my primary caretaker, Louise Vikkers, with her pinched face and her sharp nose, waiting for me outside of a large, unmarked van. The van drove us kids to and from school every day and had no seats. We sat on the open metal floor.

"Come over here!" she yelled in a shrilling, fierce staccato. I walked over and she pulled my head into her waist and started staring down into my hair, pulling it apart to see my scalp. Nerves buzzed with anxiety all over my body.

"Oh my fucking god!" she screamed. She yanked open the back of the van, telling the other kids already huddled on the floor to get to the other side of the van. "Do not go anywhere near him."

It was like the scene in *The Trial* by Franz Kafka where a man is brought up on charges for his life but never told what he did wrong. In all the years since, I have never experienced this kind of feeling of floating. My mind completely separated from my body. In that moment, when the kids crawled away and huddled together away from me in the van, I was truly in terror.

When we arrived at The Fountain, I was put into an empty room alone with a mat on the floor and a pillow on a blanket. There had been a lice outbreak in The Fountain, but what was going on in my head was special. There were so many lice eggs on each strand of hair, from my scalp halfway up my curls, that my hair looked white. There were so many active bugs in my hair that when you parted it and looked at my scalp, there was a populated, teeming ecosystem. I didn't know it, but my head was now its own planet inhabited by jumping, grotesque aliens.

I had been isolated in that room for four hours without knowing why. Even though I rarely saw my mother, she came to get me with Tiger's Milk bars. She told me that, as my mom, it was her responsibility to make sure that I was bug free, so she was taking me to Paco's house a block away on Berendo to "get all the creatures off my head."

The first step was to kill the lice. She drowned my hair with a substance called Quell—a lice killer—and then washed it. We spent from 6:30 PM till midnight purging my curls in a process that my mother invented in that moment. After rinsing my hair, she inspected it again and gasped, "Oh my god. They're still alive."

I hate to admit this, but in this rare five hours with my mother, both of us engaged in a war against this alien species that had taken over my head, I enjoyed it. I enjoyed spending time with her while she was working with me to make me better.

After three more sessions of Quell, she proclaimed that all the mean creatures were dead, and now we would have to remove the eggs. For the next two and a half hours she used a steel nit comb to strip lice eggs out, using Johnson & Johnson's baby oil as a lubricant. She did this over and over and over for hours. By the time every lice egg was stripped from my golden-brown curls, my hair was thick with blood. My scalp burned. We would repeat this ritual several times over the next couple of years—my trial of blood, oil, and steel. Into my late twenties, if I felt a scratch or an itch on my head, I would feel nerves sharpen in my body, wondering for a brief second if the aliens had returned.

X

Six weeks after all the eggs were removed from my head, I was told by an adult private navy member that I wouldn't be going to school anymore and to report to The Old Industrial Hospital for a new assignment.

Adults I hadn't met before led me into a series of connected rooms

THE BELLY OF TWO BEASTS

high up in The Old Industrial Hospital with cracked, rotting vinyl flooring in the heart of the building. And then, for the first time, I saw walls that didn't have walls but instead were exposed wood beams with a pink cotton substance in between them. There were dozens of rooms like this, the cotton candy everywhere and all around me.

It was called fiberglass, and I was told I was going to be removing it. At this point in my life, I was being penned until I grew to join the private navy. The work I was doing now seemed random and based on provisional need.

This time there was no yellow plastic hazmat suit, no respirator. They handed me a box of huge, gray industrial trash bags as big as me and thick, oversized, yellow rubberized gloves. My new mission to save the planet was ripping this cotton candy from the studs and filling up the gigantic bags. I began to pull and stuff. Every time I pulled out the pink fluff, I felt a sharp tingle inside my gloves, on my neck and face, under my clothes, and even in my mouth and throat. The tingle slowly turned to pain, and I realized whatever this was, it wasn't cotton or candy. At the end of each eight-hour day, my entire body burned. Like with the vents at the beginning, I saw it as an adventure, but once again this quickly changed.

Within a few hours, my childbody was covered in tiny sliver-like shards, stinging me from head to toe. The adults, exhaling cigarette smoke, the first time I asked about the slivers, told me, no matter what I did, not to scratch. That would push the burning slivers further into my skin, which could grow over them and then they would stay in my body. In the evenings, I would go back to The Fountain, my skin stinging, each step adding to the burning sensation of the slivers.

At this time, my older brother was never around, except late at night. My mother and my new stepfather, Randall, returned from their stations after 11:00. My younger brother was living with Paco. I had the entire dusty, decrepit estate to myself. Well, myself and the roaches.

Once inside the apartment, as the helicopters vibrated the building, I would draw myself a boiling hot bath, too hot for what my childbody or even an adult could take. If The Fountain had one thing, it was scalding hot water from the tap. I wouldn't plug the tub until the water was steaming. Every day the water seemed to take forever to fill the tub deep enough to cover the rough, dark steel bare metal and white porcelain worn from decades of use.

It would take another ten minutes for me to climb into it, my skin burning in it each day. It took another ten for the searing bath to become bearable for sitting. But when I eased into the water, grimacing and gritting my teeth, a miracle would happen. My pores would open up and the tiny, imperceptible shards of fiberglass would float out of my skin. I would open my mouth and let the steaming water seep all the way to the back of my throat, and the shards would disappear. I did this daily for weeks, but every time I did it, I would be nervous, thinking, *What if this is the day they don't float away, and my skin grows over them?* I wondered what it would be like to feel tiny shards in my skin and throat for the rest of my life.

Finally, all the shards would be out of my skin. My body now in a state of relief, I would exhale—even laugh out loud. I invented a ritual where I would make deep, long, guttural throating noises after the slivers were out of my skin. The relief from the slivers held such a powerful sensation in my childbody that I enjoyed it. In a world where I didn't exist, it gave me a feeling of deep warmth as if I was floating as an embryo in my mother's womb. The baths were the only warmth I could feel in my body. I began to enjoy the slivers. I would long for the sensation of the crucible of shards releasing from my body.

I would fall asleep in the studio apartment around midnight, before anyone came home. I slept on the floor while my mother and Randall slept on the bed. I had a pillow and a blanket, and every night I would pull my shirt over my head so roaches wouldn't crawl into my mouth.

Until this writing, I did not see this as abuse. I saw it as perseverance and endurance, ending with a cleansing. It was my trial as a young kung fu fighter. My ancestors had picked cotton. I picked fiberglass. Removing the slivers made me feel alive in an existence where I'd become numb. Even the scalding hot water made me feel alive. The ritual of the burning freed a loneliness from my cells that I had felt since The Baby Factory.

Chapter 9

ARCHIVES OF ZANZIBAR

The movement was not done with me.

It wasn't long before they asked me to do another job. This time the request came from my mother. I would work in the "Advanced Division" as a page, running files. The machine-based counselors kept files of reports and notes on anyone they had counseling with. A person going through a machine-based counseling could have hundreds of files crammed with papers that described every feeling they had: every thought, every bad dream, any action and crimes they had committed in this life or their limitless past lives.

Wearing a miniature navy uniform—blue pants, dress shoes, and a short-sleeve white shirt with a black plastic name tag—I would run from the Advanced Division to The Archives, the research facility where stacks of machine-based counseling files were kept. The machine-based counselors and their overseers needed constant access to them. I would grab a folder I had been sent for and run it to an overseer on the third floor. The overseers were the people above the counselors who directed what was needed for the adherents to continue to make spiritual advancement.

82   CHILD X

The files were cream manila folders, like anything you would see in an office, filled with the long-form white printer paper, with a line drawn down the middle and notes written along the small columns made by the line. These files remain in my mind, every detail. People get machine-based counseling for decades and their files fill up. Throughout my childhood there were shredding machines everywhere and all around me: near the dorms, in our fake schools, and in all the institutions and divisions. They became normalized in the background like a blender in a juice shop. They would never shred folders with these machines, as they need your confessionals if you ever turn on them. Why would a religious organization need or want the ever-presence of these machines?

The Archives was a spider web of rooms in the basement of the animal research facility across from The Old Industrial Hospital. I would walk through underground tunnels that went under the street. The tunnels were humid, industrial-concrete caverns lit with yellow-cream sodium vapor. Twelve feet above my head ran massive steel pipes—one hallway had more peeling paint than the other. The stairway to the tunnels ran under the Advanced Division. Behind the Advanced Division was a stairway to The Archives, which sat behind the giant industrial pit the size of four Olympic swimming pools where the large animal cages were.

Once down the stairs just beyond the industrial pit, in order to get into The Archives, you had to go through a set of airlock double doors with a security button—the movement needed to keep the files secured. In them were endless past lives and confessions. At this time, my childmind had no idea The Archives held records of millions of lives of species, planets, and battles across the universe. I just knew that I could never lose a file when I was running it to an overseer or a counselor. A file was more precious than a diamond.

Now I knew I was special. I was on a quest, saving the world while the outworld kids were naively in school. I felt like the spaceships might arrive any moment. In The Archives I would receive a new kind of education. It had an office to the right when you walked in, enclosed in the kind of glass that was wired with steel mesh. Inside the hallways and room surrounding

ARCHIVES OF ZANZIBAR

the office were stacks and stacks of files—thousands of them—on industrial shelves that towered fifteen feet in the air.

The Archives were where the keeper worked, a young Black man named Conner. There weren't many Black people in the movement. Conner was probably nineteen, not older than twenty-one. He had a thick mustache that barely hid a cleft lip, with a giant afro and mocha cream skin. He wore a naval uniform like I did—black pants, white shirt, but with a tie.

Cut into the wraparound glass was a slot just big enough for people to speak through. It was another relic from the old research hospital, a way to secure access to the animals. Conner could open the airlock doors from his station inside the glass room. He had the temperament of an old grumpy gatekeeper. Anyone who showed up at the secured airlock double doors was at the mercy of a button inside his glass chamber and his permission.

Files came out with him and went in with him. Conner would buzz me through the airlock and help me find what I needed in the complicated system only he knew. He was a Black beacon for me at a time when the world made no sense. As a small child, I didn't know why I had been given this mission. The movement assigned kids to missions based on reasons only the movement knew.

Conner had wired The Archives with speakers and a stereo system inside the glass-enclosed room where he played vinyl from his desk. Thick black rubberized cables snaked like tentacles from the desk; he had speakers placed on the ceilings, in the hallways, all over the vast Archives. This is where he introduced me to Billy Joel's newly released *52nd Street*.

When Conner sent me to get a file, I'll never forget the first time I heard a man's voice float out of the stereo speakers and sail into every corner of the vast industrial cavernous storage. It made my childbody fill with emotion. Every cell in my body stirred.

I was the grandson of a Black surgeon. I wasn't in school, and my illiteracy was mounting. My first time in a hospital should have been a medical school, not as a child slave running files based on counseling sessions run by machines.

What was surprising about the machine was that something so small could have its own gravity; everything in the movement revolved around it. It was about the size of a lunchbox, only thinner, and came in a wooden case with brass latches. The face of the machine was the blue of a baby blanket. There were large, heavy 1960s-style dials and knobs in black industrial plastic. A large window encased in clear plastic protected the needle that moved in a half arc like the seconds hand on a clock. It was something like a large version of the tricorder I would see on reruns of *Star Trek* when they beamed onto a desolate planet—but resembling a serious tool that any technician would use. They no longer look like this; now they're modern and slick, and the movement releases a new version every couple of decades. We believed the machine could read our minds, and because we did, it could.

Sometimes, I'd sit in The Archives and read Hubbard's dictionaries explaining the words he used in the doctrine. I was learning about other planets that circled other suns. The Marcab Confederacy was a powerful galactic civilization that once owned planet Earth. Over twenty thousand years they had grown deviant. The Marcabians lived around a star that I could sometimes see at night—the last star in the tail end of the Big Dipper's handle. On their world, it was a lot like my habitat: people drove cars that burned gas, wore clothes like ours, and watched TV. I wondered if it was nighttime on their planet, and if some other eight-year-old alien boy was looking up at our Sun—a tiny glinting dot in his sky.

That summer there was a heat wave in Los Angeles. The smog-filled haze over my habitat thickened. The movement had started painting The Old Industrial Hospital that blue color that sometimes matches the sky on a very rare day when a desert rain or strong wind pushes the smog away from Los Angeles.

I had finished work early at three in the afternoon and Conner let me go home. It was an unusually cool day, and Billy Joel's "Stiletto" was ringing in my head, so I decided to walk to the habitat. I walked up Vermont to the Pollywog Ponds just past the Greek Theater in Griffith Park, humming

ARCHIVES OF ZANZIBAR

the lyrics to "Stiletto," a vivid and piercing metaphor that encapsulates the destructive power of emotional manipulation.

As I rounded a corner, I could see the liquor store in the distance, its neon sign glowing against a dusky sky. I stopped at the corner and waited with my hands in my pockets. I wanted to go to buy a sports drink. I reached into my pocket, but the crumpled-up two dollars I knew I had left The Fountain with was gone. My heart stopped. I decided I must have dropped the two dollars. The money had to be lying somewhere just above Los Feliz Boulevard, as I'd checked for the money right before I crossed. I turned around and began to walk back the way I'd come.

I walked for five minutes, barely out of the sprawl, back among the film-star mansions, and just above the street there was my two dollars on the sidewalk, right in front of a beautiful Spanish mansion. I tucked the money in my pocket and smiled. As I walked back across Los Feliz and reached the other side, in that moment, I felt like someone was following me. It was almost night, at the very edge of an orange-bronze dusk. I stopped and turned to look behind me.

Billy Joel's mysterious haunting verse played in my head. A strange song called "Zanzibar" about a young man, probably the age of Conner, who finds freedom and himself every time he basks in a mysterious New York nightclub. I wondered if I would go to Zanzibar one day.

Crossing the street, from one side of Los Feliz to the other, right at the edge of the sprawl, was the low, sauntering shape of a coyote. The animal was as out of place here as I was in The Old Industrial Hospital. We both lived as animals and I was transfixed by him.

Just as I looked, the coyote stopped in the middle of the empty street, its head turned, and in an instant, the golden glow of its eyes met mine. The old sodium vapor streetlights were illuminated, washing the animal's sinewy frame in a sepia golden glow that matched its eyes. I thought to myself, *Pretty*, as I saw him in the darkening dusk, set against the gray concrete of the street. *I was raised like him.* The coyote's eyes widened as we locked onto each other as if he had heard my thought. We seduced each other. We held our gaze, bewitched. Then the coyote turned his head and sauntered down Los Feliz Boulevard.

I was sure I'd just spoken to him telepathically. Then I started walking again, singing in my head. "Zanzibar. Zanzibar. Zanzibar." *Will I find Zanzibar?* After watching the coyote's speckled black-golden eyes and brindled fur, after our minds connected with extrasensory power, I wondered if I could now speak to animals.

Chapter 10

STARBOYS

His muscles were shutting down, starved of oxygen. His body tensed, growing heavy. He smelled jet fuel in the desert heat. The young man was fused to the soft leather of the car, the weight of his slight frame fading, gradually more distant. Then a wave of euphoria crashed over him. He heard the winding hum of a jet escaping the Earth. He strained, willing his eyes to focus on the black mass of the jet now leaping through the blur of light overhead, as he drifted into the slow fog of death.

At the beginning of 1977, an everyday man concerned about the care of children wrote a letter to Hubbard, our commander, who was hastily fleeing Morocco with his small flotilla of boats. The man's letter addressed the care of children at the movement's land-bases, specifically Los Angeles. Hubbard's doctrine dictated his private navy members with children spend an hour a day with their family. The everyday man who had written this letter of concern felt like that wouldn't be enough.

This was the commander's response:

CHILD X

22 FEBRUARY 1977

Dear _____,

Thank you very much for writing me.

A program for the new Cadet Org is covered by PAC Base Order 18. If you haven't done so, I suggest that you get it word cleared [look up any words you don't understand] in qual [the Continuous Education Department].

I'm sure that you'll be able to work our [this word should have been "on" and is in here from the original document] your parent's time to be with your child which is my intention. I know how important it is as I have been experiencing the situation with my own children for many years and things have worked out fine.

Love,
RON [Hubbard's actual signature in his own hand]

Three months before he responded and signed with his own pen and ink to this man, Hubbard's son, Quentin, who longed to be a pilot, disappeared and killed himself.

Quentin had been found unresponsive in his parked car, near McCarran International Airport in Las Vegas, Nevada, where he'd been watching large jets take off and land. A simple rubber hose connected to the car's tailpipe was wedged in the car's window, which had been hand cranked to hold the hose in place. He died two weeks later in a hospital in Las Vegas. He was twenty-two years old. He was not "fine."

Quentin, it was said by those who knew him, was gay. He had been a Level 12 machine-based counselor. A Level 12 is the highest level of machine-based counseling in the history of the movement, and these very special few would be equivalent to Yoda—only fifty or so were ever made, a fraction of whom were trained on the *Apollo* by Hubbard himself. That fraction was looked up to like gods within the movement.

Despite the hose feeding the car's exhaust to the window, the coroner ruled Quentin's cause of death undetermined. A carbon monoxide test came back negative. Carbon monoxide leaves the body after twenty-four hours. The movement has always tried to claim it wasn't a suicide because there was no carbon monoxide in his system, even though it was obviously a suicide, and there was no carbon monoxide in the coroner's report because Quentin didn't die for a fortnight.

It was not Quentin's first suicide attempt. Like a medieval king securing his bloodline's future, Hubbard made his young son train to the movement's highest, most rarefied echelon. The movement's doctrine considered alleged homosexuals like Quentin "sexual perverts" who were "ill physically." A few years earlier, in deep pain over his situation, Quentin once before attempted suicide, and Hubbard placed him in the reeducation camp just like my mother, alongside others who had fallen from the movement's focus.

I had started studying the deeper, more complex versions of the doctrine. I was illiterate in every way, but I could read. Of course I could read, because dense reading of the doctrine was required. I started learning about "being cause" and using intention and spiritual decision to overcome every obstacle and barrier in life. It reminded me of the movies in Chinatown where the young bald boys studied to be indestructible. I loved it. The commander's words echoed in my head. I could use spiritual will to accomplish anything. In my heart I knew this was true and so was the doctrine. I was nine years old. I believed in the commander. I carry the belief of spiritual causation with me to this day.

X

"Huuyut! Huuyut! Forty-seven! Fifteen! Seventy-five! Hike!"

I snapped the ball to Johnny Vasquez (whose real name was Juan) and ran, my feet digging into the thick green of the Barnsdall Park grass. A slight Mexican boy with deep brown eyes and jet-black hair, and smaller than the rest of us, Johnny was coiled like a spring, but he always knew how to make us laugh. In the background was Lulu, a quiet strawberry blonde girl who had a crush on Mickey. I pivoted eagerly, ready to receive the throw that I was sure was coming. The balls of my feet stung where my Sears imitation Chuck Taylor All Stars shoes were wearing through. I felt the needles of poking grass in my skin. The ball sailed out of the bright sun.

My arms stung as I caught it. I ran.

I could feel the other kids swarming in on me. I ran.

I heard Johnny's excited voice, already tasting victory. Then I felt hands on my shoulders, the surprise of being pulled down, and the impact of the ground. I tasted grass in my mouth and the pungent smell of grass and dirt.

I wouldn't have survived The Fountain if it wasn't for my friends.

There was Mickey Tealer, my best friend and lord of the football patch. He came alive during those games at Barnsdall Park, directing each play like Napoleon. There was the blond kid with his bright blue eyes. His parents had named him Bohtan—something Hindu or Asian. It must have been part of a theme because they had also named his little sister Lhasa; she had bright white skin like porcelain.

There was another girl, Kalin, and she had a sister, Jane. Sam was there, with his sandy hair, sharp nose and cheekbones, and deep-set brown eyes. A new kid, Miles, got to The Fountain a little while after we did. He was a chubby kid with wheat blond hair, blue eyes, and a round face. When I wasn't working, I spent my days alone wandering the concrete. This gang of kids and I fell in together, like we'd been drawn in by some sort of ghetto sci-fi-navy law of gravity.

A group of us kids walked from Edgemont to Barnsdall Park, and always saw the prostitutes across the street from Los Burritos on Sunset. We emerged onto Sunset by the row of motels where the prostitutes lined up in their bright bathing suits. Between us we had a few dollars, enough to share a "wet" burrito, and maybe a Coke to sip on as we walked in the sun up Edgemont up to Barnsdall Park. The wet burrito at Los Burritos was an explosion of cheese, red sauce, and creamy, tart sour cream. It would serve as our rations for the day.

STARBOYS

The exotic ladies of the motels called out and fawned any time we walked past. "Hey, cuties." They would beam at us with radiant smiles, and I would wonder why the police would let them stand out there all day dressed in lingerie.

"You ladies give child discounts?" Mickey shouted. There was an uproar of laughter and a flurry of looks from the girls, and the pimps would smile at us. Some of the girls blew us kisses and said that we needed to come by and say "hi" more often. Mickey's fearlessness stirred something in me. The way of the boys in our pack was each one of us watched and modeled ourselves off the other. I walked taller even though I didn't understand what those kind, perfumed women did behind closed doors and curtains in those 1960s Tiki-themed motel rooms.

I was a little brown boy who faded into the brick of brown buildings, whose days were filled with chemical smog and concrete, and whose nights echoed with the sounds of helicopters beating overhead like the drums of war. Those helicopter floodlights that lit our tenement windows in the evening, while car backfires and the sharp pops of gunfire in the distant mercury-vapor-lit streets, were embryonic, a womb, a bubble. Decades into my adulthood, I needed constant noise to sleep, as honking horns, yelling, and the sounds of the street were a ceaseless melody that would rock me to sleep at night like a lullaby.

It had been a while since the movement had work for me. I was no longer running folders. Even though I wasn't required to work those days, every moment of every second I expected that to change.

One day, I wandered into The Annex to pick up Jono, and I saw a group of kids, in blue navy uniforms and lanyards, in a large room that led out to the dirt patch where the little kids played.

A twelve-year-old navy girl wearing a white shirt and gold lanyard saw me and said, "There's Jamie Mustard. He's a trouble case. He's not working with the cadets."

I was always a criminal just for existing. I spent my whole life trying to be myself despite the identities that people have tried to harness me with.

Miles, the new kid, became one of my best friends from the Barnsdall football kids. He was different than the other kids and he was a prodigy mechanic. This was not something he was ever taught; he just understood car and motorcycle engines.

Next to The Fountain was a parking structure where the adults of the movement would store cars and motorcycles. Miles would show us how to livewire the bikes, starting them and riding them to the top of the parking structure. It was the high sun of the day, and we were blasted with light. My childbody vibrated with the power of the engine. I felt like I was a master of the world. Riding the bike felt like a candy of exhilarated freedom. I didn't know how to shift. I would just roll around in first gear until Miles would wave me in to stop the bike.

One thing the world doesn't know is that poverty-stricken neighborhoods are full of genius, untapped or unexpressed—a small child who knows engines, art, or music. Genius is everywhere in poor neighborhoods. We tend to think of them as places where desperate poor people cannot get by without someone handing down a favor from up high. That is not poverty. These working-class neighborhoods are overflowing with intellectual, scientific, engineering, and artistic genius. Every ghetto, prison, and slum in the world is filled with every kind of genius that, if harnessed, might change the course of history. The people of poverty should be redefined as the most abundant natural resource in the world—the one we waste and squander.

Miles was a prodigy when it came to fixing things, but he couldn't fix himself. When Miles finally died of a drug overdose a few years ago, it didn't surprise me. We don't know for sure whether it was a suicide or not. My heart broke. It's taken me a long time to understand that what happened to us might have contributed to his death as well as the others.

Considering what all of us, as the children of the movement, went through—in or out of the doctrine—most of us were reduced to a futures commodity of labor that didn't need to be injected with emotion or with love.

X

It could be that Hollywood Boulevard, in its absurdity, saved my life, keeping me from ending up like Quentin or Miles.

In the heart of my childhood exile and entombment, *The Empire Strikes Back* exploded onto the street just before the boiling steam of summer heat settled over Los Angeles. It was so hot, if you poured water on the asphalt it would hiss and mist off.

I was almost ten when I took the bus and went to see *it* at The Egyptian on Hollywood on my own. The Egyptian was built after an ancient Egyptian tomb, with sand columns and mysterious hieroglyphics I saw as I walked down the stone pathway from Hollywood Boulevard.

The movie would change me. In *Empire*, after a brutalizing battle on the ice planet Hoth, a star boy survives and heads into space to find the one person that can explain the circumstances of his life. During those burning days, fixed on this living, moving art, this star boy crash-lands on the swamp planet Dagobah. Unfolding in front of me on the fifty-foot screen was a swampy world of thick, gnarled trees unlike anything I had ever seen in the concrete jungle of the habitat.

The silvery mist that rose from the wet marshes reminded me of the smog that hung over Los Angeles, clinging to every inch of my faded jeans. The star boy was seeking out a master; someone who could put the potential he had into context, just like the great Greek warrior Achilles from the *Iliad* had sought out the mythological centaur, Chiron—a half-man, half-horse. Built with the broad chest and sinewy muscles of a man and the powerful frame of the strongest stallion, Chiron was careful and specific in his speech. Fierce as an instructor in battle, he taught Achilles how to fight, and he taught the young warrior reason and discernment, how to hunt, and how to heal others with medicine. Maybe I would be a star boy, or like Achilles, where my mind was the weapon. I was about to find out that my father wasn't my father.

X

Not long after, rather than getting a ride or taking the bus, I decided to walk to The Annex to pick up my younger brother. It was early in the day, so I would go to Bronson Park first. I constantly switched this up depending on the heat, my life-energy, and a craving to break up the monotony of my existence. I was just grateful to be invisible as a worker for a while.

As I approached Sunset and Western a couple of blocks away, walking toward me in the opposite direction were two Black teenagers. Both were wearing wrinkled, shiny white T-shirts and faded acid-wash jeans.

They looked to be about fourteen and sixteen. They gave me a long stare from the side as they passed me, and the older one said, "You called me a nigger."

Before I could think, they were punching me. I couldn't breathe. I fell to the ground, and they were kicking me. Sucking air, I curled up to protect my body from the beating. And then it was over. In that moment, all I could think was that I was grateful that after I dealt with the bloody nose, the bruises on my body were where I could hide them. Incidents like these were a constant thrum.

I told no one.

I was responsible.

I "pulled it in." If I told anyone that I'd been hurt, I would be punished with hard labor, scorned with long periods of studying the doctrine to figure out why, in my subconscious, I made that happen to me. I felt deep anxiety, but it was no different than the anxiety I felt before the beating. Anxiety was in me like a limb, an appendage.

I only felt weakness and shame.

I decided to change my plans, not go to the park, but to see *Empire* again and say hi to Reb. I had just enough to buy a ticket and hoped Reb would give me enough for popcorn and a drink, so I wouldn't feel bad anymore.

As I approached Hollywood and Vine, there was Reb right on the corner staring at me. We gave each other five, and, embarrassed, I asked him for ten dollars. He smiled as he reached into the wad of cash in his pocket as if I'd just made his day.

"Let's grab a slice when you get out," he said.

I said okay, excited to be asked, excited to be wanted.

When I eventually broke out of the theater into the blistering Los Angeles sun, Reb was nowhere to be found. The movie had washed the beating out of my head.

It was a handful of years before I fully understood how Reb made his money standing on the corner of Hollywood and Vine in the hot sun. As a child, I had no concept of prostitution, let alone male prostitution. I didn't really know what it was.

Angels.

X

All that summer, I continued to see Reb when I could, and the other faces that made up my childworld, faces that have informed me to this day how I see poverty, the counterculture, and humans.

I returned to Dagobah on the screen too many times.

The mysterious trees and swamps of the dark planet made it seem like a place I could someday visit. I wanted to be anything but bound in concrete. I wanted to climb those trees and see what was above the canopy. I was riveted by the fog, the heat, and the dark; no environment had ever been like it in my childeyes before. No matter how many times I saw it, it felt new to me. I wanted to grow sick of it, tired of this movie, but the more I watched it, the more I wanted to see it again the next day.

Dagobah was the planet where Yoda lived—the great Jedi master who trains the star boy in the Force. The boy runs through the swamp carrying tiny Yoda on his back, while mysterious wild creatures croak and growl from the unseen depths of the Dagobah swamp. Yoda was constantly telling the boy about the nature of the Force.

"A Jedi's strength flows from the Force," Yoda says, "But beware the dark side. Anger, fear, and aggression; the dark side of the Force are they, easily they flow."

The star boy asks Yoda how he will know the dark side from the good and Yoda explains to him that *he will know.*

CHILD X

"Is the dark side stronger?" the star boy asks.

"No, no, no. Quicker. Easier. More seductive."

Yoda had a strange, backward way of speaking, childlike yet wise. The star boy, listening, stopped to catch his breath. My eyes were wide, and my mouth agape. This exotic world seized my body and electrified it beyond explanation. Sometimes I would see it back-to-back three times in a day. I saw *Empire* forty-seven times that year at The Egyptian. This was at a time where movies stayed months, as long as they kept bringing in the crowds.

Almost every time I went to see it, I would pass Reb on the northeast corner of Hollywood and Vine. We'd give each other five, and he'd ask me if I needed any money. Most days I didn't. I stole what I needed from my mother's purse in the Advanced Division while she was using the machine on paying customers. When I told Reb I had enough, he would smile.

X

At nine years old, through my machine-based counseling, it was determined that I had become a "non-reactionary" in a previous life. This is a noble state in the movement where you never get sick, don't need glasses, and never get into accidents. You are perfectly sane. A lot was made of this, and I was asked to give a talk at the Advanced Division for their weekly graduation ceremony, which took place every Friday evening. They promoted it with flyers all over The Old Industrial Hospital—"THE WORLD'S SECOND YOUNGEST NON-REACTIONARY SPEAKS FRIDAY NIGHT." I went. My mother bought me a polyester suit at Sears.

As I stared at the audience, telling them of my powers, I thought of Spock. I smiled and cheerily told them how free and non-reactionary I was, and how I never got sick or had accidents. I stared out at the crowd and saw the faces of adults smoking cigarettes, their eyes bulging, their mouths open, laughing, their heads bobbing with swollen faces, slapping the arms of their chairs, cheering me, and it reminded me of the faces of all of us kids watching the public spankings at The Red Brick Building. I quickly pushed the thought out of my head using my newfound powers. At the end of the ceremony, I looked above me where there was a picture of Hubbard looking distinguished, staring into the camera, with his hands on his chin, with a Pepsi Rolex watch proudly displayed in black and white. I turned to him and said, "Three cheers for the commander."

"Hip-hip!" I screamed.

"Hooray!" the cheering crowd clapped and screamed back.

"Hip-hip!"

"Hooray!"

"Hip-hip!"

"Hooray!"

It was an old tradition from the British Empire. "Hip-hip" was a way to grab attention and let everyone know that a cheer of "hooray" was required. Some have also said that the "hip-hip" was a reference to the fall of Jerusalem. "Hooray" was borrowed from the Mongol invaders who shouted it as a singular battle cry when they burned medieval Poland. Anytime we honored the commander, three cheers would happen without question from the swollen faces that looked like they had just swallowed a canary.

X

That same year, on a warm summer evening at the port of Brownsville, Texas, a Goldenrod Diesel locomotive raced through the Texas night. The train was speeding too fast, causing seven fully loaded boxcars to jump the track. They slammed into the hull of the aging *Apollo*—the commander's flagship in the days of the North African flotilla—tied up a stone's throw away from the train tracks in a local river.

The impact caused the ship's hull to twist and buckle. The damage was death, and the ship was sent to a wrecking yard for scrap. It being a "Goldenrod" Diesel was fitting. In the movement, any time someone is excommunicated and declared evil, the order is issued on Goldenrod paper.

The color alone strikes fear in the movement's adherents. In a strange

CHILD X

act of God, the ship that unwittingly altered my life had been destroyed not so unlike any believer who stepped out of line, publicly criticized the movement, and was taken away from everyone they ever knew in an instant.

X

In an unusual moment in our childhood, Joshua asked me if I wanted to go to Hollywood Boulevard and see movies with him at the staggering Mann's Chinese Theatre. This was a rare time in our childhood when my older brother didn't bully me. We went together and just existed as brothers.

After watching the first movie, we pretended to go to the bathroom and went to find an R-rated movie to watch. We knew this was a crime. The last movie we saw that day was a strange, wonderful, bizarre adult feature cartoon film called *American Pop*, about three generations of artists—a grandson, great-grandson, and a great-grandfather—who, despite living very different lives, are connected to art.

I lost myself in *American Pop*.

A hundred years of artists, mothers, fathers, and sons. They all fail, struggle, and get caught up in sex, drugs, crime, and war until the film gets to the great-grandson, Pete. Pete is a drug dealer with no way out. His mother is descended from vaudevillian actors, and even though she becomes a whore who abandons him, she teaches him to sing and play music. He is selling cocaine to the biggest stars in the hills above Hollywood, including the rock stars. One day, he refuses to give the rock stars their drugs until they listen to him sing. Wanting their cocaine, they angrily relent and decide they'll listen to a crazy drug dealer sing to get their coke. When Pete starts to perform, they change.

The drug-dealing son of a prostitute begins to sing "Night Moves" by Bob Seger on a solo piano to the famous rock stars in front of him. What takes place is an assaulting, pop-blues requiem of youth that invades the body—a human being simultaneously reveling yet lamenting his past.

STARBOYS

The band is overwhelmed by Pete, and they hungrily agree to record him. In the rest of the movie, Pete goes on to become an American idol. Even though Pete's mother is a harlot, and he grew up in a slum selling drugs, because he can instill this song with all his pain, in a moment of artistic zenith, these famous pop stars—who had previously dismissed him as a drug dealer—greet him as one of their own and he gets to make records and become a pop star.

As the credits rolled and "Free Bird" by Lynyrd Skynyrd played, I asked myself if it was true. Could someone really make art or something so unstoppable that it could free them from the pain of their life? I then told myself it was just a movie, but I would never forget.

My brother and I left the theater late at night, elated and overwhelmed by what we had just seen—animated characters living and dying, going to war, and having sex.

American Pop was the third movie we had seen that day. We forgot all about the other two. As we exited the theater on Hollywood Boulevard, the thick desert air washed over our skin. I breathed in the familiar fumes of Los Angeles smog. I could taste the streets of Hollywood, its scent of car exhaust, cheap pizza, and buttered popcorn.

It is a smell that I still love to this day.

Sometimes I wonder if we could all be Star Boys.

X

In the midst of East Hollywood, in all of its crime and urban chaos, sits a green Shangri-La that makes absolutely no sense. A lush thirty-six-acre hill with gentle switchbacks leads to a plateau called Olive Hill. It makes no sense because it's still here even though the land was purchased in 1919, long before the strip malls, slums, drugs, and chaos that engulfed it. In 1921 a structure was completed here that ensured this patch of misplaced green-ery would live on forever. The unusual structure resembles a giant tomb of a future ancient world, like something aliens would have built in Egypt.

The structure was at the top of the hill next to where my friends and

I would play, and we didn't even know it was a house. On the outside it looked like an oversized mausoleum or vault.

It was gray stone with sharp lines and a matching stone fence surrounding the courtyard in the back. The roof of the main building towered above like a ziggurat—a pyramid with the top cut off, like an ancient space temple. It was engraved with precise symbols and symmetrical flower blossoms cut into the stone.

Over the years its presence grew boring to us, but that didn't stop us from trying to break in to see what was inside. Before and after our football games, my friends and I would slowly try every door and peer in every small window. There were flashes of gold and mahogany, but we really couldn't see anything, and how interesting could a tomb be anyways? We would jump the back wall and check those doors too.

The exotic structure must be in one of the strangest locations of any significant piece of architecture in the world. Dirty strip malls, the prostitutes of Sunset Boulevard, and miles of concrete, neon Latin-skinned slums surround the hill.

On a slow and long day when the sun was low in the sky at the golden hour, I walked in the park alone, looking for something to do, as I wasn't in school or being made to work by the movement. I stared at the impenetrable tomb on the top of the green patch. Just as I was about to leave, it called to me.

I decided to jump the wall and approach a door in the back of the structure that I had tried to pry open with my friends dozens of times. This time the door swung open as if it had never been latched. What I was about to see would change me.

I entered a vast room, mysteriously lit by the fading light that forced its way through the many narrow windows and skylights. In a second my heart thumped with fear. The alien spaceship masquerading as a house was far larger than it appeared from the outside and made me very nervous. I was in another world. My head got light, and I felt waves and waves of fear and tiny needles in my toes. I felt like I was going to pass out.

Paralyzed by fear, I began to move within the structure as if at any

STARBOYS

moment the LAPD helicopters would be there. In the shadows, I slithered into intricate rooms, walking slowly, fearful that every imprint I left in the carpet would allow the caretakers of this forbidden structure to track me straight back to The Fountain. Even though no one lived there, some of the rooms were lit only by orange and brown lights. The corridors felt green like an alien craft.

Soon I was standing in front of an enormous unlit fireplace carved in stone. Cut into the stone was a mountain range and the sun, commanding and hanging in the sky. The gargantuan fireplace reminded me of the Sphinx and pyramids I'd seen on TV shows about ancient monoliths that some said were built by people from outer space.

Set at the bottom of a stone slab, the fireplace was very tiny. I didn't comprehend why anyone would put such a small fireplace in a multi-ton block of stone just to carve a picture into it. My mind was burning with fear of being caught, my curiosity and fear were battling for control with my fear winning.

I moved through the rooms in a trance. My whole body pulsed. As small rooms opened up to massive rooms, and massive rooms opened up into cavernous rooms with strange skylights creating patterns of light that I'd never seen. I realized this was not a tomb, but some sort of incredible expression beyond the reach of my childmind. The furniture seemed to be cut in clean lines just like the stone. The soft brown tones of the wood were perfectly smooth, without any scrapes or damage—nothing like the worn-out furniture I'd known.

Back through the huge floor-to-ceiling plate glass, I could see the broad leaves of banana trees in the courtyard. I felt the unseen presence of whoever built the house, telling me how to look at it: "Stand here, and experience this room from this spot." This wasn't a house on a hill; a god lived here.

It reminded me of a movie I'd seen at Mann's Chinese where these manufactured humans called replicants were interviewed on machines like the ones we used at The Mothership.

I realized the office building in the movie looked just like this house. Its rooms were also beautiful-future, but in the movie there was a riot of rain, with its slicked, oiled concrete out of place—both with a disjointed mess of human habitation squealing outside in a near-future Los Angeles.

In the movie, a hunter named Deckard stalks and kills replicants—the engineered, artificial people created to be industrial slave labor for a corporation that was colonizing outer space. I saw Deckard as the enemy, and my heart broke for these replicants, who seemed to have far more humanity than the "humans" that murdered them.

Why did the office in that future Los Angeles look like this house?

Why would someone put this thing here?

This wasn't a beautiful spaceship, but a house crafted by a man named Frank Lloyd Wright in 1920 for a powerful woman, before the sprawl. The woman donated it to the city so that it would remain unchanged forever. In a burning city, poisoned by poverty, within the force field of Barnsdall Park, it remained perfect.

Suddenly, a sense of guilt and dread washed over me, as if I'd stolen something and was about to be caught. I was startled out of my trance and had to get out fast.

After sprinting out of the structure, I decided to climb over a fence behind a Thrifty's that sat at the edge of the park. I scaled the fence, and as I was coming over the other side, my jeans snagged on a barb at the top. Then I was falling. It was a dozen-foot drop to the ground. I fell head first into a bed of ivy before the entire front half of my body bounced up, spinning me onto my back. My head had gone straight into a broken city sprinkler hidden by the ivy—an eighteen-inch spike sticking out of the ground had almost impaled me through my mouth. Instead, that spike had speared me perfectly on my right front tooth, bouncing me onto my back. I began to taste my own blood and realized that I was missing half my front tooth. I could smell and taste a pungent pus and a cold pain where I now had an exposed nerve.

Frozen in the ivy, my mouth bleeding, I knew I had "caused this." I knew from studying the doctrine that when you do bad things you "draw

STARBOYS

in" bad things to happen to you. I knew these laws from the time I could speak. The Spaceship on Olive Hill was not mine, yet I had violated it.

Guilt and shame grew. I knew that the broken tooth would tell the other members of the movement that I had done bad and was a victim, as I always was. I had been marked. I carried this mark for almost two years until my stepmother, who I barely knew, showed up one Sunday morning, cleaned me up, brought me clothes, took me to a movie, and made an appointment to repair my tooth, a mark of my sins. Angels.

To stay safe, I swore to myself that I would never trespass in another's beautiful kingdom again.

Chapter 11

CHILDREN OF THE REVOLUTION

[1,336 YEARS BEFORE THE BABY FACTORY] In AD 634, Charlemagne, the first emperor of Western Europe, who at the time held court in what we now call France, had laid siege to a small city in Italy called Capua. Facing certain defeat, the duke of the city begged Charlemagne to relent and offered his sons in service as hostages if the emperor would spare the city. Charlemagne, being just and known for his fairness, said that he would take one son to be educated in his court; the other was free to go home with the duke in peace. In that single moment a child's life was changed. His life would have been different had he been raised by his father rather than the life he went on to live. An entire life may be changed by a single circumstance of history.

X

"No, he's not adopted," my mother said, carefree and brusquely, like she was ordering a coffee. "He just has a different father."

My older brother's grip loosened, and my arms tingled as the blood rushed back into them. Even my brother in his anger at that age stood back with his mouth agape while his eyes saddened. Joshua had been chasing me around the room hounding me. "You're adopted! You're adopted! I know you're adopted because you're darker than Jono and I."

I felt his older childhands shoving me. I could smell cigarettes on his breath—he had been smoking since he was eleven in our City of Angels.

I just stood there in the wave of my mother's statement, which had stopped the room. In that moment, I heard my mother's voice, clear and calm, from outside of my field of view. She was saying something I would never have expected, and it would shiver through my body for years.

It turned out that my birth certificate was a lie. John Mustard was not my father. In a strange twist of *melanin-onic* irony, it turned out my true father was still White. My birth certificate, to this day, has John Mustard's name on it.

In *The Empire Strikes Back*, the star boy learns a similar truth. Darth Vader is the star boy's father. When I had learned that the star boy and I shared this catastrophic truth, it gave me hope. If he could have a false father, an unforgivable deception, and then travel to Dagobah to study with a teacher, then maybe I could be special too.

Later that night, my mother finally got home around eleven. Joshua was gone, and Jono was asleep. I had been waiting for her. By the window in her tiny, disheveled bedroom with her skin glowing in the moonlight, I begged her to tell me about my father.

She said she didn't want to talk about it. I knew not to show emotion, or she would shut me out. I wanted to scream, but I controlled myself. I would be like Spock. I steadied my childmind. With my entire being ready to explode, I pushed the feeling of pain down, gently smiled, and asked her again. This time, she drew from her cigarette and answered.

"Jamie," she said, "I am one of the highest-trained people in this movement. I am a Level 9. Your father is one of a dozen people to be trained to the most powerful spiritual level possible on the *Apollo*—trained by the commander himself. Your real father is a Level 12, and one of the rarest human beings on this planet. But he chose to leave the movement, and now he is lost to us. I think he might be evil."

X

I continued to go daily to see *Empire*. At night my mind was filled with the image of the star boy and the black knight, his father, gripped in their breathtaking, violent duel near the end. The star boy decided he would rather die than fall to the dark side. The black knight would chop off his own son's hand to turn him to the dark side. Every nerve in my body hummed inside me as I watched it, and I vowed to myself, in the silent womb and warm glow of the theater, that if Luke could choose not to go to the dark side, then I wouldn't go dark either.

Luke and I both having fathers who went to the dark side, I shared in his confusion, but I didn't respect him. The star boy let other people see his pain, which made him prey. I would not be prey. My hero, who drew me back to *Empire* again and again, was Han Solo, a man who never broke emotionally. One of my favorite parts of the film, one that would hit me right in the heart, no matter how many times I saw it, was when the *Millennium Falcon* is escaping an Imperial Star Destroyer through a deadly asteroid field. C-3PO is harping at Han and telling him their grim chances of surviving an asteroid field were a deadly 3,720 to 1. Han Solo, like a lion, defiantly quips, "Never tell me the odds!"

Throughout my childhood I would attempt to ignore the odds and only look at what I could accomplish through sheer will, like I'd been taught in the movement. This would, in certain ways, keep me illiterate and poor, rather than seeing that I needed to fix my deficiencies. I would use the spiritual will that I learned in the doctrine to overcome everything—this would leave my mind stagnant and further sever me from the feelings in my body.

My two brothers had the weakness of fathers. They had something to disappoint them. When I think about who they would become, maybe, in all the pain and neglect of our childhood, they felt that someone was coming for them. This false belief in some ways might have made their suffering worse. No one was coming for them. I knew no one was coming for me. I accepted the fact that I would have to come for myself, and I would use the knowledge that spiritual intention could defy the physical world as my tool. I would come for myself in my nine-year-old fuck-you to the world. Good people would come for me anyway, and for that I am grateful.

Angels.

X

Thirteen years later, my younger brother Jono—at sixteen years old—would be assigned to the brutal reeducation camp for having sex with his girlfriend. Unmarried sex among members of Hubbard's private navy was strictly forbidden—because we were spiritual beings, discipline over the body was expected. He would spend seven years there, until the age of twenty-three.

He would never be the same.

I wondered if my little brother slept on the roof, exposed to the sun, just under the massive sign on the now big-blue dystopian building.

For years I fantasized that my father—one of the most powerful and rarefied humans in the galaxy—would return from the otherworld and take me to live with him in a great mansion and shower me with love and touch and affection.

He never came.

X

The commander Hubbard was not alone in his taste for "reeducation." In 1968, referred to lovingly as Father by his followers, Jim Jones, the leader of Peoples Temple in Guyana, employed what he called "the learning crew," his reeducation camp, to discipline members of his "church" who deviated from his mission of building his own socialist utopia on Earth.

In the learning crew, rule breakers slept and ate separately from regular members of Peoples Temple, were required to run everywhere, speak only when spoken to, and ate slop. It was eerily similar to the reeducation camp my mother had been in throughout my childhood and that Jono was later sent to, a place where we lived in constant fear as we grew older.

CHILDREN OF THE REVOLUTION

Only Jim Jones could decide when your sentence was up, and there was no limit to the duration of his punishment. This could mean Jones had some experience with Hubbard's doctrine. Even as a child, I was uneasy with punishment and suffering being called "learning" or "rehabilitation," but I didn't question it because the commander had said that its creation was one of his greatest acts of compassion: "Other groups kick you out, but I will reeducate you."

In 1966, Hubbard knew his time in England was running out as the UK government was becoming frustrated with him. He fled to Rhodesia (now known as Zimbabwe), a British colony deep in the African continent, to find a place away from humanity to build his movement. Like Jim Jones in the jungles of Guyana, Hubbard was growing paranoid and weary of governments. He believed he could replace the Rhodesian government while colonialism was waning and independence and a transition to a Black government was imminent. The commander would step in and lead the dark nation to an even better freedom. The Rhodesians saw straight through this and kicked him out of the country.

When we strive to overturn tyranny with an ideology or self-righteousness, we eventually become that tyranny—this is tyranny to freedom to tyranny to freedom, and on and on. A revolution is like the turning of a wheel. Eventually what was on top is ground into the dirt, but what was in the dirt rises to the top, only to fall again. The children of the 1960s saw themselves as revolutionaries, only to create a tyranny that would maim many of their children.

X

It was a hot August day in 1958 when Roy Jones Gilmer died of a massive heart attack, leaving my mother at twelve and my uncle Stevie at ten suddenly fatherless. A year earlier my mother had been diagnosed with life-altering diabetes; they had just developed the insulin that would save her life.

It has taken me years—many of them in kinetic motion away from

CHILD X

the gravity well of my birth—to understand Roy's death and the illness my mother experienced. As a young girl, my mother dealt with mortality twice in two years. It was this trauma that would lead her down a dark path: to the movement, to my suffering, to the suffering of my brothers.

Back at The Fountain, at ten years old, I didn't know a lot about my grandfather—where he'd been, who he'd been, how the things he had seen and done affected him. Roy's hell in Burma was a mystery and then unknown to me. Roy came back from the war and drank and smoked himself to death. My grandmother told me that he never slept. She suspected he prescribed himself pills as he worked and partied and burned the candle at both ends in an effort to regulate his now ravaged nervous system.

Roy was not one of many in a forgotten corner of the war. He was right out of *Raiders of the Lost Ark*, an adventurer surgeon who loved his violin and the jazz clubs of Harlem, with their medium-rare steaks, bourbon, Champagne, and refined culture. Roy brought home from the war an ornate carved Burmese chest. The chest was as big as I was at ten, cut from a rich local wood, its dark chocolate color deepened by air and time. The chest carved with scenes of a glorious Burmese warrior—possibly a Konbaung warrior—carrying two swords, charging into battle on the back of a great horse. The Konbaungs were the last native dynasty to hold power in Burma. When the British Empire was expanding into Burma—then and now called Myanmar—in 1824, it took them sixty years to subdue the Konbaungs.

This ornate chest, which had been hand-carved in the eighteenth or nineteenth century, had been gifted to Roy by a local Burmese family he had grown close to during the war. It had been in their family for generations, and it had endured. It is evidence of the orphan Black Prince's love of beautiful things—art, culture, and the depth of his mind—and the meaning Roy must have had to the Burmese family who gave him this precious heirloom. Was there something about this man that would make him worthy of such a precious gift from local strangers?

When Roy returned from Burma in 1946, he wasn't the same. Outwardly he was joyful and gregarious. Inwardly, his war continued. The

CHILDREN OF THE REVOLUTION

constant pressure and death of Burma wasn't something he could simply forget about. Roy had obligations as a physician. Day after day, he was fighting a gruesome sadness in the jungle of his mind, sleeping two hours a night, living on bourbon, cigarettes, and pills.

He lived at a time when stoic men silently endured the pain of a war, which, in its totality, had claimed seventy-three million of the planet's lives. The wet jungle war that he fought for a country that killed his ancestors—yet a country that gave him hope and opportunity—also helped kill him silently at forty-two.

For the rest of her life, my grandmother lamented to me that she should have done more. She was torn between being a dutiful, loving wife, and trying to fix her wounded husband. I didn't know it when she told me this, but the reality is there was nothing she could have done. Roy was fighting something inside him that no one yet understood; the cause of his pain was beyond something that therapy could fix.

Many would try to explain the cause of my grandfather's distress. "Shell shock," "soldier's heart," Hubbard with his "somatic imprints on the body," what he called "cellular memory"—the idea that the physical cells of our body hold our trauma, unless removed by machine-based counseling. Here my mother was at twelve years old, decades away from my birth and this horrible early death, brought forth by the remnants of a war, that would determine the course of my life. Roy's cousin Amy would one day tell me that, after the war, Roy "wanted to live fast, die young, and leave a handsome corpse, and that's exactly what he did."

My grandmother once told me the story about when my mother was a little girl. She was seven when she and Roy went to a school performance at an all-White school in Connecticut. The public-school staff, teachers, and parents had gathered in the school's entryway to greet attendees. When they saw Roy enter with his family, their faces darkened. The school knew how prominent he was but also knew it wouldn't go well for him to sit in the seats that had been saved for him at the front of the auditorium.

Eventually a teacher moonlighting as an usher told my grandfather—a man who had risked his own life and saved others in the Burmese

112   CHILD X

jungle, who as a doctor and surgeon might have saved the life of their neighbor's son, or brother, or nephew—that he had to sit at the back of the public-school auditorium. Roy left. He would not be gored.

It was after that incident that Roy joined the American Communist Party—they were the only people talking about civil rights for Blacks in the 1940s and 1950s. There was something tugging at Roy's conscience. He was a Black man who came from a family that had gone beyond prominence and built generational wealth—a wealth that would be used up in the years following his death. Most of the Black men in his unit had come from nothing, and after the blood and catastrophe of the war, had come home to nothing and a country that saw them as slightly less than a human. He felt guilt for his wealth and opportunity despite how hard he worked. Joining the party made him feel he was doing something to help his people and made him feel he was part of something bigger.

When Roy would have first attended one of these rallies in 1952, during the height of the Red Scare—a time when hysteria over the threat of communist influence in American institutions and culture spread like wildfire—he would have heard about how the American war machine had fed itself on Black American lives. He would have heard about how the G.I. Bill—aimed to help American veterans adjust to civilian life after the war through benefits, loans, and education—had been denied to Black people. Roy didn't need the G.I. Bill, but what if he had? This wrong burned deep inside him in every moment following the war.

My grandmother told me that as young teens, my mother and Stevie worked hard to make their clothes look tattered, worn, and real. They pretended to be poor because the counterculture made them ashamed of their wealth. As young Black Americans they couldn't have transcended or been from families that had exploded out of slavery and into prosperity—the counterculture promoted a myopic story of Blacks in America as only one of oppression.

Stevie was more interested in communes and free love than Black militancy. My uncle, who would at times be a surrogate father in my life, would go on to live for many years as a functional heroin addict. Even

CHILDREN OF THE REVOLUTION

113

when addicted to heroin, he retained his Greek god–like physique and held the warm glow of empathy as he taught his kids about fishing, hunting, and humanity.

In the early 1960s, kicked out of a boarding school in Switzerland for smoking pot, Stevie ended up at the Stockbridge School—a progressive Jewish school in Massachusetts for bright teens who didn't fit in. Arlo Guthrie, son of famed musician Woody Guthrie—who would go on to become a celebrated folk singer, recording with Pete Seeger, Judy Collins, and Willie Nelson—was my uncle's close friend. "Alice's Restaurant," a 1967 rambling folk ballad that aimed a sonic middle finger at the Vietnam draft, was Guthrie's anthem that would help define the counterculture and serve as its highest tribute. The songs were made from the scene where Stevie lived and his adventures with Arlo. For years, when I was living with Dorothy in New York, the house phone would ring, and I would hear her say, "Oh, hi, Arlo!" I was an adult by the time I knew who he was. For many years, when he was anywhere near New York on tour, he would call his childhood friend's mother to say hi. As I listened to my grandmother talk to Arlo, he seemed otherworldly and distant to me. He may as well have been from Mars.

Throughout the 1960s, my mother attended, and dropped out of, three fine art universities until she settled on a fourth, the Pennsylvania Academy of the Fine Arts. She would eventually drop out of that one too. She had been a promising young oil painter, mentored by Elaine de Kooning, wife of the Dutch-born father of American Abstract Expressionism, Willem de Kooning, an artist who would eventually be an influence on my life and my desire to spend it trying to make beautiful things.

In my early twenties, I would go to see Willem de Kooning's work in a museum in New York City. On the wall was painted something he once said: "You have to keep on the edge of something all the time, or else the picture dies."

When my mother joined the movement, she quit painting. What's strange is that she quit exactly when her art was getting somewhere. Her work had been collected by a few art museums—those with a hunger for young Black artists. What I love about my mother's work is also what I love about the work of James Baldwin, Zora Neal Hurston, the painter Jean-Michel Basquiat, and the actor that played him in the film, Jeffrey Wright. Their work transcends race. The greatest artwork, whether containing ethnic content or not, goes beyond any sort of category and becomes something accepted in the world as simply beautiful, moving, and human.

I can say with great certainty that my mother, the woman who never wanted me, created work that moved me. Had she not fallen prey to a complex, dark ideology, what would she have done in the world?

During the 1970s, some American Blacks felt that slavery and Americanism had robbed them of their roots. Some adopted African names and natural Afrocentric hairstyles and wore African colors. This "Back to Africa" movement culminated in 1976 when Alex Haley, my aunt Lucy's friend and classmate in their poor Tennessee town, published *Roots: The Saga of an American Family*. Haley's book was a cultural phenomenon that told the story of Kunta Kinte, an African man sold into slavery in eighteenth-century America, and his descendants, down to Haley himself. Haley's Pulitzer Prize–winning work was turned into one of the most successful television events of all time and made him one of the most known authors in the world.

In his twenties, my uncle Stevie took every last drop of a chunk of money he got in trust from Roy when he turned eighteen and booked a months-long trip to Lagos, Nigeria. He wanted to "go back to the motherland and discover his roots." My mother used her small trust to travel to a pseudo-naval compound in the lush English countryside. My grandmother lived comfortably off this money for more than twenty years, but eventually it would run out.

Stevie was a lean six foot three and muscled like a pro athlete. He wore an afro, goatee, and a colorful dashiki of white and gold. As he traveled the streets of 1969 Lagos, local Nigerians kept insisting there was a particular bar he would like in Lagos called The Gathering House. Everywhere he went, handsome and beautiful dark Nigerians told him this is where he would find his people.

CHILDREN OF THE REVOLUTION

Eventually Stevie did decide to go to The Gathering House bar to "find his people"—the reason he went to Nigeria. When he found the bar and went inside, he was shaking with joyful anticipation only to find he'd been sent to an expat bar full of White Europeans. To my uncle's shock, the Nigerians didn't see him as an African, but as an American expatriate in a foreign land with more in common with the resident colonials. I often thought my uncle probably chose to go to Nigeria because of his relationship with Tunji, but I don't think my ancestral past emanates from Nigeria. When my uncle set out for The Gathering House that day, he imagined a gathering of Africans telling stories over drinks. But in fact, The Gathering House was a haunt for CIA agents and spies, and postcolonial elites living in Nigeria's capital. Oh, the ridiculousness of it all.

X

One evening on my tenth birthday, thanks to Paco, in the basement of a 1920s movement-owned building on Hollywood Boulevard, between the smog-blanketed streets fraught with pimps, hustlers, and whores, between the Korean restaurants that served everything from doughnuts to teriyaki, I was sat down in a blacked-out playhouse with other movement members to see one of its biggest stars in *One Flew over the Cuckoo's Nest*. Somewhere in the play I saw a large Indian chief dressed in all white standing on a stage. A dark man did his mute character's monologues by turning the entire theater black with the giant rumbling, pounding sound of a heartbeat and strobe lights, so that you could understand that this was his inner world. He's speaking of the system as a machine. The deep bass of his voice shook my entire childbody. My head got hot. I began to float and the world fell away.

I burned.

I didn't know it until years later, but he wasn't an Indian man, but a Fijian prince who had found his way into the movement. They owned the slum upstairs, where members lived. This man not only starred as the King of Hawaii alongside Julie Andrews, Max von Sydow, and Gene Hackman,

116 CHILD X

but also played the great Chief opposite Richard Harris in *A Man Called Horse*. This large man was Manu Tupou. There is no way that I could've known that, someday, this man would become my greatest teacher and the reason I am an artist.

X

A year later, my older brother was still smoking cigarettes.

I went to sleep around 10:00 PM on the top bunk long before my brother came home from the streets. Around midnight, before falling asleep, my brother was having his last cigarette of the day in the bunk below me. Cigarette smoke was always everywhere and all around me, and I'm sure I smelled of it. The smoke was gathering near the ceiling. From the top bunk I could see it hanging in the blue-white mercury-vapor streetlight that flooded the room from outside as I faded in and out of sleep before falling deeply into a nothingworld. When my brother decided to go to sleep, he put his cigarette out in the white fluff just above him hanging out of my mattress.

In my dreams I heard a loud banging. I awoke in the arms of a giant man wearing a brick-red metal hat and a thick coat that felt like rope. The door behind him was broken and falling to the side. The gigantic man was staring down at me, eyes wide, and touching me all over my body, searching. We were surrounded by other large men in thick rope-like jackets and pants, staring at me with gentle concern. The room was awash in a halo of gaseous smoke illuminated and made beautiful by the gold fluorescent lights radiating above us.

I looked back at my bunk bed and saw it engulfed in flames as my nose and throat were coarse with the smell of burnt fabric and chemicals. I felt weightless in this man's arms. The fireman then raced me out of the room into the lobby of the building and down the front stairs into the cool air of the Los Angeles night. I was floating. He must have grabbed me one second before I was sleeping in a bed of fire. I didn't have a single burn.

Angels.

CHRYSALIS

flesh cauterized acid tears of the sun our skin bloodied

as the bad men did their work

in the dark invisible, burning

and in death I would become mummified.

Dried ancestors bubbling and popping in my cells

when we die we die long in the dark

Shrouded

long is our bill

—THE BAD MEN

Chapter 12

OREGON

We left The Fountain at three in the morning and slept on the floor of the airport. I was told only a couple of days before that I wouldn't be seeing my friends again, and that we would be leaving in secret. Randall and my mother told me that she had medical circumstances that they couldn't tell me about, and the movement wasn't allowing her to tend to them. I was told that if I told anyone of our plan, the movement's secret police would stop us.

I wanted to stay, and I thought I would miss my friends. But I was also excited about the conspiracy of my first escape and what was ahead of me.

Oregon was all green. All water. All wet, heavy mist. It was an alien landscape, and I an alien in it, but I was finally far away from The Baby Factory, The Red Brick Building, and The Fountain.

I was twelve years old, had recently learned the truth of my birth father, lived through one of the largest domestic raids in US history, narrowly escaped a devastating fire, and was leaving LA and the sun behind.

In those winters in Oregon, this new alien land, the cold blanketed my body with a new pain, seeking out any exposed skin with a cold burning. Seven days a week I was up at 4:30 to work. I would see a man racing across the horizon at the corner of Twenty-Fourth and Agate Street and disappearing into the dawn light. Some mornings the sky would crack open with thunder, and the rain that followed fell so hard it stung my skin. At times the weather felt emotional, but I could *feel* finally.

I was learning how to breathe this new air as I entered the street just before dawn each day for the paper route I walked for the *Eugene Register-Guard*. In winter, most days, it poured all night, every night. I would do my paper route, waking at four thirty in the morning, in temperatures just above freezing, wearing only a T-shirt and my thick canvas paper carrier, which didn't cover my arms. The cold burned. The cold allowed me to feel my body in a way I never had in the desert. I could have worn a jacket, but I wanted to *feel*.

I didn't understand what green was until we moved to Oregon. The shades of green within the trees and grass and parks seemed endless. My desert, green-starved eyes were run over by the invasive workings of chlorophyll. Early in the morning, everything was covered in glassy droplets of water that bent the light of the streets and gave life to the most boring things—cars, houses, mailboxes—all beaded with tiny watery diamonds. There was always a gray glow that I could enjoy for a moment or two before the sun rose and the dark gave in to daylight. My stepfather told me that the running man I would see every morning like a dawn clock was a legend—one of the fastest men alive.

I'd arrived on a colder biosphere than Dagobah in *The Empire Strikes Back*. I was a sun-based life-form adapted to drought, dust, and concrete. Now I felt like I was wrapped in a cocoon of water and had no idea of the dark road that lay ahead.

X

For the first three months away from the movement and its constant churn, we lived like most people. My mother and Randall tried to act as involved parents.

Randall smiled a lot but took no interest in me. He worked as a janitor and then a waiter in a Mexican restaurant on Willamette Street, the main

OREGON

artery that went through the city. My mother found work for Fair Share, an organization that went door to door to raise money to fight for better tax law for American and Oregon citizens. The two of them were bringing in enough to pay for the small house halfway down the block from Agate on Twenty-Fourth Street. The house, which was squat and the size of a mobile home, was a slightly-brighter-than-olive-green Sears house from the 1940s, the kind that you could order off of the back of a catalog. Everything was small, but at least it had three rooms. Jono and I shared a little room. Joshua had his own tiny room. And my mother and Randall had a small room.

My uncle Stevie, the one who threw me in the air using extraordinary words so many years ago, had moved to Eugene years earlier and found us the house. When he didn't find his people in Nigeria, he did find them in the counterculture. Eugene, Oregon, a mecca for the children of the revolution. Jerry Garcia and his legendary band the Grateful Dead ended their tours there every year in what was a sublime hippie celebration of phantasmagorical euphoria.

Even though I was never raised to brush my teeth or shower, in Oregon I slowly adopted some of these behaviors. I figured out how to shower, daily. I learned through the ritual of removing the fiberglass from my skin the exhalation of daily washing. I still didn't know that people brushed their teeth. It was something I saw in movies, but without context, I didn't know it was something people did daily, and I had gone so long without brushing that maybe it didn't matter.

On Monday morning, I stood a mile down the street from our tiny house in front of Roosevelt Middle School, a 1960s fortress of steel, brick, and solid glass. The building had been designed during the Cold War to be a safe haven and bomb-resistant in case of Soviet nuclear attack.

It was 1983, and starting late into the new school year made my strange clothes and my strange presence even stranger. I wasn't aware that teenage alienation was normal. I thought it was me, coming from a strange desert. I had clean clothes—simple T-shirts, corduroy bell-bottoms, and collared button-down shirts my grandmother had bought me from Meier & Frank.

My five pairs of dark corduroy bell-bottom pants were not going to serve me well. I was still an alien in an alien land, and now with my first months in an American middle school wearing corduroy bell-bottoms every day, I not only felt but looked like one.

X

John Podpeskar's science classroom sat just inside the inner courtyard, with rows of floor-to-ceiling windows in 1960s steel, lined with metal blinds. I looked outside at the water-soaked rows of low shrubs and the endless beadlets of rain collecting on the steel piping that lined the walkway. There were large squares in the open courtyard packed with ferns and small trees.

We called Podpeskar "Pod." He was built like a bear, with combed-over '80s hair and a thick brown mustache. The classroom was divided into two sections. Half of the room had rows of school desks where we sat; the other half had rows of microscopes set on high science tables where we worked standing up. They were covered in glass test tubes and beakers.

Those first days were madness. In my first week standing at a high science table in front of a microscope, I saw four heavy metal girls walk in and move toward me. The lead one had flaming feathered red, blown-out hair and a Def Leppard T-shirt. With a slight smile on her face, she looked at me and said, "Look, there's Jamie Mustard. He used to have friends, but they couldn't ketchup."

Pod rolled out a 16 mm projector on an industrial office cart, while excited kids noisily jumped up to turn the blinds down and darken the room.

"Hey, guys, I know we live in a place where it seems the rain never ends," he said. "I thought, because it's the beginning of the year, we would watch a science fiction film by Ray Bradbury of a story where middle school students on another planet also never see the sun."

As rain bombarded the windows of the darkened classroom, the

OREGON

projector began to flicker. The soft whirring of the projector and the droplets hitting the windows filled the room with a gentle sea of sound.

The film was called *All Summer in a Day*, and it invaded me. A red-headed girl with a strange mullet moves with her family to the colonized planet of a water-drenched Venus where it always seems to rain. The sun only comes out once every nine years in this dystopian land of gray steel and concrete; it was a rain version of Los Angeles, like the movie with the sad replicants. An Earthling, the main girl is old enough to remember what the sun looked and felt like. Her stories make the kids born on Venus jealous, and they grow furious. On the day the sun is set to come out, a boy born on Venus cruelly locks her in a closet after the other kids run outside. With the distraction of the sun, no one misses her.

When the years-long storm breaks, and the sun emerges in a powerful Venusian sky, all the children are overwhelmed by its shimmering warmth and power. When the red-headed girl with the mullet is let out of her captivity in the closet after the eternal storm returns, she is devastated.

All Summer in a Day overwhelmed me. It was my story in reverse: I came from a world drowning in sun, longing for rain. After years of drought in Los Angeles, my body longed for water. The film looked and felt like my new world, with its lush evergreens.

Back then, Eugene got up to sixty inches of rain a year. It rained every day. As the days went by, I continued to realize I'd never seen so much water. Moisture interacted with everything; it shined the streets; it matted the bark on the trees; it collected on the branches and the leaves; it soaked into and darkened my clothes; it got under my shirt and rolled down my back.

It felt as if the water filled in my body, from deep inside of me to the surface of my water-soaked, glistening skin. It allowed me to exhale. None of my classmates could ever comprehend the world of dust and concrete from which I'd come.

X

124   CHILD X

At Roosevelt, there were no interventions or special programs for someone like me who hadn't been educated. In math class, I sat at the back
without glasses. The blackboard was a blur of amorphous white characters
bathed in black. Even if I had glasses, it would have been easier to go to the
moon than understand algebra.

My teachers scribbled notes in bright red telling me that if I applied
myself, I would do better. These teachers didn't know, and I wasn't going
to tell them, that I'd been living in a spaceship in the desert, being conditioned only to save the world. In the movement I would only need to study
and apply the doctrine to move up its ladder to my previous state as a god,
and all would be solved.

Often my mother and Randall weren't home until late. I walked from
school to the corner store with food stamps before going home. The owner
was an old, plump, bald White man in polyester pants, a crisp off-white
collared shirt—complete with a pocket protector—and circular wire-
framed glasses who sat at the counter, surrounded by a jumble of cigarette
cartons and snacks wrapped in plastic. As I presented my food stamps and
made my daily purchase of canned refried beans, cheddar cheese, and tor-
tillas to heat up for dinner, he looked at me like I was something he could
tolerate, but never welcome. The old man always seemed to scan the food
stamps for a little longer than needed.

X

I couldn't do algebra, I couldn't write, but I could dream, and I could read.
I'd learned to read early to study the doctrine. There was one class at Roosevelt Middle School called Novels where all I had to do was read. I didn't
know what a novel was, or what literature was, or that you were supposed
to read books in a certain way. To me reading only consisted of tools that
would lead to saving Earth. Cultures having a language of symbols that
communicated humanity's experiences wasn't something I was aware of.
I might as well have had a red mullet and been from Venus. I'd never read
books about subjects outside the doctrine—it would be a waste of time.

OREGON

The first novel we read in that class was a true story called *I Know Why the Caged Bird Sings*. I was going through puberty, and this novel was my first reading, or seeing, of any sexual experience outside of the adult cartoon sex in *American Pop*. In this book about the life of a young girl, Maya Angelou describes her sexual molestation at the hands of Mr. Freeman in detail: *And then. then there was the pain. a breaking and entering when even the senses are torn apart.*

With my own sexuality emerging into my body like a silent storm I couldn't interpret, and no one talked to me about, the words of an eight-year-old girl being raped were hypnotic. I was horrified and moved, and I thought, *How come this didn't happen to me?*

It did happen to at least three of my friends from The Red Brick Building, and at least a couple of them have committed suicide. As I read *Caged Bird*, turning each page in witness of Maya's destruction, one of my constant thoughts was, *Thank God I haven't suffered anything like that.*

I wondered, what crazy adult made the decision to teach these books to thirteen-year-olds? There was a street vengeance where her devil was murdered after her sexual assault. I have often wondered if immediate justice helped Maya rise.

The second book we read in that class was *Les Misérables*—a French novel from the 1800s about how injustice always haunts the poor. Poverty sends a guy named Jean Valjean to prison unfairly. Reading about this strange, dark European world, I felt grateful that my life had not been unjust.

The third novel, *A Separate Peace,* was set in a wealthy boarding school in New England during the 1940s. The school looked just like The Red Brick Building on Melrose, but beautiful. In it there is a shy, introverted boy. This boy's best friend was everything that he wasn't—free, athletic, and liked by everyone. One day the two friends go on an adventure to climb a tree by a river. While in the tree, the introverted boy shakes the branch his best friend has climbed on to. The popular boy falls to the ground, breaking his leg, and is crippled for the rest of his life. They are never truly friends again.

126 CHILD X

Decades later, when they meet to try to fix their friendship, another accident happens. Stumbling as a cripple, now a man, his friend falls and breaks his leg. This time a piece of bone from his broken leg gets into his bloodstream, travels to his heart, and kills him. I didn't know you could die from a broken leg. When I finished the story, all I could think about was the possibility that rich kids could also be damaged and suffer like me. While I pushed this out of my mind and told myself it was just a book, it continued to haunt me. I had been raised in a strange naval doctrine with intergalactic space travel underpinning it all, a child X housed in the inner city, and novels made me realize there were things about the world that I didn't know.

In my life at The Red Brick Building and The Fountain and on the streets of LA, I had been separated from society through the sensory deprivation of forced illiteracy. I was among the living, but I was experiencing a slow death within my own mind. It was a death where you never die—a form of psychological torture that I have no language to describe. It's like falling from a tower waiting for impact, knowing the end was supposed to come, but it doesn't come.

In Oregon, among the green and the water and the power of those novels, I felt like a human at rest finally. For the first time in my life, I wasn't under constant physical threat. I exhaled. I had been paroled.

X

In my new town, there was a theater in a church called the Bijou Art Cinema, which was set in a remodeled nineteenth-century Mediterranean Revival church that had been converted into a cinema in 1980. We'd watch films from the religious pews, the sound intensified and crackled as it bounced off of the stone walls. The Bijou would change the way you experienced a movie, and I wondered if other places could do that too.

I lived one mile from Hayward Field—the most legendary running track in the world, made famous by middle-distance runner Steve Prefontaine. Rather than just winning, Prefontaine saw racing as a work of art. He felt how you won a race was its own form of creation.

OREGON

Sometimes, you see a movie, you leave the theater, and walk a little differently because you've taken something from it that helps you see the world. In Eugene I saw a movie called *Rumble Fish* that took place in a working-class town. It looked very much like the Eugene I was in, but with a more busy downtown. It was about these poor kids that looked cool and got into fights. The main kid had a mysterious older brother like mine. He was called the Motorcycle Boy, and he was played by Mickey Rourke with a cherubic face with the haircut of a Caesar. He was mysterious because he was indomitable and seemed to hear whispers from another world that no one else could see. It was called *Rumble Fish* after Siamese fighting fish that, if you put them in the same tank together, will violently fight until one of them dies.

Rumble Fish was set in black and white because those were the only colors the Motorcycle Boy could see. The only color in the movie is when they walk by the town's pet store and there are these fighting fish in a small tank separated by a barrier in screaming colors of red and gold. I wondered if S. E. Hinton, the female author of the book the movie was based on, was trying to say that when you grow up with nothing and absent parents, you are destined to fight, even when there is no reason. At the end of the movie the Motorcycle Boy violently breaks into the pet store, grabbing the fish, and freeing them in a concrete river like the cement LA River back in Los Angeles, by the entrance of Griffith Park. I wondered if my brother Joshua and I would spend our lives fighting—everyone, not just each other.

At fourteen my body was changing. I was building lean muscle. In our new house someone was watching TV in the sparse living room. I heard the opening beat and strings of the hit song "Human Nature," and Michael Jackson's ethereal voice. I looked over at the TV. There were images of emaciated Black children, living in tents in the dusty deserts of countries I'd never heard of. They had bloated bellies while flies circled their faces, landing on their open eyes and mouths in slow motion. The shot dissolved into Michael's face, and in his most caring voice he said, "What about the children?" Upon hearing his words, the first thought that entered my mind was, *What about the grown adults?*

128   **CHILD X**

The spring that Nu Shooz released "I Can't Wait," I met Coach Craybaugh, a tanned-skinned, red-haired, walking block of muscle who at sixty couldn't hear in one ear. Every day in gym class we ran a mile-long loop, then progressed to doing it while holding a five-pound and eventually a ten-pound weight overhead.

Over a few months, I transformed. I put on lean muscle as I grew, and my shoulders broadened. But I was still an other, a Mulatto mongreloid freak, uncomfortable under my own skin, who believed in aliens and spaceships.

Around this time, one evening my Uncle Stevie called when I was watching TV. He told me he just got back from staying at a hotel with the Rajneeshees on their compound, a place I'd never heard of. I had no idea what a Rajneeshee was. I was electrified by the story when he said that when he went through the security gate, the guards had machine guns. Several years later I saw on the news, in an act of terrorism, the Rajneeshees had been accused of poisoning more than 750 people in the Dalles, Oregon.

Watching this, I was grateful that I was never involved with a movement that hurt people.

X

I started at South Eugene High School in fall 1985. There was a tall and pretty mixed girl named Sophie with big eyes who always seemed to smile at everyone. When I would see her in the hallways, she would smile at me, and I always thought she was looking at somebody else. I was afraid of her. While her smile scared me, I thought she might be the nicest person in the world.

Eugene's biosphere was special. Our "family" had moved to a small house directly adjacent to the county fairgrounds. One morning during my bike ride from the fairgrounds to school, before the winter rain started and the sun was low, I stopped at Eighteenth and Olive Streets and marveled at the cloud formations towering above the valley.

OREGON

There is something sensory about the skies over Eugene that I have never seen anywhere. The high mountains of the Willamette Valley sit above a flat, endless plain. Above the bottom of the valley explode the overwhelming, beautiful monoliths of clouds stacked like anvils starting only a hundred feet off the ground. It was as if the valley sucked the elaborate formation toward the ground. These forbidding clouds may have been an omen for what was about to come.

In January 1986, Hubbard died. In the small living room of our little house bordering the county fairgrounds, I watched the coverage from the back of our small living room. The local news explained that science fiction author and founder of the movement, Lafayette Ronald Hubbard, had passed away. Reporters speculated and questioned the movement's future.

The TV screen flashed with pictures of the mysterious man in all his guises—a portly middle-aged man at a typewriter, a young explorer in the jungle, a young thin man at a typewriter, a middle-aged man on the high seas. The news clip ended with an image of an aging man on the high seas, staring at the horizon, wearing sunglasses, the commander of his own navy. The news clip faded, and they went on to the weather.

I thought of what I had found in Eugene. I thought of the novels, the Bijou, Sophie, and that Oregon sky. I was scared to think of what was next.

X

With Hubbard gone, the movement would need all the help it could get.

I was just beginning to find my footing in this strange, tiny green city with its hippies, its mountainous clouds, and its constant and abundant water, when I was told that we were returning to The Mothership.

The movement flew someone up, a chatty man named Sol with sandy red hair. Mentally, my mother and Randall were already back at the Advanced Division. Right before we left to return to Los Angeles, the Chernobyl nuclear power plant exploded in the Soviet Union. The disaster was all over the news and it gave me a tight feeling at the pit of my stomach.

In the months before leaving that spring, I sat down to lunch in the noisy expanse of the school cafeteria. Suddenly, Sophie sat in front of me. She flashed her warm, terrifying smile and looked at me like she wanted to make a confession. My body was completely frozen.

"Will you go out with me?" she asked.

When we met someplace, Sophie didn't ask a lot of questions, and made me feel totally accepted. As a result of the commander's death, I wouldn't be going back to school in the fall, so Sophie and I would only see each other into part of the summer. She was kind, and it was easy. Sophie had cream skin; long, black, curly hair; and brown eyes. Her hair reminded me of Shirley Temple if she had long hair. I started visiting her house on the hill. Her Black father was a psychologist, and her White mother was a housewife. They were kind to me. We made out in her bedroom, but I felt as if I was outside of my body.

The last time we met before I left, she spoke to me in a way that would change me. We walked to Skinner Butte Park on a warm summer's day and sat on the children's playground, which was abandoned for the day.

Sophie knew nothing about the movement, spaceships, fallen spirits, my physical defilements, my shame. She only saw me for what I looked like, an athletic, physical specimen—mixed like she was. The internal me could not have been more distant from the external me.

We sat there with the sun shining in our faces, and Sophie said to me, "Have you ever looked at your eyes?"

I was confused and didn't know what she was talking about. I had never looked at my eyes. "You have tan skin with bright green eyes," she said with radiant kindness, and a smile on her face. "It's very unusual. We're both mixed. You should notice how beautiful your eyes are."

"We're both Mulatto," I replied.

Sophie's face changed and turned sad. Then she looked at me sternly, grabbed my hand, and caressed it. "Don't use that word. 'Mulatto' comes from when you breed a donkey and a horse—that's what makes a mule. A mule can't reproduce. They used to call mixed people like us Mulattoes because we shouldn't reproduce."

I realized in that moment that the way the world saw me and the way

OREGON

that I saw myself didn't necessarily match. I became obsessed with understanding how the world saw me. I wanted to know, as I realized my new status as mixed and Black, if this skin and this label would hinder me. I wanted to know if it would affect my ability to move through the world.

Something was happening to me in Oregon. Many who lived in the damp valley, with its rain and dark skies, said that the gray overcast brings them down. Not me. I had been a fragile larva transmuting into a pupa inside a chrysalis, gestating, suspended below a branch in a wet forest. In the three and a half years I spent there, I never missed the sun, not once. My illiteracy was overwhelming, but something was different. I was changing. Soon I would return to the concrete and sun. I would have to leave my protective chrysalis too early. I was scared that the winds ahead might be too much.

As Sophie and I got up to leave, a burning was spreading throughout my body, fighting against the cool breeze rising up from the Willamette River. I felt rage at my real father. I felt humiliated about my association with a sci-fi navy in a desert slum that had been my universe for my first twelve and a half years on Earth. I promised myself that, no matter what, I would never tell anyone that I was a part of that movement—not ever.

I was about to turn sixteen, and for the first time I thought about the promise I made to my nine-year-old self: "If I go dark, they win." I made this promise to myself again. But first I would again have to face the beast.

Chapter 13

RETURN TO THE JUNGLE

Before I went back to Los Angeles, Dorothy asked me to come see her and bought me a plane ticket. She had a day or two with me in her house near White Plains, New York, before leaving to visit her childhood friend, Alex Haley, at his Tennessee farm. She pushed education and my Black roots as something I should care about.

Every day the phone would ring. It was Haley calling, and Dorothy would talk to him for what seemed like nearly an hour. Once she put me on the phone with him.

"Hello," I said.

"Brother James, I've heard so much about you. Your grandfather was the town doctor and everyone looked up to him. I looked up to him. Your Aunt Lucy was one of my best friends in elementary school, and Dorothy and your family have always been part of my family." He then startled me and said, "For what is the purpose that you have entered this world?"

I paused, tongue-tied, and said, "Mr. Haley, I'm trying to figure it out."

He laughed and quickly responded, "My name is Alex, please." I could hear him smiling over the phone. "But let me know if I can help."

We would never speak again before his death, but that conversation would bring me closer to where I came from even though I didn't know it at the time, and his words would go on to save my life. Dorothy asked me to relax in New York for a few days and gave me a hundred dollars for food and video rentals while she was gone. I would stay there with my step-grandfather, Robert, who was always grumpy, but seemed to love having me around.

The doctrine can be a prison with bars in the mind more powerful than steel. In the teachings, what we exchange is everything, and if you take something without planning to give far more in return, you could be a criminal. I didn't see any way I could exchange with my grandmother, and as much as my illiteracy haunted me, it wasn't as important as the fast-moving decline of our world. Maybe there would be time for education in future lives, in future bodies, with future parents, and so maybe illiteracy was what I had been called for, to serve something higher. My grandmother had nice things. Being around those things didn't make me feel like they were attainable. It just made me feel inadequate—that I wasn't contributing to her.

A few days later my grandmother returned with a copy of Haley's Pulitzer Prize–winning book, *Roots: The Saga of an American Family*. I had never seen a copy of the book before. It's a massive, hardbound thing that feels like a testament when you hold it. In the front of the book, Haley had written a personalized note to me: "To James, with brotherly love, Alex Haley."

All I could think as I looked at the book was, *I'm not Black. I'm an ancient spirit in a temporal mixed body. How is any of this relevant to me?* Maybe my grandmother hoped it would ignite a fire, get me to see and care about this side of myself that I didn't know. At the time, the fact that Alex Haley's words would eventually save my life wasn't even on the border of my imagination.

Before my grandmother left for Alex's farm, she made me an offer and asked me to think about it for a few days: "If you're willing to stay here, and work on your illiteracy," she said, "you can have access to a car, weekly

RETURN TO THE JUNGLE

135

money, everything you want you can have, but you have to be in school for rent." It went over my head. I was looking forward to being back in Los Angeles, being in the sun, getting back to my friends.

Reading. Writing. Arithmetic. I don't need education. It's a waste, I have the doctrine, I thought while her eyes glistened and she waited for my response. The thought of trying to learn how to write and do kindergarten-level math as a teenager made me feel sick. I turned her down and went back to a city of angels.

X

On the flight to Los Angeles, sobriety set in. I remembered the feeling of going back to the streets after being cared for in New York by my grandmother as a child—having ginger snaps and warm milk and honey and having my life saved. Then going back to the burning slum with its blinding light and neglect—thinking the whole time that I was doing it because it was my duty to my mother. Then the cold, creeping dread invaded me. I thought of the industrial food, the emotional and physical violence, the poverty and filth. I was flying back into all of it.

The jet engines whined like the screaming of spirits as we descended into Los Angeles. I felt the deck of the airplane drop under my feet, heard the machine groaning as the flaps extended, and I looked outside, wondering if my concrete habitat was the same as I had left it.

"I Can't Stand Losing You" by the Police was playing on my Walkman, Sting crooning in his symphonic voice, a lament about a man contemplating that if he died the people that he cared about would finally miss that he is gone and feel shame in their lack of love.

The sun was waning, dipping into the dark blue of the Pacific Ocean. The familiar smog that hung unmoving over the millions and millions of dots of light that make up LA glowed in a deep orange-amber.

It's a blanket of light, I thought as we descended into LAX.

X

136   CHILD X

I stood in front of The Fountain, muscled and lean, alert like a wild cat, surveying the movement fortress, The Mothership, with my eyes wide and intent. I was scanning for how the environment had changed and hoping I might see one of my friends. The long, cinematic, symphonic percussive intro to Dire Straits's "Money for Nothing" played on my Walkman at full volume, drowning out all the sound around me.

As I stopped and looked across the street, what I saw stunned me. The big, blue Brutalist Mothership with the huge movement sign on top was thirty yards to the right of an array of futuristic motorcycles, like something you would have seen in a Formula 1 race. There were the shops of my childhood set back from the street, creating a large concrete platform exposed to the sun. I recognized some of the faces as some of the older kids that had been raised in the movement. Here, a dozen of these colorful, powerful motorcycles and their riders, sitting on the stained concrete next to The Old Industrial Hospital, looked like a scene from a science fiction version of Jean-Luc Godard's *Breathless*—a New Wave French black-and-white film from the 1960s about a criminal car thief on the run; cash and a girl; and sex, betrayal, and death on asphalt.

Some of the bikes were parked, while other motorcycles cruised up and down the platform just outside The Mothership in the Mexican slum. Just as I thought it couldn't get any weirder, I heard a large roar. A massive motorcycle raged by me with one wheel up high in the sky. The bike turned around and joined the others.

I took in the bikes. Kawasaki Ninjas in candy-apple red. The Kawasaki GTR1000s in matte blue. Yamaha FZ750s in electric blue with their silo tubes and matte chrome tailpipes made brighter in the sun. Even at rest, their sculpted lines exalted power and motion. My eyes danced over a black-and-chrome Suzuki GSX-R1100 with a mirror-shine finish so flawless I could see my reflection growing bigger as I crossed the street.

I was confused. I saw older kids I recognized from growing up in the movement. These motorcycles cost between $6,000 and $10,000 in 1980s dollars. These kids had no education, no family, and—since it was a weekday morning—likely no jobs. They were older than me. None of them recognized me, as my body had transformed. I was wearing fitted, faded denim jeans, a white T-shirt, and a perfectly battered pair of red and black Air Jordans. I would come to learn that many of these kids were homeless, couch-surfing, or huddled together with five of them living in a one-bedroom apartment. I would also come to learn that some of these brand-new shiny machines of astonishing design weren't acquired in honest ways.

I saw a kid named Tor who, although older than me, was unmistakable in his square-faced, dark-haired Viking handsomeness. He was never nice to me, but I always knew him to be reasonable. Tor was leaning, half-sitting on the seat of his bike, talking to a sinewy girl who weighed about ninety pounds and was clutching her own helmet in her hands.

"Tor?" I said.

Tor didn't seem to recognize me, nor did he seem to be confused or concerned with the fact that I knew his name. I asked him if he knew where Mickey Tealer was. He pointed down Berendo and said, "The first apartments on your left, just past the parking structure, apartment three. They're bungalows. You'll see the number on the door."

He quickly turned his head, dismissing me, and started talking to the girl again.

My first thought was that the bungalow was a shithole not so different from where the movement had put us on our return to LA. In an ill-thought-out, somewhat humorous attempt to surprise my long-lost friend, I didn't knock and jerked open the door. In the darkened living room, I saw the form of a figure sleeping under a pile of blankets on a worn-out mattress on the floor.

"Rise and shine, motherfucker," I yelled.

The figure popped up, throwing off the mismatched blankets, revealing my friend Lulu, her breasts hanging freely in the lint-filled sunlight. Her eyes were huge with fear, and I realized that the last time she saw me, I was twelve. This sixteen-year-old, brown-skinned, muscled athlete standing in her living room now, while she was naked on a mattress on the floor, had to be a shock.

138   CHILD X

"Oh my god, I'm so sorry," I said, just before I looked away, as I stared at the wide-eyed fear on her face.

"Jamie?" I watched the recognition spread across her face.

"Lulu, this is so embarrassing. I wanted to surprise Mickey. Where is he?"

"Jamie, where have you been? He's going to be so happy to see you. Where have you been? Where did you go?"

"We went to Oregon. I wasn't allowed to say anything."

Lulu stared at me with a knowing glance. I asked her where the gang was, and she told me that Mickey went to see his mom, and he should be back in an hour if I wanted to wait. I turned around while she dressed, and she walked to the studio's old, rounded fridge and poured us two glasses of Tropicana orange juice. We sat down at a card table with two folding chairs and began to talk like two people intimately connected by some invisible umbilical cord where no time had gone by; puberty and age had changed nothing.

Lulu explained to me that, a year earlier, all of us kids between the ages of fourteen and eighteen were told we had to sign the billion-year contract or get out, while the Night Stalker raged across the streets of Los Angeles. Our group of friends had scattered. A couple signed, but most everyone else went out on their own and were working around The Old Industrial Hospital to be closer to their parents, since this was the only world they knew. They weren't part of the movement anymore, and with their loud motorcycles, crime, and drugs, they were rhapsodic in an act of machine-based defiance—hanging around the beast, homeless, destitute, with no education, forming a community of their own. It was a no-money, 1980s version of *Rumble Fish* where poverty and expensive motorcycles coalesced to define an era.

In movement doctrine, there is a chart of emotional effectiveness. The chart goes from below "body death" at total failure to "serenity of being-ness" at the top. There are forty emotional vibrations where human beings live. You can't survive as a human below 2.0, which is "antagonism." The people in the movement across the street would see these kids that they terrorized and abandoned as "victims." A victim is 0.1 on the chart, well below anyone who had any chance for survival in the world. On the chart, the victim sits just above "body death." It's a form of being a sickening grotesque in their stigma. Below body death exist emotional states like "controlling a body," "needing a body," "being nothing," "total failure." At the high end of the spectrum, seventy tones away, are emotional vibrations like "exhilaration," "action," "cheerfulness," and "enthusiasm." I lived in a state of constant cognitive dissonance. I didn't think these kids were monsters, but I didn't necessarily think they *weren't* monsters. Outside of parties, I kept my distance. I needed to survive.

In Hubbard's doctrine, and in his principles of the mind, he describes how our cells have memory and that when we go through emotional or physically painful events, our cells store that memory. This is the source of all of our neuroses, fears, mental illness, and even physical sickness. With machine-based counseling, you use the machine to help spot those incidents and theoretically the machine tells you when the cellular memory has been cleared out, restoring you to a state of mental and physical perfection.

When you look into the doctrine, with the reeducation camp, the promotion of yelling at each other, hard labor, sleep deprivation, the shaming of sex, the unacceptability of displaying emotion, the psychological equivalent of a bullwhip used to get people in line, keep people in line, to keep work flowing—you have a system that constantly damages the cells the master is claiming to repair. What I now know is really happening is the destruction of the nervous system. But to me then only machine-based counseling could fix these symptoms. They harm you by psychologically and sometimes physically destroying you, and then only they have the cure.

The motorcycle kids and I weren't aware that this was what had been done to us, but we could feel the effects. They resented the movement, and they used it to justify all sorts of self-destructive behavior. The movement would then judge that behavior, compounding and worsening the problem, ultimately condemning many of these kids to lives of crime, or deep frustration and anger.

X

I moved into a broken-down Spanish Mission–style apartment on Edgemont, one block west of The Mothership and one block south of Sunset Boulevard. It was another tiny one-bedroom, only about five hundred square feet. My mother and Randall lived in the living room, while Jono and I shared a tiny bedroom with two twin beds and a small space in between.

My mother and Randall went back to work at the movement but didn't bug me about the billion-year contract because we didn't live inside the fortress. They were highly valuable to the movement because they had trained for years as machine-based counselors—the equivalent of what you would call a PhD in the otherworld. What it really meant was money. The counseling they could deliver on a weekly basis was tens of thousands of dollars a month, necessary fuel toward the movement's quest for planetary salvation. And, in the wake of Hubbard's death, money was as important as ever to drive the movement's future.

I was desperate to get back into school. My illiteracy was a piercing needle that wiggled inside my heart. I didn't know what to do. I didn't have the strength to do it, but I would have to do something.

There was a private school run by high-level members of the movement out of a former Russian Orthodox church. I asked if I could go there. It cost $1,000 a month. Barbara Heper was the woman who ran it, and I thought she might be a lesbian. If true, like Quentin, that meant she would be considered in the vibrational tone of concealed hostility matching Charles Manson and Hitler. This would not work for someone currently on Level 7 of spiritual return.

She told me that because of who my mother was, she'd let me attend the school for free in exchange for work. I would have to work from 3:00 to 6:00 at the after-school program with the younger kids, never be late, and never leave early.

I said yes.

I had no money and no car. In the doctrine, you are taught from birth that through the power of decision alone, you can cause the physical world

RETURN TO THE JUNGLE

141

to bend to your will. I visualized that I could have a motorcycle. I met a guy on the concrete platform where the motorcycles hung out, who saw me staring at his 1970s Honda 350 Enduro. He looked like James Dean, and he smiled at the way I was eyeing his bike. He had just bought a super-bike and was needing to get rid of the Honda. We made a deal.

The Enduro had a tall front wheel. It wasn't a superbike, but to me it was cool. With expired tags, no idea how to ride, or what a clutch was, I sat on the bike at the corner on Berendo, staring directly at The Fountain, my childprison. In that moment I released the clutch too quickly; the front wheel rose up and almost threw me off the bike while I was flanked on both sides with the Advanced Division on my left and the giant building of the fortress on my right, now painted a ridiculous baby blue. I thought them painting it from the militaristic tan to the baby blue was some attempt to make it more friendly and less weird. It was weirder—Marilyn Monroe's haircut on a pig.

I taught myself to ride the Enduro in exactly the same way I had taught myself to ride a bicycle in the carpeted hallways of The Fountain. I practiced on quiet streets, and after hours of messing around, I could ride.

To this day, outside of the confines of the doctrine where I learned it almost as a form of magic, when I want something to materialize, I visualize it. I make it true in my mind. When you make something true in your mind, it can cause the world to bend to your will. In the movement I learned hard work is not enough; you need to visualize a defined future with complete "certainty" to accomplish anything. I still believe this, but for me now, it is not certainty, it is faith.

When I was twelve years old and in machine-based counseling with my mother, I had my first past-life memory. I was an American GI killed by Viet Cong after stealing a motorcycle off a Charlie in Vietnam. I believed because I had ridden motorcycles in a previous life that that was why I could do it now. I also knew, without a father, after teaching myself how to ride a bike, if I ever wanted to ride a motorcycle, I would have to be my own father.

I kept asking myself, how did these kids who had grown up in the movement's slum neighborhoods, with no real education, get the money to own these bikes? Avo was a lanky Armenian kid with a busy black afro and a pencil-thin mustache. Avo had a brand-new 600 Kawasaki Ninja, a brand-new Corvette, and $25,000 worth of DJ equipment. He couldn't have afforded any of this as a cashier in a Los Angeles corner market and a liquor store in a slum.

X

I was leaving New York George's restaurant when forty Filipino gang members approached me from where the motorcycle boys hung out. The leader stopped just inches short of my face. He was tall, bulky, and had a single tuft of black hair erupting from the base of his skull.

"Who are you?" he challenged me.

My nerves tingled. In that moment, I thought of Alex Haley, and I didn't know. I realized these guys were seeing a muscled brown Mulatto kid that everyone knew in the neighborhood except them. It made them uneasy. If I was antagonistic in any way toward these gang members—who were just like me, poor, illiterate, and futureless—if I was fearful, he'd smell it, and they would hurt me. I had to be nothing. Fear, aggression—both were weakness, like blood in the water.

"Jamie," I said evenly. "I'm from here." I could feel my heart beating and blood rushing through my head. In the three years I was gone, the sons of Santanas had grown up to be this angry gang of kids.

The leader studied me, craning his neck back, chewing on the inside of his cheek.

"You're not worth it," he mumbled, brushing past me. They walked away, down the street. From then on, they left me alone.

X

There are many LAs. They are broken up into many mixed neighborhoods—Filipino, Korean, Mexican, Armenian, Nicaraguan, Guatemalan, and Black. They are all different and carry their own charm. Echo Park, a now hip neighborhood, consisted, in the '80s, of small casita-like bungalows in the hills that were the home of working-class Mexican families and gangs with their tricked-out cars. Sitting between Silver Lake and Downtown LA, Echo Park had Deco bridges and streetlights that simmered with orange and yellow sodium vapor.

Repressed kids from the movement, as teenagers living on their own, were now going wild. I would eventually find myself at a party thrown by Tor and his friends in the then-Mexican-gang-filled Echo Park, now a queer bohemia. Avo always DJed our parties. I went to one of the shared houses of the motorcycle kids who lived there because the rent was cheap. Emanating from the house before I entered it was "Erotic City" by Prince, coming from Avo's giant speakers in the humble Midcentury home with floor-to-ceiling windows, caressing the night on the East Side of Hollywood. "Erotic City" is an ethereal, beautiful, seductive, sweaty poem about sex in purple hues.

The kids at the party consisted of a few of my old friends from The Fountain, the motorcycle kids, and some upper-middle-class children of the movement I'd met at my new school. We were all mixing, and I had no idea why. Tor and I watched Avo behind his turntables—DJ gear fit for movie stars that he hauled to every one of the parties on the Mexican side of the Angels. The sounds of the '80s entered my body. I burned.

I stood talking to Tor by Avo's DJ booth. Tor explained the motorcycle economics of the new neighborhood to me. Avo and his collaborator Jack would get a request from a chop shop about a superbike that had been totaled by the insurance company. The shop would tell them what kind of bike they would need brand-new to restore the damaged bike. Avo and Jack would then steal the exact superbike the shop wanted. They would just lift a bike and shove it in the back of a van. Then, they'd haul the wreck to the chop shop, keep a factory model of the same bike, swap out the essential parts from the fresh bike to the wrecked one, and sell the damaged bike as "practically new." Jack, Avo, and others would make a few thousand dollars every time they did this, and they did it weekly.

The motorcycle kids next to the movement acquired bikes all sorts of ways. Some borrowed money from their long-lost fathers and mothers, and others stole bikes and sold drugs to live their lives. I had one friend who was seventeen who hung out with a twelve-year-old girl whose mother—who he was having sex with—bought him a brand-new $6,000 Ninja. The kids that acquired the bikes by being a part of Avo's scheme seemed to never get caught. I don't think Avo saw himself as a thief, but rather as a businessman. The new bikes were insured, so the people he was stealing from didn't lose anything. The restored totaled bikes would be sold slightly below market, giving people a deal. All of this could only be good.

As Tor and I finished the conversation, the Smiths' "Death of a Disco Dancer" faded out in the back of my mind, I thought about death.

It was a song about dying young and how outside circumstances can, at any moment, reach in and change your life, making idealism kind of pointless. Tor said that the song was either about AIDS or bombings in some place called Belfast—a movement where Irish sometimes used bombs to blow up dance clubs. Tor and I had this entire conversation with him staring at the door. He was completely uninterested in me and told it to me like he was reciting it to himself.

Then Tor became a blur of blue jeans and leather, moving across the crowded living room and into the apartment's small entryway, seizing space under the archway of the door frame like a gargoyle statue. Then I saw what he was glaring at. A group of Mexican teens in wool zoot-suit pants, flat-black penny loafers and wingtip shoes, plaid flannel shirts, and jet-black hair slicked back with pomade—Cholos. Some say the word "Cholo" comes from the Spanish Caribbean; it means roughly "wild dog" in Spanish. The Spaniards who had colonized the islands hundreds of years ago used it as an insult for anyone who wouldn't work. Of course I didn't know this at the time. All I knew was that they were kids in the surrounding neighborhoods that you didn't want to mess with, but I knew some of them and loved their style and their hydraulic fucking cars. These guys I didn't know. Soon they were in the house, smiling and drinking with us.

Growing up in the movement's slum educational facility called the

RETURN TO THE JUNGLE 145

Apollo Training Academy, we saw the graffiti of the gangs that built this culture left over from the '70s. Two famous gangs from that time were the Mexican Barriox13, called B13, and Santanas—the oldest Filipino street gang in Los Angeles that had been around since the 1920s. Growing up in the movement with their old gang graffiti everywhere, many of us kids glorified and looked up to them like invincible unseen gods when we saw their marks and symbols in the streets. The gang in our neighborhood that threatened me at sixteen was called B3 and was said to have been the younger brothers and children of the mystical Santanas.

LA Cholos and their subculture arose from second-generation Mexican immigrants born in the US wanting to differentiate themselves from newly arrived Mexican immigrants. They were saying, "We defined an identity in a hostile land long before you got here." The Cholos were not so different from the children of the movement, and we stuck together in bands.

Morrissey faded into the background as Avo began the next song before the last song ended. I heard an electronic wail, a clashing and colliding beat, and a descending guitar as Oingo Boingo's "Private Life" enveloped me. A bubbling, paranoid song about a person who feels their private life is a need.

As I sank into an oversized old armchair, my eyes floated over the crowd of people gathered in the shifting, smoky light of the small house, the orange glow of the Echo Park streetlights creating a cinematic glow through the window. Then, sitting by herself, I saw a living vision, a White teenage girl I didn't know. The pale flesh of her face was pristine, and her beautiful clothes seemed bespoke and out of place. Slim, slight, and elegant with big medium-chestnut hair, she had thick bangs that threatened to veil her haunting eyes. I thought, *She is the most beautiful girl I've ever seen*. She was beautiful in the way of a girl who seemed older than she was and knew all the world's secrets. I stared at her like she was otherworldly.

In that moment, my friend Devin entered from the kitchen; then he was suddenly grabbing her hand and walking her toward me. He kept holding her hand as they approached.

146   **CHILD X**

"Hey, Devin," I said to Devin as I looked at this angelic being.

"Hey, Jamie, this is my friend Lisa. Lisa Marie," he said.

I quickly realized it was Lisa Marie Presley, the most sequestered child in Hollywood. Devin had been friends with her growing up. His parents were artists and all I could think to myself was, *What is she doing here?*

I had barely said hello when the aura and energy of the party shifted. "Close to Me" by the Cure was exploding in, a fast and up-tempo vibrating bass line, topped off by synths that could have been a child's xylophone. It was an exhalation of sound. There were odd breathing sounds just under the mix, and something else that could have been a snare drum or a door slamming repetitively. Lisa Marie would die of a "broken heart" thirty-seven years later while she was at public odds with leadership of the movement.

She would become addicted to opioids after the suicide of her son, who had been raised in movement schools. Like the rest of us, Lisa was a child X brought young or born into a narrative where her needs would need to be secondary to the imminent task of salvaging humankind and achieving a return to our original state as fully realized gods. In Lisa's case, her X would come from her young mother, who likely joined the movement as a form of protection in an uncertain world in the wake of Elvis's death.

Lisa was just one of the kids and, eventually, adults who were part of our tapestry—one of us. Even though this song would not come out for three years, today, whenever I hear "Lovesong" by The Cure I see Lisa's face, a daydream that never ends.

Tor wanted the Cholos to leave. As the music blared, Tor and his friends politely asked them to find somewhere else to be. As a crowd of nervous, drinking kids watched from the stoop of the small house, the Cholos in their cinematic uniforms started walking out of the house down the driveway but weren't moving fast enough for Tor, who started to threaten and move toward them. As Tor and some of the other kids, Jack, Big Keith, and Salvatore, got to the driveway, the immaculately dressed Latins ran to the street. As they got to the street and stopped, one of them pulled a .357 revolver from the waistband of his wool pants and either waved it or fired

RETURN TO THE JUNGLE

a bullet into the sky. We all froze. I swear I remember the echoing blast of the gun lighting up the asphalt beneath him. It was a warning, and Tor and his friends backed up. The Cholos laughed and disappeared into the night.

In this tiny house in Echo Park, we were the children of the movement—pseudo-navy kids, movement rich kids, and the motorcycle boys—all very disparate situations that had one thing in common. We all had parents who were making their children's needs secondary to salvaging the planet and achieving their own spiritual salvation. We normalized the emotional disconnection between us and our parents. All this because our parents *knew* with absolute certainty that past lives were a fact, making this life less important. When I think about Heaven, living a life of deprivation now to live in a glorious afterlife, it always sounded preposterous to me, but we children of the movement were doing the same thing.

The parents had lived millions of lives before and would live millions of lives in the future, their kids would be their parents, and their kids would be their husbands and their lovers and their wives. Any relationship of this life was but a drop of water in an ocean of interactions between eternal spirits—they had lived countless lives and would continue to live future lives. It wasn't faith, or belief to them—it was *science*, as irrefutable as gravity.

I witnessed children understanding that they are one being out of trillions of lives. Being born one of millions of children one has had before, and would have in the future, leads to depression, suicide, eventually self-harm in some form no matter who you are.

The kids of the private navy and the non-navy kids are the same in this way: while their brains were still forming, through the "mind-training" they learned to detach from and deny the body. Emotions were not allowed. They were told they were trillions-of-years-old gods at five.

To this day, former members of the movement will not acknowledge the destruction of their children, insisting it was the commander and his doctrine that did the damage. The psychological manipulation has often turned our adult minds, as the children of the *Apollo*, into paranoiac rage.

148   CHILD X

I know now parents are the first line of decision against children. That's why I believe that the children of the revolution are ultimately responsible; *the parents* who chose to join the movement. *The parents* who chose to believe their children were the commander's children. The parents who clamored for machine-based counseling as the solution for the natural chaos of growing children.

The *former members* that built the movement were saying to their children that the parents' own freedom was the most important thing in the world. The inconveniences of this lifetime and the pain it created for their children were nothing in the shadow of their own infinity. That certainty, like cigarette smoke blown in your face, is a silent killer. What would it do to a person to be the child of a parent who thought of them as one of a million children over a millennium—what would this do to their self-esteem, their state of mind, when they're too young to process it? To make a save-the-world omelet, the movement might have to crack a few skulls.

However, I believe today that it is the *former members* who built the movement in the 1970s, denying our pain while pretending to be on our side, who are killing us. They believe we are all just ex-members like them. They believe our child experience means nothing. Their denial while pretending to be our allies crushes our minds. They are devils.

X

In 1986, after David Miscavige appointed himself the movement's new commander, I started at Heper Academy's aftercare watching the younger kids. It turned out to be a collection of movement kids in an abandoned lower parking lot playing until 6:00 PM. Completely open to the sky, it was more sun and more concrete. These non–private navy kids were still from the same alien world that I was, and we spoke a common language.

The first friend I made there was a handsome kid with freckles a year older than me named Francis Caldwell. He was lanky like Robert Smith from The Cure, with beautiful dirty brown hair. Francis's mom was from Scotland and a member of the movement. In her early forties she met

RETURN TO THE JUNGLE

149

Lightning Nicky Hopkins, widely considered to be one of the greatest studio pianists in music history, having recorded with The Beatles, The Who, The Rolling Stones, The Kinks, and many others, and they married and moved to Nashville. Nicky Hopkins, also a member of the movement, was from England and considered the greatest rock session piano player in the world. Francis moved in with a friend of the movement who had a daughter his age. They let him come and go as he pleased. Like many movement kids, whether involved in the pseudo-navy or civilians, as trillion-year-old beings, Francis lived unsupervised.

Francis as an act of mercy brought me, illiterate and all, into a small pack of middle- and upper-middle-class kids of the movement. We connected on some level of intelligence where he could see past my illiteracy. Francis asked me to come downtown with him to see a friend of his mom's, also a movement member, named David Campbell, who I now know to be a rock music arranger, known for string arrangements for famous bands. Francis told me he wanted me to meet David's kid because he was a genius. I didn't know what a genius was.

We ended up at David Campbell's house near the Knickerbocker. The walk up the street to the building was very Bukowski. We entered a hot pre-war apartment. Francis was close to David's son, this quiet introverted kid sitting on his bed. He was kind.

I had a new girlfriend, Cara. She was a childhood friend who left to live with her father in Seattle around the time I went to Oregon. We came back at the same time.

Cara had gotten cool-cultured in Seattle and shoved me into thrift fashion and independent films, insisting that I see *Room with a View*, which would fuel my love of Victorian parlor dramas, novels, and films, for the rest of my life. Why the hell does a Brown kid growing up in the slums of Hollywood like Victorian parlor dramas?

We saw *She's Gotta Have It*—Spike Lee's first film—at The Vista where Hollywood, Sunset, Hillhurst, and Virgil meet in a schizophrenic five-way intersection. Not long after with Francis, I saw *My Beautiful Laundrette*—a film about a Pakistani man named Omar living in London and his eventual romance with his best friend, a mixed half-Pakistani half-English street punk named Johnny, played by Daniel Day-Lewis in his first leading role. *My Beautiful Laundrette* haunted me because it made me doubt my ability to ever do anything beyond manual labor and languishing in my habitat, in the shadow of the movement's fortress.

I had no money and whatever money I did make went to movies and food—my nourishment. Most of the other kids I had grown up with at The Fountain weren't using movies to frame their reality the way I was. Movies would become my mother, books and fine art my father. These forbidden fruits of outside knowledge had been implanted in me and would eventually serve as my mind-worms, giving me what I needed to carry through.

Many of the kids I met and knew in those years would go on to create the art I loved so much. Juliette Lewis's older brother, Lightfield, had a brilliance. He made movies on VHS documenting our teen years at parties. Many of these kids—some in the movement, some not—running around LA would go on to be famous, including Juliette, Beck, Cuba Gooding Jr., and Giovanni Ribisi.

When I met eleven-year-old Giovanni Ribisi, it was a kind of poem.

One day I was walking down to the baking lower parking lot of Heper Academy, the light concrete reflecting the sun up at me from the ground. A few days earlier Cara had told me, "There's this new kid in the school—he glows. You have to meet him." This glowing kid wasn't at school every day, so it was a few days later, when I was walking down to the cement playground, that Cara appeared out of nowhere, her face rapt with excitement.

"He's here!" she said, grabbing my arm. "You gotta come! He's here!" I thought it was kind of ridiculous for her to be so excited for me to meet an eleven-year-old.

She led me into the blistering sun, and I saw a blond kid playing football. His hair wasn't just blond; it was cherubic, a mane of curls that radiated light from the sun. He saw me standing with Cara, who beamed. We walked up to him, and he looked up and smiled.

"I'm Vonnie," he said.

I felt instantly open. It almost felt like love. In those days, he was like

RETURN TO THE JUNGLE

151

that toward everyone. Even though he was younger than me, he would become my friend during that time in Los Angeles, and we would all spend our lunches together the next year when he graduated into a high school run by members of the movement. From the second I felt his presence, he was different.

Somewhere around then I went with a friend to see Oingo Boingo at The Palladium on Sunset in the middle of Hollywood. It was the most pulsive rock show I'd ever seen in my life, with its multi-piece horn section and its enigmatic lead singer. Toward the end, Danny Elfman sang "Not My Slave," a song about a man who has a love that he is losing and exalting. He possesses another but does not see them as a slave. With its driving beat and pained lyrics, he wails that his possession is not his child and not his slave.

After the show, we went into the backstage catacombs with passes that my friend had gotten. Right away and up close we saw the electrified man from the stage in front of us, with his flaming red hair. He was covered in sweat, wearing a white wife beater, dress slacks, and black work boots. My friend knew him and that's how we'd gotten the passes.

"Hey, Danny," said my friend. "This is my friend Jamie."

"Nice to meet you." Elfman looked at me and flashed his famous mischievous-but-kind smile from ear to ear and then vanished back into the green room like an apparition.

I didn't know it at the time, but the death service of another man also with flaming red hair had been held at this very same venue just eighteen months earlier—Lafayette Ron Hubbard. The new leader of the movement, David Miscavige, told a massive gathering of the movement at the iconic Hollywood establishment The Palladium that "at two thousand hours Friday the 24th of January A.D. 36, L. Ron Hubbard discarded the body he had used in this lifetime for seventy-four years, ten months, and eleven days; the body he had used to facilitate his existence in this [physical] universe had ceased to be useful and had become an impediment to the work he now must do outside of its confines."

When I think back, I'm moved by how much happened. When you're

CHILD X

a kid, one year feels like ten. When you're in middle age, ten years feels like one. Music always anchors me to that time. KROQ-FM—we called it "kay-rock"—exploded out of its Pasadena Hotel suite with bare-bones equipment and blasted across the landscape of Los Angeles with a fireball of post-punk sublimity, New Wave, and pop. In 1986 someone bought KROQ, and it became the epicenter of my artistic education, in direct conflict with the mechanistic form of the movement. This was the music that Avo played at every party . . . the sonic fascia that held our lives together, even though we thought we were fine.

X

In the movement, everyone's a throwaway except for who is useful. Anatoly Levertov was my mother's boss as the commander of Los Angeles's Advanced Division and was said to have been descended from Russian royalty. His eldest son, between eleven and nineteen, spent years in the reeducation camp and a worse version of the reeducation camp called the reeducator's reeducation camp.

Years later, Niklaus Levertov, the son of a Russian prince and movement executive, would blow his hands off and lose an eye in a horrible accident using home explosives. I heard conflicting stories as to why it happened; he was making fireworks, or making bombs to blow up newspaper stands because the media is "Evil," as the movement would say. Niklaus was declared psychotic and shunned. The movement would pretend this never happened and act like Niklaus never existed. They still do to this day.

As I was floating around LA with no prospects making new friends, trying to survive being on my own at sixteen and denying the future, Niklaus was in a hard labor camp getting machine-based counseling that would set up a series of decisions that altered the course of his life. He would eventually become a nonverbal homeless man with no hands, sitting in front of various locations around Los Angeles for the next two

RETURN TO THE JUNGLE

decades. We would see him down the street from the movement places like Figaro, the Skylight Theatre, and the Los Feliz Theatre. He would bark like a seal, throwing keys up in the air with his stumps for pocket change. He had a fascination with tossing and catching keys.

When I first saw him on the street, "Love My Way" by the Psychedelic Furs crossed my mind. It is a song about loving someone just the way they are.

Niklaus had two brothers. One is still alive. The other died of a health condition, and I wonder if it was due to the neglect that we suffered.

After the French Revolution in 1789, as the working poor beheaded their rulers, they called the new era "Year One." In 1975 in Pol Pot's murderous Communist Cambodia, the period immediately after the revolution was called "Year Zero." In our movement, time was described as "A.D."—After *Dianetics*, which came out in 1950.

Revolutions seem to like creating a starting date where the old way of life, the old way of organizing society, and all of a people's history, are wiped clean. The revolution's doctrine then takes over, and from that point on, nothing existed before the revolution. You need to take one's history away to control them.

No longer with the movement, Anatoly Levertov, Niklaus's father, was one of the most successful leaders in terms of growing a movement institution in its history. The children of the revolution, the Baby Boomers, who were recruited in the 1970s and built this thing, never said or did anything as they saw us roaming the streets around The Mothership without our parents. Looking away was a crime. Today, these "allies" are hurting us far more than the commander as they assign a lack of empathy to their beliefs at the time. They say things to us like, "Our experience is the same, and we're over it," as though what was done to the children wasn't special. When you do choose something, it has a different reverberating effect. To this day these former members pretending to be our friends deny our pain in their complicity. They won't admit what happened to us because of what it says about them.

Beliefs do not commit crimes. People do.

I don't blame the machine for what happened to us. I hold accountable our parents, and the other believers who built, oiled, and tended this machine as it burned us as fuel—while they lapped up their machine-based counseling, swallowing down the doctrine, and hungrily looking away from our slow annihilation.

Chapter 14

THE CRUMBLING

A half mile away from The Old Industrial Hospital was an abandoned garage. I would go there to see homeless Mickey Tealer and Johnny Vasquez, who were living in it. The garage had a couple of scattered old cars and a packed dirt floor. KROQ played from a small stereo. I followed the sound of "Institutionalized" by Suicidal Tendencies as I ducked out of the abundant Los Angeles sun and into the shade of their concrete bunker in the heart of East Hollywood.

The first thing I saw was a 1970s Chevrolet Chevelle rotting in the open cavern structure. It had once been a beautiful brown, but age and neglect were breaking it down into rust. The top had been cut off by someone. It was their bedroom. Mickey slept on the front bench seat, while Johnny slept in the back. These homeless teen children were the kids of what the commander called "the most ethical group on the planet."

Not long after I got back from Oregon, one of the kids from my young pack had gotten into deep trouble with the movement and was kicked out. The movement had spread horrible rumors about him, making him an untouchable among the other children who were living around The Mothership. I moved him in with me and he slept on a little sliver on the floor

156

CHILD X

between Jono and me for a couple of months. I had to get him out of Los Angeles. I called Paco, who agreed to take him in and give him work in New Jersey until things settled and it was forgotten about.

My mother and Randall had completely returned to the fold. I met a guy who said he'd let me live in his guesthouse if I drove his kids around to doctor's appointments, friends' houses, and school whenever he needed. He was an upscale member of the movement, and his kids were attending the Heper Academy. It felt like the last chopper out of Saigon, and I grabbed it.

I moved out of the tenement one-bedroom with my mother and Randall. I was sixteen years old. I had graduated from the motorcycle to a 1976 Chevy Nova V8 with faded silver paint and a completely crimson plastic, polyurethane interior. I liked it because I could clean anything out of it fast. I used to say to my friends that I could hose nuclear waste out of it after a rough weekend. I bought the car for $700 from a movement member and took a year to pay it off. I was on a payment plan for a $700 car when I couldn't afford to buy the gas, renew the registration, or buy insurance, but I was mobile.

Francis had gotten a cream 1960s Mercedes from David Campbell— Beck's dad. David had told Francis it had a doomed engine and would only last a year or two, but the car was a sculpture, and now it belonged to him. David gushed when he saw the smile on Francis's face as he gave him the car. Francis was an artist waiting to happen, but those dreams would be derailed by the movement.

I was trying to graduate from the Heper Academy when my grandfather's cousin, Amy—Tunji's wife—came to visit. Amy reached out to my mother, and we all agreed to sit down for a meeting. I can't remember where it was. Amy had a regal presence with African garb and thick dreadlocks with a wrap around her head, making her look like a queen. She spoke like a queen with great deliberation and asked me what I was going to do with my life. I told her that I had no idea, that I didn't know how to write, and I was self-conscious. She said, "Oh Jamie, you can write," and then pulled a pad and a pen from her purse and asked me to write something. I wrote

THE CRUMBLING   157

the chicken scratches of a three-year-old and had crossed out letters where I'd made mistakes.

Amy looked down with a wide smile and kind eyes, with nobility, took the pen, drew a flower on one of the crossed-out letters and said, "Jamie whenever you make a mistake, turn it into something that is beautiful and purposeful." She turned to my mother and told her that, if I wasn't getting educated in Los Angeles, she would like to take me with her, where I could learn under her supervision while she traveled the world as a spiritual teacher. I seriously considered it. I was terrified. I didn't go. Maybe I should have. The Movement's School gave me a high school diploma certified by the State of California when I had no useable education. Such is the standard of the Movement—achieve the product no matter the cost.

The Heper Academy graduated me while I was illiterate based off a 5000-word essay that I wrote on the war in Vietnam. It was an absurd, incomprehensible, decrepit mix of words—a cacophony of run-on sentences, lack of grammar, lack of paragraph structure, only legible because I got someone to type it out. At 17, three of us graduated that year. Me, my friend Olivia, and a kid named Quinn. We had a graduation ceremony at the Movement's Artist's Centre. We gave speeches for parents who came for Olivia and Quinn. No one came for me.

Francis got a job where he had to drive all over the city. Since I was working at Heper Academy, Francis and I would trade cars, and I would take the Mercedes during the day. He loved driving my V8 all over LA and I loved driving his work of art, even though I was always anxious the engine could stop at any moment. When you have no money, you have to buy things that are used and might break down, and you spend your life praying that this used thing you're relying on will just keep going.

We spent our weekends roving around Los Angeles in Francis's Mercedes, from Downtown to Venice Beach. After escaping a superheated twilight, I sat with Francis at Alcohol Salad—an underground Downtown Los Angeles club that served alcohol to minors—watching the dance floor shift and writhe in this darker version of John Hughes's America.

As we were laughing and drinking beer, "Once in a Lifetime" by

Talking Heads emerged like a flash of lightning into the club, and even more people got up to dance. The speakers blasted a flurry of rapid notes, flying up and down in scale like birds to an off-rhythm beat.

It is a driving and powerful musical challenge to all of us about a man who wakes up in the middle of his life and doesn't recognize himself, his wife, his car, his purpose, and it asks us if we chose this. Every time I would hear this song, I would feel a shudder down my spine and say to myself, "It can't be a choice." David Byrne anxiously sing-shouts that you might find yourself living in a small, fallen-down shack, or in another country expatriated, or you might have a beautiful car, or a grand house with a beautiful wife and still question if it was a choice?

I felt completely paralyzed.

I didn't want to wake up in thirty years and have it just happen to me. It seemed, for over a year, wherever we went in Los Angeles, whether it was in a shop, or a café, this song blared on the radio, taunting me. It has cursed me like a ghost. I can say this musical elegy may have altered the course of my life in its contemplation of living in a rotten shack, which seemed more appealing than a grand house with a beautiful wife with a beautiful car, which I had been groomed to believe was inherently bad—something for the wogs.

"What are we gonna do with our lives, if we're not doing this?" I asked Francis.

"I'll probably end up married, working for the inner movement."

His answer scared me.

Even with his loving parents and famous-artist stepfather, he didn't know where to go either. I thought about the Mexican immigrants I grew up with and how hard they worked, but I didn't see them building stability. I knew there were unseen things I needed to learn. I was illiterate. Being able to read at a high level may not seem like illiteracy, but without the ability to write, or understand even basic math, I had no path to a job that didn't require manual labor. When you're slipping into a mental oblivion from not developing your mind, you can feel yourself being slowly buried. I felt the best I could hope for was to be a server.

THE CRUMBLING

As I entered deeper into the mechanical beast of the doctrine in an autumn that felt like summer, I stayed up late in the guesthouse reading a battered paperback copy of *All Quiet on the Western Front*, its cover half torn, its pages dog eared and yellowing. It was a 1928 novel by Erich Maria Remarque, a German veteran of World War I—a war fought in trenches that slashed across Europe. If a human being could have looked at its destruction from orbit, it would have looked like a black smear across the continent; like the fingernails of a dark god had scratched a scar into the earth.

In the novel, Paul Bäumer, aged sixteen—around the age I was—and his teenage schoolmates are pushed by their teacher to join the German Army or be forever cowards. Paul shoulders this cause with complete innocence for what this war would do to his life; how it would change him, how it would maim him, how it would kill him. The way the book described a coward reminded me of the way the movement described a victim. This was the first mechanized war in human history. I read it with complete lack of irony, and it made me feel lucky for my circumstances. Maybe our parents used the doctrine as an apparatus of mechanized psychological destruction of our minds the same way World War I used innovations to destroy the human body, just because it was innovation.

In Hubbard's doctrine, he refers to humans as "terminals," and the emotions people express as "indicators." One has either "very good indicators" or "bad indicators." There is no inner life. Machine-based counseling takes away emotional concerns that slow down production. They took our choices away, until there was one direction where we remained for life. We might have to be destroyed so that humankind could survive.

On the Western Front, Paul endures years of gunfire, mud, gas, bombs, hunger, disease, and skin-consuming gangrene. Tank treads crush bare human skulls covered in a roughened gray patina. The once green fields of France are churned up by unceasing shells and bombs; trees were a distant memory. Unburied bodies, bloated and torn apart, lie where they fall for weeks or months; gray rats gnawing on gray corpses, in endless gray mud. The putrid stench of death saturates everything, from the uniform

160 CHILD X

Paul wears to the food he eats. His friends are killed by horrific machines of war. It was as if the Industrial Revolution was trying to find itself by seeing how many ways it could inflict mass death—gas, chemicals, flame-throwers, bombs falling from the air, tanks whose treads would rip a body apart, razor wire, and machine guns that spit lead with the sole purpose of disassembling a human body. The generals and soldiers used this new industrial killing apparatus because that's what the Industrial Revolution provided just because they were there.

Paul doesn't understand why the war needs to be fought, but he fights it passionately, because he believes in the people who tell him it needs to be fought. He doesn't know that his body is meant to be thrown away as one of millions of carcasses in this new industrialized warfare. The movement's doctrine and policies of emotional violence were deployed with the same dispassionate utility as the innovative killing machines of World War I. The disciples of the movement wanted to know how their apparatuses of mental pressure would affect the psyche and the human body just because they were there. No matter how much damage they wrought, they saw it as moving the universe toward salvation.

The commander believed his unchangeable set of therapies, which worked every time, could make a fully predictable and mechanical human. Like Paul Bäumer, I was not a person; I did not exist. I was seen by the movement as an asset—an X with a function that had been pre-determined for me before my birth by a hive that had no interest in me beyond what I could produce for them. No "I love you"s. No care when you were hurt. No concern for your well-being. No safety. Depriving emotion numbs the childmind. We had been machined.

I thought for the first time in years about the billion-year contract that I had signed, without my parents, when I was a five-year-old kid with no underwear. I didn't feel that I was coerced into signing it. My illiteracy guaranteed I was only able to do manual labor until my body aged, broke down, and eventually quit. Night after night my head tightened with anxiety—a feeling that was becoming hard to suppress with my friends in the nightclubs, alcohol, and the girls we hung out with.

THE CRUMBLING

I needed the movement. I had suckled on its breast. I didn't know how I was going to survive in the outworld of day-jobs and houses and wives and kids. I didn't have a bank account. I didn't know how to open one. I didn't know I had been infantilized, conditioned to depend on the movement for a place to live. Even the subsistence amount money in my pocket, all came from businesses that were connected to the movement.

I knew we had to do something different, yet I couldn't see a future.

Francis told me he had a plan. Francis always had a plan. He and I were best friends, misfit toys who would be friends for life. We were enslaved for eternity by grooming and lack of options, and we transmuted our desperation, twisting it within our heads, shaping it into our own personal desire to stop the decline of the world. Francis convinced me to join the private navy. The recruitment office was a satellite to the right after you walked into Lebanon Hall, inside The Mothership—the exact same entrance we used the night of the invasion with all of the FBI agents. We were going deeper into the belly of the beast.

We signed up for a billion years, then we were instantly on a plane to Clearwater, Florida, the movement's spiritual mecca. When we signed up, the recruiters asked us what we did, and we told them we wanted to be artists. The pretty Australian recruiter in her accent said, "Well, I'm glad you signed up. There won't be any art if we don't have a planet to make it on."

When I had time, I loved to hang out with Miles where I saw him in the abandoned garage with a smile beaming across his face. One night that summer, Miles and one of the motorcycle boys, Jack, got into trouble. Jack stole motorcycles for Avo. Miles and Jack got drunk on the top of a water tower in the hills above Los Feliz. The police arrived and told them to leave. Miles came down. They cuffed him and put him in the police car. Jack refused to come down, so a cop climbed up to get him. When Jack resisted, the second cop went up to help his partner.

Miles sat handcuffed by himself in the back of the squad car, watching the police go in on Jack. He realized the water tower was high. It had taken ten minutes for the second cop to climb to the top and would take at least fifteen for one of them to get down. They were distracted beating Jack.

Jack was White. Miles decided to slowly get out of the police car, with his hands cuffed behind his back, and run to Colin's house in the hills a mile and a half away.

Colin had a daughter, Katie, whose best friend was another fourteen-year-old girl named Salan. Both were living on their own with other girls who had been cast out by the movement for not signing the billion-year contract. Katie lived with her father in the hills and would go see her friends in the streets. Colin met Salan through his daughter.

Colin married Salan. She was fifteen. Katie's best friend was now her stepmother. Things like this happened. A thirty-nine-year-old man dating a fourteen-year-old girl was irrelevant for a trillion-year-old immortal spirit. No one in the movement batted an eye.

Miles showed up, cuffs behind his back, at Colin and Salan's house, where Colin sawed them off. The next day, Colin and Miles went together to the police station to bail out Jack. A few years ago, Miles died of a drug overdose. Inside I burned.

Thinking Miles would live forever, just weeks later in 1988, I was on the maiden voyage of the movement's new cruise ship, the *Freewinds*, where the movement's Advanced Level 8 courses were delivered. I was working eighteen-hour days as a dishwasher in the ship's huge industrial galley.

One bright afternoon, I had a one-hour reprieve on the beach on the island of Aruba where the woman who was in charge of us, and a few others, asked us to enjoy our "pleasure moment"—a doctrine term. As we walked toward the water, I never made a connection to *All Quiet on the Western Front*, but at the time hearing her words ruined that brief moment of sand and sun. It was a pleasure they had machined for us. It wasn't human beings enjoying a beautiful place. It was a ration doled out to us, necessary only for the same reason that one temporarily halts a car that is overheating.

We were the perfect mechanical soldiers.

Chapter 15

ASYLUM

I didn't know, when I moved back to Los Angeles, that I was destined to become a slave and then a fugitive in need of asylum.

[3 YEARS BEFORE THE BABY FACTORY] At 11:50 AM in late 1960s Chicago, with a blustering wind whistling off Lake Michigan, my grandmother's first cousin and close friend John Marshall Branion arrived at his apartment on Woodlawn to rendezvous with his wife, Donna, for lunch and spend the day Christmas shopping. He had just picked up his son Joby from Hyde Park Neighborhood School. John inserted his key in the door, turned it, and stepped inside.

His wife was nowhere to be found. In the eerie silence, John called out for her. He searched the bedrooms, finding them pristine and undisturbed. Finally, he checked the utility room. Donna's body lay on one side, carmine, red blood pooling on the floor under her. Her bloodstained sweater, the tan one she was wearing when he left that morning, was hiked up just below her breasts, revealing her bare, unmoving abdomen. Her legs were sallow and gray. Donna Branion, wife and mother, lay dead in her own home.

It was 1967, and this Black couple was wealthy. The Branions owned two beautiful cars, a brand-new Corvette along with a Buick. They lived in an upscale first-floor apartment at 5054 South Woodlawn in the wealthy "Black Belt" of Chicago's South Side, which Donna had smartly appointed in beautiful, French Provincial style after the couple's extended time in Switzerland, where John had attended medical school. The Black Belt was an enclave of Black elites.

Annie Dell Scott, Dorothy's aunt, had met John Branion Sr.—John Marshall Branion's father—at Rust College. He was on his way to law school. Annie and John Sr. fell in love, married, and eventually moved from Mississippi to Chicago. John Marshall Branion Jr. was born there, not long after John Branion Sr. became the first assistant public defender in the city's history. John Sr. could have been the district attorney of Chicago, but because he was Black, they invented the position of assistant public defender—the modern equivalent of a district attorney. With strong Mississippi roots, my grandmother Dorothy had spent much time as a child with her cousin John and loved him. They always stayed in touch.

By 1967, the second John Marshall Branion was a tall and imposing Black man of forty-one with chocolate skin. He was built like a wrestler, yet his visage looked soft-Irish, his face lean with expressive features. He had a booming voice. Larger than life, he raced cars, owned horses, and cooked gourmet meals for his friends. Cousin John was social and loved to chat to anyone within reach—philosophy, jazz, sports, and horses, every subject a feast for his complex and voracious mind. A highly skilled physician, John worked in obstetrics, delivering babies. He learned fundamental German in five days before starting medical school in Switzerland. He was said to have loved bringing life into the world. By the time he finished medical school, he sounded like a native Swiss.

In the 1940s, dozens of prominent jazz musicians had also moved to Europe, mostly France and Denmark. Copenhagen had been the home of Dexter Gordon, a long-time heroin addict, for a decade. In the time before civil rights, Europe was the only place where Black artists were appreciated and not treated like animals.

ASYLUM 165

The Branions would stay in Switzerland for five years, starting a family there. Their first child, a daughter they named Jan, was born in Fribourg. By this time in the mid-1940s, Dorothy's husband Roy, unlike her rising cousin John, was in Connecticut slowly dying from a war that had subversively besieged his soul.

When the Branions moved back to the Black Belt of Chicago, they were only two blocks away from Elijah Muhammad—the controversial Black religious leader and exotic civil rights lightning rod. Reverend Martin Luther King Jr. had moved from Alabama to a walk-up apartment on Hamlin Avenue nearby. Muhammad had developed a strange, scholarly affectation and cadence in his voice in his ascension into being a religious leader.

By the 1960s riots broke out every summer in the other Black neighborhoods, ripe with crime, overcrowding, despair, and resentful policing. Their neighborhoods often burned as a denied people cried out with frustration. In 1966 King had led a march near the neighborhood around Marquette Park and was met with a fury of sticks, stones, knives, and bricks. His friend Dr. John Branion marched with him.

At one point during the march, John threw himself on top of King, shielding him from rocks hurled at them from all sides.

"He was trembling," John later said of the incident, describing King. "I was amazed. I could feel him actually trembling, but that's what courage is, isn't it? To go ahead even though . . . it frightens you."

Throughout the 1960s uneasy Blacks were growing weary of King's nonviolent methods, and Black militancy was on the rise, personified by the Black Panthers, who had formed in California. Militancy was simmering and spreading across the nation.

The Panthers drove muscle cars, carried semiautomatic rifles, and dressed like a stylish paramilitary militia, hip in their uniform of black leather jackets, black berets, and mirrored sunglasses. They projected an aura to go where Martin Luther King wouldn't.

A man that never lost touch with his Southern roots, John secretly and regularly treated Black Panthers for bullets and other wounds the

166   CHILD X

Panthers didn't want reported to the police. By law, doctors were supposed to report gunshot wounds. John chose not to, protecting the identity of his Panther friends. Even before John's wife's murder, the FBI suspected his activities, because of his affiliations, but they couldn't prove it. From the FBI's perspective, the Panthers needed to be stopped.

A forensic investigation into Donna's death wouldn't be held until a month after her murder. The delay was chalked up to the lack of working rooms at the Cook County Morgue—there were only four morgues in the whole county and Chicago was a violent city, one for every shell casing that was found under Donna's body. Three bullets were found in the walls, which had all passed through her body. A fourth bullet remaining in her body was retrieved. The shell casings—clearly stamped 9 mm—would be mislabeled .380 caliber shells by forensics by mistake. This particular mistake revealed an impossibility: a .380 pistol could not have safely fired the 9 mm ammunition. It would have malfunctioned on the very first squeeze of the trigger or exploded in the gunman's hand.

To his own detriment, John owned an extensive gun collection—also to his own detriment, he was known to have kept them loaded.

When Chicago police searched the Branion home, they conveniently found two boxes of .380 ammunition—not the 9 mm casings that forensics would prove killed Donna a few months later. From the .380 ammunition, four shells were missing, the exact number that killed Donna. Despite this distinct discrepancy, John was arrested and charged with murder. If it was a setup, the framers took the wrong ammunition to frame him for murder.

Donna's body told a story: she had fought for her life. The evidence receipt showed head hair, nail clippings, an oral swab, and blood samples had been collected and handed to the Cook County Coroner's office. The nail clippings were never analyzed and have since never been found. A mere two days after Donna's murder, John flew to Vail, Colorado, for a Christmas break with friends. It didn't look good.

Distraught yet eager to cooperate, John asked Nelson Brown, Donna's brother, to get his .380 handgun from his collection and hand it over to the police for analysis. Nelson gave police John's Walther PPK, a .380

ASYLUM

167

handgun made famous as the weapon of choice used by Sean Connery's James Bond. Again, not being able to fire 9 mm bullets, it could never have been the murder weapon.

Despite the discrepancies, a verdict came down on a scorching hot day in June 1968, two months after Martin Luther King was killed.

Guilty.

John Marshall Branion was sentenced to not less than twenty years and no more than thirty. His appeals were quickly submitted and even more quickly denied. John was officially in a state of an arrested life. Awaiting and during the trial, John had relocated to Wyoming. He'd sold off all his possessions and wanted peace to mourn his wife and lament the friends he had lost over the scandal. The time in Wyoming felt like purgatory. During his solitude, John became convinced that there was no true justice possible in the United States. With his famed friend now assassinated for his work with nonviolence, John felt, in 1960s America, he would have to take his life into his own hands.

Without telling anyone, John immediately retreated back to Wyoming at the start of the jury's thirteen-day deliberation. Even before that guilty verdict in Chicago came, John had a bad feeling. Escape options were limited. The authorities had confiscated his passport. He could brave the deadly expanse of the Mexican Sonoran desert, a route where Dorothy and Roy had driven twenty years earlier on their honeymoon. Or he could flee to the dense woods of Canada.

To the Swiss-trained doctor, the entire United States felt like an open-air prison. Since he had sold off most of his belongings in Chicago, including his beloved Corvette, he had enough money to hire a forger to create a fake passport. But he wasn't sure where to go. Then it struck him. He remembered a friend, Arthur Lord McCoo III, had recently passed away. Arthur liked to travel. Within two weeks John had applied for and gotten his hands on a copy of McCoo's passport. The two friends looked similar enough. A new photo wasn't needed.

John was soon on a midnight flight to Paris. He left his children behind.

168   CHILD X

From his time in Switzerland, John spoke German and was also fluent in French. Soon Paris would be his gateway to Africa.

Through his wife, John had met the only true Africans he'd ever known: the Browns. They were a prominent Black family known to host African diplomats and world leaders through their connections in DC. John decided to seek out these familiar African diplomats—*they* would understand the injustice done to him in Chicago. John resolved to disappear into the vast unknown of the African continent, well beyond the reach of American authorities.

Once in Paris, he bought a seat on the first flight to Algiers. Waiting for the plane, he sat alone at the far end of a deserted restaurant in the airport with five excruciating hours to pass. He sat in focused silence, overcome with anxiety, praying no one would recognize him.

His destination, the great continent of Africa, was named from the ancient Phoenician word *faraqa*, meaning "separate colony." Covered in thick jungle and the most expansive deserts in the world, Africa had been impenetrable by Europeans, Asians, and others for most of human history. Homer, the Greek poet, thought that Africans were dark skinned because Africa was so far to the edge of the world that the sun was closer to them. In America, Africa at this time—and maybe to this day—had always been thought of as an otherland. This was just before my life as a Mulatto, ignorant and abandoned, before I was raised in sci-fi for salvation. If I would feel anything in my early life, it wouldn't be the pride of my Black heritage, but the shame of being an "other" from my own otherland.

In Franz Kafka's horrifying *Metamorphosis*, it has long been misunderstood that the young man Gregor Samsa wakes up as a cockroach. If one reads this book in the actual German, the literal translation for *ungeheueres Ungeziefer* is "verminous outsider." He wakes up an outsider.

This is what I felt I was after I escaped the movement. I had been programmed to feel this way since my birth. In the shame and humiliation of experience, I decided no matter how long I lived, I would die with this secret. This is what I felt I was—but inside I still believed. My calculation was

X

that if I was ever to be free, I would have to keep the story of my existence and the first chapter of my life hidden until I died, or the world would see me as a verminous outsider.

By the 1960s, Algiers was what Casablanca was in the 1930s: a way station for political dissidents fleeing trouble at home. Antiwar demonstrators, draft dodgers, and criminals inhabited the maze-like streets of the radiant white city. Nestled in sweeping North African hills cascading into a deep blue sea, people had lived in the old city of Algiers since the days of Carthage two hundred years before the birth of Christ.

John landed in Algiers with a large amount of cash. He disappeared into the city, constantly looking over his shoulder for familiar faces from Paris that he thought might be following him. Amid the city's bustling bazaars, he moved into a dirt-cheap hotel and relaxed. He knew he needed work. He missed practicing medicine, and he knew being a doctor made him valuable.

The Algiers of the late 1960s and early 1970s was still built on the old cobblestone Roman roads—narrow, winding, ancient streets thick with people and animals as it is to this day. Algiers had won its independence from French colonial rule during a violent uprising that had collapsed the French government almost a decade earlier in 1962. Now no one owned Algiers but the Algerians. For the moment no one owned John but John.

If the North Africans were rich in anything it was heat. While stopping to catch his breath, John saw a teenage girl and a young boy of five or six playing in the square in front of the old post office, smiles bright, their laughter echoing off the building's grand Moorish arches. John thought of Jan and Joby and questioned, "Did I abandon them?"

By the time John arrived in Algiers, the famed civil rights leader Eldridge Cleaver, a leader in the Black Panthers since 1966, had also landed there to escape attempted murder charges in the US. He was operating a Black Panther compound in the Arab Sector—just a ten-minute drive

170 CHILD X

from the US embassy. John walked to the compound, his heart pounding in his chest. Even though no one in the world could possibly know where he was, practically invisible as a Black man in Algiers, he constantly felt eyes crawling all over him.

John didn't know Cleaver personally, but felt the Black Panthers owed him a favor. He had operated on and aided and abetted so many of them during the Chicago race riots. When he arrived at the compound, Cleaver stood in the doorway of a cramped shack loud with radios. He looked indestructible in a bright green dashiki, open at the neck, with an AK-47 slung over his shoulder. Glistening with sweat, John stood in the severe Algerian sun and made his case to Cleaver for help.

Despite John's overwhelming and risky contribution to the Panthers, Cleaver harbored deep suspicion behind his mirrored sunglasses. Fidel Castro had warned Cleaver of CIA infiltration in the Panthers. John was entirely out of place in Algiers. Even with his guilty verdict and his story of flight, it was too good to trust. Also, during this time, the Panthers were gathering weapons and training for a possible land invasion of the US. Feeling vulnerable and exposed, Cleaver wanted John Branion gone.

With his opportunities evaporating in Algiers, John decided he needed to move. Having burned through his cash at the hotel over several months, he borrowed enough from a friend for a one-way ticket to Tanzania. He walked to the Houari Boumediene Airport in 90 degree heat, checking every face for a threat. He smelled soot and jumped at backfiring cars. His neck burned. He was convinced he would be caught.

Before leaving Chicago, John had met Julius Nyerere, the president of Tanzania and the godfather of the pan-African movement—a nationalist ideology that promoted Black cultural unity. When John landed in Tanzania, he drew anxious deep breaths. The air was thick and humid. But John felt soothed as he smelled grass and horses, familiarity burning in his veins. John would say about arriving in Tanzania, "Here was the same red earth, the same wooden houses raised off the ground. In the villages I passed through there were singing and drums. It was Mississippi in 1935 . . . this was Mississippi when I was a child . . . I could almost

ASYLUM

171

feel my father there." The same Mississippi where he was raised with my grandmother.

At first, President Nyerere listened sympathetically to John's story. He needed the means to survive and make a living. John met with the health minister, but it turned out the man didn't like Blacks from America and would never offer John work. His passport was promptly stamped "persona non grata." John had to leave again.

John would fly halfway around the world to Brazil and spend another five months there only to fail again. John felt constant anxiety with a feeling of being trapped. In Rio, an ex-CIA agent offered to help him return to Algiers. Despite being terrified that law enforcement might be there waiting for him, John was out of money, and risk was his only choice.

John returned to Algiers. He walked back to the Black Panther compound with his head low and shoulders hunched in nervous exhaustion. His neck ached whenever he threw an anxious glance at the busy street behind him. Anyone could be an agent. He worried the man in Rio had sold him out. He walked faster.

The Algerian government had been accusing the Panthers of drug running. The word in the bazaars was that the Panthers were to be expelled, adding pressure to any foreign American Black man in Algiers at the time.

Still, John once again sought out Eldridge Cleaver. This was a mistake. An agitated and paranoid Cleaver searched John, took $1,000 from his pocket, and threw him in a locked room. Through the door, John listened as the Panthers discussed what to do with him. After an hour of discussion, they decided either to ransom John to US authorities for cash or kill him.

However, over the next two days, John befriended two of his Algerian captors. On the second day, in the dark of night, his new friends came and unlocked his makeshift prison. Cleaver had decided John was too much of a liability and ordered the Algerian men to kill him. Instead, they rushed him to the street and urged him to escape. John Branion raced into the night.

Constantly finding friends to lend him money, including my

grandmother, John landed in Cairo, Egypt. The widow of Civil Rights activist W. E. B. Du Bois, Shirley DuBois, was living in Cairo. John had met DuBois and Shirley years earlier in Chicago and struck up a friendship. Mrs. DuBois wanted to help and offered to connect John with physicians in Cairo; the modern, cosmopolitan city was short of doctors. Also, Anwar Sadat's Egypt had maintained neutrality during the Cold War. To John that meant no extradition. He still couldn't find work, but he expected to be safe.

In the coming months, Egypt's stance on the world stage, like John's future, was on the edge of a knife. It became clear granting asylum to an American fugitive was unlikely to last long. Mentally and physically exhausted by months of flight, John left—this time for Sudan.

There were more problems in Sudan. John's medical certificate and passport didn't match. The passport was confiscated. He was then locked up in a Sudanese cell with three other men, in a visually cinematic ancient British fortress on the Nile. It was hell. The days were 112 degrees. There were no toilets, and vermin infested its urine-soaked floor. Claustrophobic, short of breath, his body too malnourished to stand on the floor's only clean, dry corner, John expected he might die there. He was forty-five years old.

During this same time, I would have been a toddler in MacArthur Park, shielding myself from the sun in yellowed grass garnished with heroin needles, looking for candy from the candyman.

After his capture and sentence, Chicago newspapers ran a headline: "Murder Fugitive Caught in Sudan."

The FBI and CIA machines jumped into action. The US had no extradition treaty with Sudan, but now John Branion was on the grid. For the FBI, it was only a matter of moving enough cash into Africa to activate assets. They needed a little bit of time. Before this, John would get lucky, and his Sudanese jailers would release him and fine him merely $10 for entering the country illegally with his fake passport.

John questioned how long his luck would last. His lower neck ached. He knew his detainment in Sudan would send up flags in the capital city

ASYLUM

173

of Dar Es Salaam, and it would be swarming with agents. Before he could leave the ancient city, friends introduced him to the health minister of Uganda, who was looking for foreign doctors. A day later, John was on a growling bush plane to Uganda.

Physicians were rare in 1973 Uganda. The landlocked African nation, once an ancient collection of fiefdoms not unlike Europe in the Middle Ages, had a decade earlier been consolidated into a nation by the British— it was the same thing the Romans had done to ancient and primitive tribes in Britannia. For now, the country had its newfound independence. Old kingdoms that had ruled since ancient times were so recently gone, the newly founded state felt uneasy. Tribal rivalries had not been swept away until an enigmatic general named Idi Amin seized the nation.

Upon arriving at the airport in Kampala, John was taken by Mercedes-Benz to a lavish public reception in a poor rural village to meet the six-foot-three, two-hundred-pound dictator.

"So, this is our doctor in Mbarara," Amin blustered. "Welcome, brother, welcome."

The two men shook hands. John's hands trembled. Mbarara is the second largest city in Uganda, second only to Kampala. Soon, John was to become General—now President—Amin's private physician.

Uganda was already disintegrating. Indians, a prosperous minority population there who had built businesses, were being expelled. As Hitler had done to the Jews thirty years earlier, Amin was pointing to the successful Indians as the cause of all of Uganda's problems. In response, the United States cut diplomatic ties. John was now officially beyond the reach of American authorities. He could breathe once again. His hands stopped shaking. In this way, a Black Amin had blamed Uganda's problems on a class of successful Brown people in business—a sequestered upper class. This is not about race. It is what all humans do to each other—"you're poor because they're rich."

While Amin's people starved and many were tortured, the dictator wined and dined John. Desperate, the doctor appealed to Amin for Ugandan citizenship. It was granted. While Ugandan villages died, John was

174 CHILD X

issued a Ugandan passport with a changed last name, from Branion to Businye—a Ugandan word for "peace"—a feeling he hadn't enjoyed in years. During his reign, Amin was known as "the butcher of Uganda," and John should have suspected his peace would not last long.

Idi Amin's army often terrorized the Ugandan countryside. In one village, the people were rounded up and accused of plotting to assassinate him. Some were shot. Others were tortured. Men were hammered to death in minutes. Women died quickly—guards simply cut their throats. Rumors of electrocution and cannibalism at Amin's hands saturated the foreign press. Amin, the liberator, was soon feared as a voodoo warlord who dispensed death. While John's peace came at the expense of Africans' deaths.

John stayed in Uganda until 1975. Always an innovator, and under Amin's approval, he built the country's first ever ovarian cancer protocol, at the same time corpses of women in the countryside, killed by Amin's soldiers, lay rotting by the roadside under a burning Ugandan sun.

A heart attack sent John on leave to Kenya, where there were physicians capable of helping him. Uganda was quickly collapsing into civil war, and opposition in the countryside grew against Amin and his atrocities. John's chest was sore from the heart attack, but he could walk the length of a room before he ran short of breath. John could not have recovered from the heart attack, and John didn't want to go back to Uganda.

A friend offered John airfare to Sudan in exchange for services, only to promptly strand him with no fare, no cash, and a four-week hotel bill. He hitchhiked 1,300 miles to Sudan. The CIA were closing in, already ahead of him. Nearly fifty years old with progressing heart disease, he fled again.

Ivory Coast. Botswana. Zambia. None presented safety.

He was out of money and out of options. With his nervous system on fire, John returned to Uganda in 1979. Idi Amin had left a year earlier with his people in uprising, fleeing to exile in Saudi Arabia and leaving his country in chaos. In 1983, John would be arrested by Ugandan authorities. It has often been speculated that Idi Amin ordered that John

ASYLUM

be turned over to US agents in exchange for the CIA relenting in their pursuit of him.

John was in essence ransomed back to the United States. Shirley Hudson, a mistress of John's during his marriage to Donna, later remarked, "I thought slavery had been abolished in Africa. But here you see, Black men are still being sold," referring to an African selling John out to the FBI at the hands of Idi Amin.

Dr. John Marshall Branion returned to the United States in police custody. He would serve seven years of his sentence in Illinois before being granted an early release as a result of his heart condition. He died in 1990. His suffering was over. Angels.

Four years earlier, in a cruel twist, it emerged that Judge Reginald Holzer, who had sentenced John in 1968, had received an eighteen-year jail sentence. Charged with extortion and racketeering, the corruption made national headlines. According to writer Barbara D'Amato's book *The Doctor, the Murder, the Mystery*, Judge Holzer received a $10,000 bribe in 1968 to persuade him to not send John to prison. Immediately following the bribe, Holzer condemned John to decades in prison anyway.

The world is a beast.

Chapter 16

FORTRESS

The warm rain began to bombard the streets as if it was the end of the world, hitting my skin like the stings of angry bees. The sky darkened. Looming black clouds gathered above the expanse of downtown. White flashes of lightning tore through the stone-dark cumulus, splitting the air; the black sky had blotted out the sun. Then came the shake of thunder, to me like the seven trumpets of the apocalypse.

And then suddenly the sun tore through the blackened clouds, casting beams of white light onto the water-battered rooftops. The sun would not relent. The return of the sunlight swiftly heated the saturated concrete, drawing up steam from the brightly colored 1980s cars in the street. A rising mist of hot rain brought with it the heavy smell of asphalt.

I stepped out of the hanging trellis where I had taken shelter in the wet air, now bright with the full force of the sun. I smoothed my navy whites, looked down on the black scuffs marking my pearly white naval dress shoes, and walked.

I had been in Florida for a month with Francis, who had been traded to the massive movement headquarters in Florida. Not long after I came to Florida, he was sent back to Los Angeles for a year to do the movement's

178

CHILD X

equivalent of a business PhD. His focus was a Byzantine-deep study of Hubbard's thousands of pages of management teachings.

I know people who the movement genuinely helped; many of them had no idea what happened to us kids. At this time, I had no idea what had happened to us. I really do believe that I feel like I saw people become better people at times, but at what cost? After more than three and a half decades, Francis is still in Hubbard's navy. When we were teenagers, he was a brilliant artist, and his love of art amplified my love of art, helping to alter my life. My heart breaks for the art the world will never see because Francis wasn't in the world to make it.

I was officially part of the *Freewinds* and working out of the *Freewinds* relay office, which was just up the hill from a repurposed waterfront motel owned by the movement called The Sandcastle.

Freewinds was an ironic name for a ship where people were often sent with their passports confiscated and held against their will. Sandine Jansen was responsible for raising the money that funded the *Freewinds*.

I was working then as her gopher, and she had sent me to her brother's house to pick up a personal item when I was caught in the storm.

I looked down the now sunny street and saw two of the skinniest kids I had ever seen. One, a young man in his twenties, wore fading acid-washed denim cutoff shorts and a secondhand T-shirt. The other was a woman about the same age, in a '70s flower-printed dress and worn aviator sunglasses. They were standing in front of a Volkswagen minibus painted in two-tone blue and cream.

Then they saw me. I must have looked like someone from another world, an eighteen-year-old Mulatto kid in a white navy uniform, standing in the middle of a Florida street watching them. The girl waved, beaming, her eyes wide. They looked right out of the Manson Family, and yet I thought I was out of place.

"Hello," I said as I waved back. I don't remember the decision to walk closer, but suddenly I was standing next to them.

"Hiiii," the girl in her trance-like state practically sang back. She was

FORTRESS

holding a small yellow flower and twirling it slowly between her slender fingers.

I looked over at the squat brown house they were mesmerized by. There was absolutely nothing there. It was a small two-bedroom brown bungalow probably built in the 1940s with absolutely no flourishes. It was a brown box.

"What are you guys staring at?"

The boy paused for thirty seconds before he answered. It felt like an hour. "This was Jim Morrison's house. He lived here with his grandparents when he was a kid."

The girl said, "We're on a road trip around the country and we came all the way here to see it."

They both seemed nice and incredibly interested in me despite my distracting them. The fact they were talking to a complete stranger—a Brown kid in a naval uniform—didn't seem out of place to them compared to the brown box which captivated them.

"Really?"

"Really," the young man said without turning to me, unblinking, with a soft smile.

We stood on the baking sidewalk, silently looking. Then the boy quietly said, "Jim said that we're all gods, y'know?"

I had just walked two minutes from a refurbished motel where I was working for the movement aiding fundraising where they just happened to be returning fallen mortals to their godlike state. As I listened to these out-of-time flower children, all I could think was, *Jim Morrison was right*, and how much I had in common with two treacly hippies who were so completely different from me.

"Really nice to meet you," I said.

"Yeah, you too."

I walked on.

Years later, I would come to find the hippies had been in the wrong place. The Jim Morrison house was across the state in Melbourne, Florida,

CHILD X

but it didn't matter. It made me think about the power of meaning. When we believe something wholeheartedly to be true, that faith can propel us to do remarkable things. I thought, *Maybe belief is more important than reality if that's what gets you through the day.*

X

One morning, I was walking from my small bunkroom at The Hacienda Gardens to The Sandcastle when I heard the revving of engines. I looked to my right and saw two red Chrysler LeBaron convertibles, packed with quasi-navy members in uniform, racing to the Fort Harrison Hotel. Two men in bright blue navy dress uniforms were sitting on the back of the lead car, high up with their feet in the seat, one with three and one with four commander's stripes on their epaulets and cuffs. They were smiling and laughing. I figured they must be the movement's leaders, and for the next few days I saw a convoy of LeBarons going back and forth surveying downtown Clearwater. Seeing pseudo-naval commanders in overly styled Chrysler convertibles in full naval regalia even at the time seemed strange. I pushed it out of my head.

Seeing the commanders' uniforms made me think of a time when I was, oddly, in the Boy Scouts as a kid. I would walk the streets of LA by myself in my desert khaki shirts complete with red epaulets, olive-drab green shorts, neckerchief, and red beret—designed by famed fashion designer Oscar de la Renta. A movement member had started a troop to keep us from splitting psychologically and collapsing.

There was a one-mile walk to the scout meeting at a local elementary school that took me through a gang fight, a writhing mass of three hundred Black and Brown men with sticks, bats, and knives. I saw a couple of men fall.

Within seconds a voice on a loudspeaker blared, "Disperse and exit the area!" Two LAPD helicopters descended and hovered about forty feet above the fight. The men scattered, some faltering, some bloody, some assisted by their brothers. And then it was over. The street was quiet.

FORTRESS

181

I straightened myself up and walked quickly into the school as if nothing had happened. Completely unaware of what I had just encountered, my buoyant scoutmaster asked me how the walk was. I told him it was great. I knew better than to tell a member of the inner-navy, even one I trusted, that something bad had just happened.

Florida seemed safe. My office at The Sandcastle was an old cabana with a large entrance and a door leading to the motel, and a large sliding glass wall overlooking the courtyard. I would always see who was coming and going. There was an older Mexican immigrant named Fernando who spoke no English—yet had signed the billion-year contract—and who drove the powder-blue van that shuttled members of the movement between The Sandcastle and the palatial Fort Harrison Hotel—a 1926 Mediterranean Revival hotel, a pearl in the crown of the movement. The Sandcastle, for Level 7s only, was on the water and had been highly renovated with a restaurant and café that serviced the movement's most affluent and important members.

Whenever the van arrived, I would look up from my desk and out the window to see wealthy and famous members of the movement, who, determined to move up the ladder to shed their flesh-body and return to their omnipotent state, would eventually find themselves at this small, repurposed motel. Sometimes I would think that life outside a body would be devoid of pleasure and the joys of humanity. I would quickly push these thoughts out of my head.

My job was to intercept anyone who was on or had completed Advanced Level 7 at The Sandcastle and have them pay for Advanced Level 8 so they could go to the Caribbean and do the advanced spiritual machine-based counseling on the *Freewinds*. The commander's claim was that on Level 8 you would learn the primary reason all of us fallen gods had forgotten who we were over the last billions of years—on Level 8, "truth would be revealed." It was hailed as the first level that would begin to restore your god-like powers. Advanced Levels 1 through 7 were only to remediate damage that had been done to you as a spirit. Level 8 would begin to make you a god again.

182   CHILD X

In Clearwater, I met a member of the movement named Jeff. He was born with a spinal deformity causing his back to be permanently curved. He walked completely hunched over, dragging his right foot. He was a strange man-child who joined the movement to better understand why he had been born that way. One day, while walking to the ad hoc cafeteria during lunch a block from the Fort Harrison, he told me that he wasn't really disabled, but had been very important in his past lives. Due to his congenital injury, he slurred his voice and spoke in a drone-like manner to get his words out. He told me that in his machine-based counseling, he discovered that he'd been John F. Kennedy in his life before this one. "My spinal deformity was exactly where I took the bullet," he said. He told me he was born in 1963, right after the assassination. It was the dramatic spiritual residue of his assassination that caused him to be born imperfect.

In the movement, it is strictly forbidden to discuss your machine-based counseling and the specific discoveries you make there with anyone. You're only allowed to talk about how you are a better version of yourself. The commander claimed that by discussing your past lives, you could upset others. However, it seemed that many people in the movement had been famous in their previous lives. I think Hubbard was trying to avoid two Jesus Christs or Marie Antoinettes meeting each other.

The commander is in the *Guinness Book of World Records* for having published more works than any other human being who ever existed. Sometimes I would think, *If someone went through this much trouble to write this much specific information about everything in the world, and write it all down, and so many brilliant and successful people followed him, then it must be true.*

Gottfried Helnwein was a lean, dark-haired, hawk-faced man who looked more like the frontman for a hard rock band than a painter. The Austrian visual artist pushed the boundaries of every medium he has ever touched. He became well known for his oil paintings, innovating airbrushing techniques to create staggering, photoreal, haunting imagery, forming a twentieth-century extension of Caravaggio—paintings as realistic as photographs.

FORTRESS

There is an oil painting of Helnwein's called *Epiphany III*: a small girl-child on a table—dead or asleep, it's hard to tell. Surrounding her are men in bespoke suits—Victorian vivisectionists, with deformed pig-like faces. The child is perfect, completely pristine and innocent. This painting could have represented my childhood. I was like the little girl, pristine and curious, with grotesques standing above me, manipulating my life—a failed experiment in making a better man. Gottfried may be one of the most skilled and visionary anatomical figure painters alive. He has and does continue to inspire me. I would see Gottfried walking around The Sandcastle wearing a headwrap and sunglasses, sometimes with his beautiful wife, Renata. She was brilliant. She ran his business. She ran his image. She ran the public's access to him. Both were kind. I thought, *If the doctrine of the movement was not true, there's no way geniuses like the Helnweins could be a part of it.*

Kurt Listug—a co-founder of Taylor guitars—was a man of presence, gentle buoyancy, and humility. Kurt began Taylor Guitars in 1974 in a small guitar shop in El Cajon, California. Kurt and his partners would do the musical equivalent of reinventing the wheel. This tiny, boutique guitar company would revolutionize the way guitars are made, innovating the five-hundred-year-old standards of the instrument's construction with distinguished tonal woods. It's not easy to improve on an instrument that has been around for thousands of years, but Kurt and his partners did. Daryl Hall and John Oates played "Adult Education" on Taylor guitars. Kurt was kind, intelligent, and sane. He gave money to Sandine and me for Advanced Level 8. I thought, *If he's here, how can this not be true?* It could be that these people were unaware of what happened to us kids.

In the second century, Christianity was considered a cult. Roman forces would execute anyone that would proselytize the religion, only a hundred years after the man had come back from the dead in a desert. The persecution of Hubbard's movement seemed mild in comparison and based on history, through time, it would be accepted. A man coming back from the dead is no stranger than being a fallen god living on a prison planet.

184 CHILD X

David Gaiman had a large physical presence. A gentle giant, tall, elegant, and imposing, but quiet and humble with kind eyes. He had been the movement's official spokesperson in the United Kingdom and was an unindicted co-conspirator in Operation Snow White—the largest domestic spying operation on our own government in U.S. History that lead to the largest domestic FBI raid in U.S. History at that time—the raid I was in as a kid. The raid led to the exoneration and dropping of the indictment of Holocaust survivor, journalist Paulette Cooper, where Hubbard's intelligence service had lifted her fingerprints to make her guilty of bomb threats, a crime she didn't commit. Despite his calmness, he felt like an electric shock walking into a room even if you didn't see him. David went on to run the movement's Secret Police as the head of its Intelligence Service worldwide.

His son, Neil, would go on to direct art with the same quiet presence that David directed the movement's espionage in England. Neil Gaiman redefined dark fantasy in literature in the 1990s, taking the world by storm with books like *Sandman*, *Good Omens,* and *American Gods*—where the gods of old, like Odin and Thoth, have fallen to Earth and live their lives in decaying apartments and smoke-filled bars. I was a fallen god who grew up in slums, with smoky and pickled drug addicts. Neil was born and raised deep in the movement, and I sometimes wonder if he made it out unaffected.

I spent time with Neil's brilliant father, David, at The Sandcastle, thinking, *There is no way this brilliant man would be involved in something that wasn't true. He's too smart, wise, and kind.* David's presence made me feel that, despite everything I had experienced growing up, I needed to stay in the movement to keep going and help the world.

Through a mutual acquaintance outside the upscale Hibiscus Restaurant in the Fort Harrison Hotel, I'm uncomfortable to say that I met John Travolta. He was nice, but he scared me. His life was big and mine was so small. He was wearing fitted black jeans and a bright red V-neck long-sleeve shirt made out of some kind of beautiful material. I thought about how much he looked like a painter. He reminded me of the people that I saw in the Village when I was with Shade and Modupe. He was standing next to the young, angelic Kelly Preston, who wore an intricate white dress that, with her elaborate hair, made her look like a mermaid, completely out of place in the Central Florida Deco hotel.

So many who came to do the upper levels were so virtuosic in their fields—doctors, lawyers, professors, mathematicians—but I felt like a slave. In that year in Florida, I kept asking myself, if this is slavery, these brilliant people wouldn't spend their lives pursuing it. Some of these people were so accomplished that to this day I sometimes wonder if they were right.

Often Sandine would tell the wealthy visitors who were doing their upper levels that the release of Level 8 on the *Freewinds* had changed the world. With the fall of the Berlin Wall and the end of apartheid, she would explain, Level 8 had put so much raw spiritual positivity onto the Earth that these established systemic evils came crashing down. They needed to pay her and do Level 8 because we were so close to saving the planet. This concept was met with universal applause.

The commander had said that, whenever the evil persons of the world began to scream, it was a sign that we were winning. These days I see it as an Orwellian thought-stopping tool to get people to stop asking questions.

In 1985, the state of Oregon entered a $39 million judgment against the movement, which was countered by members converging on Portland by the thousands to wage a war that they called "the battle for religious freedom." It was a spectacle, with Chick Corea, Al Jarreau, and Edgar Winter performing. Stevie Wonder called in and told the protestors that he loved them and passionately crooned, "and I mean it from the bottom of my heart."

Travolta flew in to join them. Mesmerized, I watched him being interviewed on the local news. He said, "Once in a while you have to stand up for what you believe in." His words hit me like a baseball bat. At the time, Travolta's sincerity would help keep me in the machine.

For a movement that documents everything, they didn't document the rearing of the children. Our story has gone forgotten, outside of those of us who rage in our dismissal. I spent my whole life promising myself I would never tell this story and living in my shame. However, after all the ruination I've seen, despite the humiliation of my childhood, now it's time for me to "stand up for what I believe in" and tell the story of the children of the machine, the disintegration of thousands. A complete disregard for the human heart. There should be a reckoning for these children.

X

When I was seventeen, I had my first and only direct interaction with the movement's new leader, David Miscavige. He'd come into my office where I was an intern with executives who were responsible for ensuring that the *Freewinds* was packed with members at all times to do its courses and Advanced Levels.

A diminutive man walked into the room, past the shredding machine, wearing full naval regalia, with a gold lanyard, four commander's bars on his shoulders and four commander's bars on his sleeves. At the time, it had a commanding power. On reflection, it was full Captain Crunch.

These serious men that I worked for jumped to their feet in fear. At the time, I didn't know who the man was and the most senior executive in the room, Bill Johnson, a successful businessman before joining the movement's inner core, stuttered, "Sir, how can I help you?"

I was confused why everyone was so afraid of this smallish man, but eventually I would understand.

The man was all smiles and told everyone to relax. Bill exhaled. I could feel the small man's delight that he experienced from the unease he injected just by walking into a room. Today he was happy, as he was about to launch the movement's ocean liner and its most advanced level ever, Level 8.

"I do have one question," he said. "Who was the weird kid in the hallway? That kid was weird," he said in a strange urban accent I didn't recognize.

FORTRESS

187

Bill Johnson responded, "I dunno, sir, but I'll find out and let your assistants know."

Three days later it was figured out that the "kid" was a forty-five-year-old man named Chet who had encountered the leader in the hallway. Having no idea who he was, Chet did not treat him with reverence and fear when directing him to Bill Johnson's office. Chet was an old hippie who should have never been in the core of the movement. You could tell he'd done way too many drugs in his youth. He was always a little disheveled, and overly happy with any interaction you had with him. Yet you could feel he had an inner life of confusion and had mentally remained back in 1968.

This is the best way that I can describe the leader. Every moment of every interaction in any time or any place *has to* be a crescendo. It *must* be a crescendo, and it has to revolve around him creating a feeling of dread in anyone below him in status—which is everyone. He can separate anyone from their family, excommunicate anyone, or send them to the reeducation camp for years on a whim. He brings paranoia and fear that can cause mistakes, and then all mistakes are punished. Any insult is dealt with, and he could be insulted by a dozen roses.

Chapter 17

WEST SUSSEX

[1,558 YEARS BEFORE THE BABY FACTORY] *The Earth shook as they marched through high grass wet with rain, driving a mass of black crows cawing, swarming, and soaring into low-hanging thick clouds. The men emerged from the gathering fog at dawn, five thousand spears and large round shields painted in bright colors. Saxons—invaders from Northern Germany, driven by conquest and plunder. Five thousand marching in unison, beating iron-tipped spears against their shields, a great wave of inevitability sweeping forward—disciplined and certain.*

Watching in restless silence, six thousand native Briton defenders stood at the crest of a low rise, the woods at their backs. The last of their Roman rulers had left long ago, emboldening other men to carve up Britain like a roast at harvest. Briton hands gripped their spears, javelins, and axes. The shields overlapped, forming a wall of oak, iron, and flesh. A war-horn bellowed, casting a deep howl across the wet field, as thousands of Saxon invaders lurched forward, marching in clean, even lines through wild wheat and high grass.

The Saxons screamed, brought their spears down, and the battle lines collided with a discordant clamor of iron crashing on wood, breaking bone, and the wet gurgling of men torn by swords and axes, all amplified by the frightened cries of the dying. Spears on both sides split through chainmail armor, opening bellies and piercing wet hearts. The grass grew dark, stained with blood. Wide blue eyes glared from faces slick with dirt and sweat. Peering from the mud, the dead stared with unseeing eyes, as they watched their Briton shield-wall break and the Saxon horde scatter their conquered brothers toward the forest.

Now, just outside the small hamlet of East Grinstead in West Sussex, England, a different kind of foreigner had taken the land, this time in the form of a savior with no beard. The name "East Grinstead" comes from those fierce Saxon conquerors fourteen hundred years before, the name of the town literally meaning "the place where one shows one's teeth"—

The bump of the landing gear striking the wet English tarmac jarred me awake. I looked out through the porthole, fogged with streaks of dew and condensation. I wasn't sure what time it was. The sun was dampened by a thick and unmoving fog of dense gray clouds. They loomed low in the sky.

"Ladies and gentlemen, on behalf of our aircrew and British Airways, we would like to welcome you to London, Gatwick International Airport. The local time is 9:07 A M, Greenwich Mean..."

I shifted my focus away from the blonde stewardess's lilting voice as the plane whined and taxied to a busy terminal. The streaks of water on the porthole distorted the tailfins of airlines I never knew existed. I felt as alien as I had during my first days in Oregon as I departed the massive aircraft that had been home for the last seven hours. The air was thick with wet, I could smell the dank breeze of fuel and soil even as I stepped out of the airplane and into the jetway.

I was headed to West Sussex, England, to sign people up for upper Level 8 in the advanced spiritual classes available on the movement's ship. The classes were available to anyone and were said to have information that would speed up the progress of returning to "native state," your true form as a fallen god. These classes had names like "Route to Infinity" and "The Power of Simplicity."

The palatial estate of Saint Hill Manor lies twenty minutes southeast

WEST SUSSEX

of Gatwick Airport. It's a place I had only ever heard of secondhand—referenced by the pseudo-navy members, in their countless memos and policy letters, and in the files I used to run at The Archives as a kid. I was still a kid. I didn't know anything about Sussex, where the name came from. I didn't know that it was an ancient place that had seen the rise and fall of kings and had been invaded and conquered again and again by ambitious men from Rome to Scandinavia.

I was nauseous from the plane ride, hunger, and the smell of jet fuel. As we drove toward the compound, the gentle curving road from the airport was lined with thick, gnarled trees. The canopy of branches reached in wide, sweeping arcs over the road that created a tunnel of darkness in the bright daylight, and I was moved by it. I never knew that trees could make a cave.

Saint Hill had been Hubbard's home until he left for the high seas in 1966. Now it was where members of the movement did Advanced Level 5. The Gothic Romanesque manor commands a manicured green rise halfway down a long curving driveway, surrounded by green gardens and flowers. When I arrived in 1988, the massive reproduction Norman castle from the Middle Ages, complete with rounded-off guard towers and battlements, was still being built. The castle's main entrance was designed to look like a barbican—a defensive military structure where two large towers dominated the entryway, and an iron-spiked portcullis gate could barricade the castle against invaders. It looked like something out of the movie *Excalibur*, cinematic and beautiful. I'd seen John Boorman's masterpiece as a kid on movie nights in Lebanon Hall in the days before the movement got even more oppressive.

In front of the barbican would eventually stand a bronze sculpture of man—like Michelangelo's David without genitals—clutching a shield and holding a torch to the sky. The sculpture seemed to be saying that whatever was beyond the massive doors of the barbican was promethean in greatness. Prometheus stole fire from the gods and gave it to humanity as a gift. The commander had once said that his regression therapy from his first book in 1950 was a greater discovery than the wheel and fire.

192   **CHILD X**

I was immediately placed in a dorm called Brook House, now called Brook Manor, a massive Gothic building of red brick and glass that looked like something out of a Charles Dickens novel. Finally, there and exhausted from travel, I crawled into the bed I'd been assigned where the sheets hadn't been washed in months. I could feel the residue of someone else's body on them and smelled the stench of cat urine. I slept for eighteen hours.

X

A week after I arrived, I finally adjusted to the wet and rain, which felt different than in Oregon. One morning upon my arrival, I walked past the movement's castle, slowly being erected. The Castle Project supervisor, a tall, lean, middle-aged American Black man named Harry Jefferies, pointed a lone sinewy finger toward the flat gray sky and smiled. Harry must have recognized me as one of the kids running around the dusty, urban streets of Los Angeles next to The Mothership.

"This what they mean by *pissin'*?" he said to me as I walked past through the drizzle on my way to eat breakfast in The Stables—the movement's spacious ancient stables that had been converted into the staff eating rooms—which sat beyond the manor. Distinguished, Harry walked down a muddy path in the pouring rain, in the middle of the English countryside, wearing a full naval class A uniform—or "dress blues." He had lieutenant commander stripes on his sleeves and an air of power and authority.

There was a structure chart inside the Advanced Division in the compound at Saint Hill. When I saw it, I thought back to the giant chart at The Red Brick Building on Melrose that we'd been forced to memorize as children through repetition. Hubbard once said the structure chart was the most effective ever created, as it was used effectively by an "old galactic civilization" that had lasted for "80 trillion years."

I talked with a kid named Barnaby, standing in front of the castle. I

WEST SUSSEX

knew him from Los Angeles, and it was good to have someone there who was familiar. Suddenly, a man walked up and said hi to Barnaby, introducing himself as Woody. When he left, Barnaby explained to me that the man was Woody Woodmansy, David Bowie's drummer, at least for *Ziggy Stardust and the Spiders from Mars*. These are the things I would say if I ever had doubts or didn't like the way I was being treated: I would think, *What a brilliant, nice man. If someone as talented and kind as that is here, then this must be right.* Every time I had doubts, I would push them out of my mind. Francis's mom and Lightning Nicky Hopkins would get married at Saint Hill. Francis would come to Saint Hill for the wedding, which was attended by rock legends, including Paul McCartney.

Dougray Cathall was a pseudo-navy member with a billion-year commitment who wrote a song after the success of Band Aid, Bob Geldof's Africa fundraising project in 1984. Cathall's song, "What About the Children," sung by Yolanda Adams, had a luscious and moody melody. He'd shown the song to Nicky Hopkins before Nicky had moved to Los Angeles. Nicky brought the song to Paul McCartney, who said the song was perfect for a Christmas special coming up, either on Channel 4 or the BBC, that he'd been asked to contribute to, and that he'd like to arrange it. This would be good repute for the movement, so Nicky brought Dougray to meet Paul, and Dougray sang him the melody. Paul McCartney was so blown away by Dougray's voice that he arranged for him to sing it on national television in England on Christmas Day. If members of the private navy were singing on *Top of the Pops* across the UK on Christmas Day, with an arrangement by Paul McCartney, Hubbardism had to be real. I'll never forget the artwork on the vinyl single, showing a cartoon English countryside where it rained violins. Back then, growing up in Hollywood, anything said by a celebrity was said by a god. Paul McCartney was more than a celebrity.

I was eventually moved to a better-than-normal room because, as my supervisor told me, "You work with the ship," meaning the *Freewinds*, "so you get something nicer."

194   CHILD X

The doctrine says our bodies are a flesh prison, on prison planet Earth. During these advanced levels at Saint Hill, you could begin to shed both prisons and return to your godlike state.

The commander had published the beginnings of the doctrine in 1950. Within a few years he needed a new way to make money. He started the movement and built it around a new version of the doctrine—proof of past lives and a method for freeing humanity from the "reactive mind." When a member of the movement becomes a non-reactionary, eventually they then do machine-based counseling on themselves. This can go on for years until they are ready for the next level of their spiritual development.

In machine-based counseling, a counselor and a patient sit across from each other at a desk. The counselor has a physical machine in front of them and is the only one that can see its dials. The patient verbally answers questions, predetermined by Hubbard, holding two long thin cans (similar to unmarked soup cans) with a bright chrome finish that are attached by wires to the machine. The patient is attached to the equivalent of a galvanometer machine, a device that measures electrical current. The machine is only able to measure a fraction of the biological signals that appear in the nervous system; respiration, digestion, the dryness of the mouth are only a few of the signals that the galvanometer can't detect. Machine-based counseling, the movement's foundational therapy, is built on a small sliver of biological signals. Hubbard's doctrine explains as science that what this machine is actually measuring is the physical mass of your thoughts—this part is non-scientific.

Movement members believe that it is scientific with the same certainty that accepted science believes in gravity. They believe, when the needle reacts on the machine, that a thought is being measured, and that they can lead you to painful incidents and past-life memories by using the dial to tell you when something has entered your consciousness before you are even aware of it. The needle reads, and the counselor says, "That, right there," and you start looking, and you may have a memory, or a past-life memory. The movement believes these are real memories, but they are just as likely memories that are being fabricated by the person receiving

WEST SUSSEX

counseling. They are being told this machine is insisting they're there, so they likely start creating memories that they now believe are completely real because the machine says so.

The promotion of false memories causes the needle on the machine's dial to move a certain way, and the counselor sees it: "Yes, that right there." This confirmation from the counselor that the needle is matching your thoughts gives you a hit of sweet dopamine—confirmation that you are remembering something that *really* happened. You want to feel that way again and again and again. The more dopamine hits you get, the more you need in order to feel the way you did that very first time. Machine-based counseling eventually gives you a dopamine addiction in the form of masquerading as euphoric memory.

For the counselor, the smiles and elation they witness in the subject confirm that these memories are real, and they feel powerful, like an important scientific magician, and also receive a slight hit of dopamine. Further, and more importantly, one is never allowed to leave a counseling "sitting" without the needle saying they are at peace through the floating motion. All throughout a machine-based counseling sitting, one is having positive and negative emotional reactions. Often, all one wants to do is get up and leave. The danger is that the machine, through false confirmation, is separating you from your physical self and actual memory and reality. This creates an illusion where both the counselor and the patient think it is making both of them and the world better, but in reality, it is facilitating a micro-addiction to dopamine. No sitting ends without both patient and counselor flush with dopamine. No human being on Earth under the right circumstances would be immune.

These sittings can go on for hours. It is strictly forbidden to leave machine-based counseling before the needle is smoothly going back and forth, telling the counselor that the patient has thoroughly confessed or has gone through their trauma and is totally serene. To reach this state, one must constantly deny their nervous system and their body. When our body says "leave," it is doing that to protect us. When we deny the body continuously as a form of repetition and conditioning, we are training ourselves to further sever the connection between our feelings and our actions. The body tells us when something's wrong. It is this constant denial of feelings in their body that allows a member of the movement to ignore the most heinous of atrocities that they may see before them and dismiss it as necessary for saving the planet.

I came to realize this is how so many good people saw what was happening to me and my brothers and my friends and went about their day. It is unnatural for any human being to deny their internal feelings when they see a child in pain. When we do see a child in pain, we feel it in our bodies. Members of the movement have often severed the mind–body connection, and when they see a child suffering, feel nothing. The fact that this works equally well in both the counselor and the one receiving the counseling simultaneously—with a scientific certainty experienced by both parties—makes it the most sophisticated and effective mind control system in history.

The non-reaction training has a similar effect. It is a series of practices where one doesn't react, blink, or flinch (and this can go on for hours), no matter how uncomfortable their body is. The understanding of this within the movement is you are training to keep your composure when something startling or upsetting happens. What actually occurs as you train to not react to bad, jarring, and alarming things is that you've just trained yourself to not react to the pain and suffering of others. They are conditioning you to ignore your body's sensations and feelings when a reaction is required. You are trained not to react. By not reacting, your mind–body connection is once again severed. This is how I think machine-based counseling and the training works. I could be wrong. We can see somebody murdered in front of us and we are forever changed biologically. No one has touched us, but our biology is altered by the overwhelming sensation of the traumatic act. If you separate our ability to feel what happens in front of us, that which makes us human, you destroy us.

Many inner navy kids that grow up with the commander's doctrine dictating their life for so long become locked in an infantilized or childlike emotional state. This can result in adults who, decades out of the doctrine,

WEST SUSSEX

197

have to deal with people through force and threat while losing control of their emotions.

Severing this mind–body connection is the same fundamental mechanism behind chattel slavery. By displacing someone physically and stripping them of all means of support, the slave must ignore their body and thoughts and comply in order to survive. One does it physically, the other creates the same effect solely within the confines of the mind. If we are forced to deny the body either mentally or physically, it is a death even if we remain alive.

Hubbard was constantly secluding himself, sitting alone in a room doing research. Any other scientist would have data, papers, formulas, even microscopes and test tubes. There is no research. The commander sat alone in a room and whatever came into his head, he would decide how truthful it was and create a doctrine from his thoughts. Whatever he decided he believed must be true. Sometimes it was and sometimes it wasn't.

Not very humbly referring to himself as "Source," Hubbard stole use of a galvanometer for counseling from Sigmund Freud, Carl Jung, and Volney Mathison. Even before he started using the machine with his regression therapy, the commander claimed his insights had surpassed Jung's and Freud's. I don't think Hubbard considered the brain or the gravity of dopamine. I think he thought the dopamine hits, verbally and on the patients' faces, were scientific verification that his constructs were real. I could be wrong.

If you approach the post–World War II babies who built the movement—our parents, the children of the revolution—to this day they will respond to this suffering of the kids of the momvement with steel-eyed indifference. Even after they've left the movement, most have no compassion or empathy for us kids. That is another travesty of what happened: its detritus lingers in you for a lifetime even after you leave it. These women and men have become deformed, languorous monsters of self-righteous detachment. They'll say they care with a wry smile of superiority. This is my mother, and tens of thousands of others.

The movement has a book of ethics that is sacred to all of its members. Movement ethics consist merely of one thing—anything that protects the movement is ethical, and anything that threatens it or hurts its reputation is unethical. Buried in the book of ethics is a poetic essay that the commander wrote about Simón Bolívar—the former leader of Colombia who was known for freeing South America from the control of Spain—as well as the story of his concubine, Manuela Sáenz. Both lost power and died with nothing. The poetic novella on Bolívar is the commander's way of telling his followers how power is lost and maintained. Intricately written, what most adherents glean from the essay can be summed up in one simple phrase: ignore the crimes of the leader.

On a warm summer in 1631, a flotilla of warships descended on Baltimore, a coastal village in Ireland. In an instant, a horde of fearsome raiders from North African Algeria and the Ottoman Empire swarmed ashore and into the village, brandishing curved swords and early muskets. Craving blood and treasure, they burned houses and stole valuables and livestock. Then they rounded up the White Irish villagers, separating husbands from wives, fathers from daughters, mothers from sons, and marched them at gun and sword point back to their warships.

The men were pressed into service for decades as laborers and galley slaves who rowed the ships. The women were placed in North African harems as exotic sex slaves of the local nobles. The raiders were even led by a White man, Jan Janszoon van Haarlem, a Dutch sea captain who himself was a slave of the dark-skinned Algerians of North Africa.

The Irish women were separated from their homeland and native language, placed in an alien environment they didn't understand, dependent on their captors to survive, and abused physically and mentally. These captives had to break themselves of everything familiar to endure their bondage. Anything that separates the mind from the body as a form of control is slavery.

In the Western world, when we think of slavery, we think of Africans being brought on boats in chains and taken across vast oceans to work the cotton fields. We think of whips, beatings, and death. This is not the only form of slavery. You can only be controlled when your past, present, and future are taken from you—you obey. By giving you past lives, having you sign an eternal contract, and isolating you in a psychological cage, even in the middle of Los Angeles, Hubbard created a Middle Passage of the mind.

The commander used the severing of the mind–body connection through a doctrine to create a staggering labor machine—a plantation to enrich himself through spirituality. The plantation owners of the American South, who believed that the economic system of chattel slavery was a Christian enterprise, also enriched themselves. In 1967, Hubbard lost the tax-exempt status of his movement because the IRS proved that funds were being passed to him for personal gain. Slavery is about money.

X

Even though I wasn't doing the hard labor I had been as a child, I was still working eighteen-hour days and couldn't leave. If I wanted to leave without escaping, I would be subject to months of physical labor and interrogations. If I escaped without warning, I would never be able to see my family again.

When the FBI raided The Old Industrial Hospital in 1977, when I was seven, it was because the movement's secret police—called the Guardian's Office—were committing the largest infiltration of the US government in its history. As a child I believed that this militaristic intelligence arm of my religion was necessary to protect it and ensure its future. What I didn't know was that, during the Cold War—while the commander was sailing the high seas off North Africa—people in places like East Germany were suffocating under the same strangle of a secret police that used the same tactics.

Any time a member of the movement breaks any rules, other members are required to report it. This means a husband reports on their wife, a wife reports on their husband, a child reports on their mother, a mother reports on their child, and so on and so on. Everything you do is monitored by those close to you. The result of these reports can range from a day's bodily labor to being sent to the reeducation camp. This is what the movement's Stasi culture created: common in all fascist, communist regimes, "snitching" allows the regime to unjustly preserve itself.

One common thing from my childhood that was no different in the English countryside is the amount of quasi-navy members who smoked. Cigarette smoke was the milieu of my childhood. Its texture in the air, its odor, its patina on walls and furniture, and its soaking into the fabric of bedding and clothes. Nicotine calms the nervous system. If the doctrine worked, why would all these people be salving themselves with cartons and cartons of cigarettes?

X

It was a quiet morning in the Sussex countryside, and the air was scrubbed clean from recent rain. I was having breakfast with Peter, a sad-eyed old man with silver hair, whose job was to deal with external threats to the movement. A threat could be a negative report in the media, a rogue ex-member planning to corrupt or influence current members, or a government investigation. Anything that could lead to a potential threat against the movement. In East Germany the Stasi—the State Police for the Communist Party in East Germany—wiretapped people's phones, surveilled them, and encouraged neighbors to report on each other.

Over breakfast at The Stables, I was talking to Peter, and he was speaking quickly, telling me how he measured his progress through "threats handled." Since I was new, he said, I could help him find threats by observing movements around the organization. If I found any, could I please come tell him about them? Listening to him talk, I wondered what happened when all of the threats were handled. In the movement, everything was managed by statistics—your value is determined by your output.

Peter was explaining to me that to be considered successful, he always had to handle more threats the following week than he had the previous week. I thought, *What if there are no threats, and the only way Peter can prove his value is by handling threats?* You would have to invent threats.

WEST SUSSEX

201

So, inadvertently, the secret police, which had changed its name from the Guardian's Office to the Office of Special Affairs after Hubbard's wife went to jail for government infiltration from the 1977 raid, *is the movement creating its own threats?* I quickly pushed this thought out of my head.

I had no days off. I was at best the equivalent of a house slave. I was owned, an asset ready to be deployed. My movements were completely controlled. During my time in the English countryside, taking payments for courses and Levels to be done on the ship, I sent every penny each week to a bank in Luxembourg. I wasn't doing hard labor like I was as a kid or being a domestic servant, but I was working eighteen-hour days.

X

At Saint Hill I saw greens greener than I ever thought green could be. I saw rolling fields rolling farther than I ever thought fields could roll. I saw reflective ponds reflecting light in a way that I never saw light reflected. There was the constant echo of frogs. As I took in this visual exaltation of nature's curation, I burned inside with its beauty. What I wouldn't understand for decades, was that this beautiful, magical, sublime, ancient green place had been the birthplace of my pain.

In 1967 my mother, heavily pregnant with my older brother, and John Mustard, the man who for years was passed off as my father, had been here at Saint Hill. They traveled here just missing Hubbard's hasty departure by weeks. England's Home Office had soured toward the commander and what they perceived were strange ideas. He was furious to leave the grand lord's manor that he'd called home for eight years and where he had raised his children—Diana, Arthur, and Quentin. He justified his flight from the government and the tax man as an evolution.

He went to the one place on Earth where governments didn't exist: the high seas between nations, searching for a place to further establish and build the movement. He still had to come to port to refuel, gather food, and get supplies. His ship, the *Apollo*, was stoned by locals off the coast of Madeira with claims of being a CIA spy ship. As the mysterious man grew in reputation, the governments of the planet, which the movement was working hard to salvage, began closing off their ports to Commander Hubbard—vexing man's greatest friend.

My older brother Joshua was born in England not long after Hubbard had left. He would eventually be smuggled into America and remained stateless for the first two decades of his life. He had no birth certificate, social security number, or papers that said he existed.

My mother and false father, when boarding the *Queen Mary* for their return voyage to the United States, were stopped by a Royal Scots Grey guard, known for their unwavering reserve. The unflinching soldier eventually took pity on my weeping mother and let them board the gargantuan ocean liner with their tiny undocumented child. It was only a few years later, when I was little older than an infant, that I would be taken to visit the *Queen Mary* on a rare reprieve from The Baby Factory. As a toddler staring at this massive oceangoing structure, I would have no idea that my stateless older brother had been its secret passenger, ensuring he would never exist.

X

In my teens, I felt like his lack of a nation-state had amplified Joshua's lifelong unrest. He was no one. He wasn't someone. He didn't officially exist. When my brother was eighteen, my grandmother became obsessed with getting him US or dual US and British citizenship. My mother kept saying it was no big deal, but Joshua couldn't get a driver's license, health insurance, or a job, or register legally with any American institution.

Many years later, I was reading Jules Verne's immortal science fiction novel *20,000 Leagues Under the Sea*. In it, the enigmatic Captain Nemo had abandoned his previous life and taken on a new identity. Nemo's lack of identity had been a choice that infused him with the strength of not being tied to a place—he was self-defined. No man's identity is something others can choose for him. Nemo means "no man" or "no place" in the

WEST SUSSEX

dead language of Latin. For my brother, lacking a place, a state, or a sense of belonging haunted him.

I love my brother and look up to him for having the more rational reaction to what happened to us, but to me he is like an apparition. I didn't see him often. He was out there doing who knows what—rebelling, existing, I don't know. I don't elaborate on who he is in this book, because he wasn't really in my life, and I don't want to try and define what I didn't see.

When we got older, he told me that he loved me, but he didn't want to know me because I reminded him of what happened. The world never knows what someone can become. Whether the daughter of a primitive villager in a jungle, or the son of a Mexican immigrant fading into the brick in Los Angeles, you can never tell the vastness of a human before they've been "skinned"—by "skinned" I mean defined by the place where you're born and the color of your outer shell.

In Saint Hill, as my time drew to a close and I was about to be delivered back to Florida, it was becoming clear to me that I had been made a slave.

Chapter 18

THE ESCAPE

At eighteen years old, supervising fundraisers with millions on the line seemed a bit much. It didn't matter, because I had done it in millions of lives before—I just had to remember.

I'd been called back from England suddenly and put back into my fundraising role, and now I was failing at my job. In the movement, you do what is assigned, not what you want to. It wasn't going well.

A rare commander named Declan Shaughnessy flew out from headquarters in the California desert and pulled me into a meeting. I sat across from him in his navy blues with epaulets on his shoulders and three gold bars.

Declan was the highest-ranked official I'd ever seen, outside of the group's leader, David Miscavige. He was in charge of the ship. I felt like I was alone in a room with General Eisenhower. I was trembling. Declan sat behind a large desk, and I sat in a small undersize chair in front of him. He quietly peered at me, unflappable in his demeanor. He was a handsome man, in his late thirties, with raven black hair and piercing blue eyes. He calmly asked me, in his cool Irish brogue, "Hi, Jamie. How do you think you're doing?"

He was referring to my new job as a supervisor.

206 CHILD X

I quickly responded as confidently as I could, "I think I have potential."

Almost without pause, as I finished the last syllable of my last word, Declan pleasantly said, "Hitler had potential."

The room twisted and revolved around me. If I hadn't been sitting, I would have fainted. I thought for sure I was going to the reeducation camp where I would be doing hard labor for five to ten years. They also had a child's reeducation camp, which I'd managed to avoid, but now here, right now, I was going.

Under the Cultural Revolution in China, Mao Tse-tung's poor revolutionary followers believed in a path to redemption in the form of years of hard labor. Digging ditches and any labor that put stress on the body cleansed the Chinese soul. This was done in the name of Mao's benevolent ideal of communism. I promised myself, if sent to the reeducation camp, I would escape.

"How would you like a change of scenery?" Declan's words jarred me from my fear. "We're sending you down the hill to work with Sandine."

And then it was over. I had been spared a gauntlet that would have changed my life forever, one I might never have recovered from.

X

I was getting two to three hours of sleep a night. I had never had a bank account or made more than a few hundred dollars in a week, yet I sat there in my posh prop office and took money in the tens of thousands of dollars from some of the wealthiest and most famous people in the movement. The size of the checks were inconceivable to me. I never had enough money for food and couldn't pay my car insurance, or parking tickets, before returning to the fold. Every morning, I would be up before dawn, expecting this to go on for years. Once again, I had the feeling I might be a slave. Every day, bleeding into the next with no days off, just collecting money—modern-day servitude to fuel the movement's machine.

Now, as I think back at my time in The Sandcastle, I remember the exact night when I realized I might be a slave. I was listening to the shake

THE ESCAPE

207

of thunder at sea. Another storm was forming on the coast. When I reflect back on that moment now, I see my sixteen-year-old younger brother, a few years later, being sent to the reeducation camp for sleeping with his girlfriend. I think about him in a black boiler suit with a yellow armband. I think about him doing hard labor, calling everyone "sir," eating slop from industrial trays.

I wasn't thinking that then, but I was thinking that night that I might be a slave. In fact, I was becoming certain of it. Finally, like sediment falling from clear blue water, I was starting to see. I walked constantly through the streets of downtown Clearwater, the lush green palms swaying in the wind, the bright pastels of the resorts and houses, cars in bold reds and yellows that crowded the streets, and again my bright navy whites, brightly shining in the sun.

My new boss, Sandine Jansen, was a South African Jew with a brown Princess Di haircut and bright skin. My literacy hadn't improved. I didn't know any grammar. I didn't know how to use a period or a comma. She never complained about having an illiterate aide de camp; she liked me because I could stir emotions from those prominent members and could help those who had handed her fortunes. If I raised money on my own, my five-year-old writing level made the invoices I filled out impossible to read.

I was saved in the form of a fourteen-year-old Mexican boy called Nacho, who barely spoke English, but had the ability to rewrite my invoices so they were legible. I blacked out my illiteracy as unimportant in my necessity to contribute to planetary salvation.

Eventually, it all started going wrong with Sandine. I didn't even know what was going wrong, but Sandine had the ability to impact a massive swath of the movement's weekly global income, and she was failing to do so. She was too valuable as an asset to the movement to be wasted on a sentence to the reeducation camp like my brother Jono would be. I was the next best thing. I was told I was being sent to the *Freewinds* for "correction." It reminded me of that day when I was seven and all the kids in the van were told to stay away from me, but I didn't know that it was because of what was crawling around on my head. This was another Kafkaesque noir happening as my anxiety grew.

In under an hour, two quasi-navy members in navy whites drove me to the airport. I was soon on board a flight to Aruba to do penance on the *Freewinds*, which was docked there. As the plane floated into the rising sun, every person on board yelped joyfully with the anticipation of arriving on a tropical island, but I knew I was going to experience something very different.

In 1984 the movement was looking for a completely safe, aesthetic, and distraction-free environment for its Advanced Level 8 students. Hubbard had administered the first Advanced levels aboard the *Apollo* in the late 1960s. A corporate entity was assembled in the 1980s, purchased *The Bohème*, and in 1988 the movement rechristened her *Freewinds*.

X

Arriving on Aruba, I ran up the gangplank of the towering alabaster cruise ship to the deck, where I found a woman in full navy whites, model brown and blonde, her eyes behind mirrored aviators, holding a mop, bucket, and jumpsuit.

"Jamie Mustard," she screamed. "Get over here, get this jumpsuit on, and follow me."

Lily was the commanding officer of Hubbard's "Couriers," the senior-most officers on the ship. I changed in under two minutes and was quickly marched along bustling decks, through cramped compartments and staterooms, to the engine room, a metal cavern full of deafening growls and wet heat.

With me was Kent Weatherly, an Australian who headed up the engine room. A large tree trunk of a man, Kent had been the head of the engine room on the original *Apollo* with Hubbard.

"Put this person in the deepest, darkest bilge you have," Lily screamed to the sunburned Australian, who nodded an assent.

Hubbard had ordered, for decades, that someone sent to clean the

THE ESCAPE

209

ship's bilge represented the utmost form of correction and punishment. A ship's engine constantly emits oil, which leaches into a mix of seawater and grime. Whatever you clean out is immediately replaced with a new slurry of gunk. Kent, this centered man responsible for the engine of a very expensive ship, pointed to a crevice. Under it, frothy oil drooled from the beast of an engine towering above me, a behemoth mechanical sculpture.

"Yer gettin' into it, and cleanin' it," he said politely in a thick Australian drawl. He knew what he was asking: go under the lip of the ship's engine, a two-foot wraparound enclosure along the side of the engine, with a half to one inch of engine oil floating freely in the bilge at all times, and make it clean.

Cleaning the bilge was a Sisyphean task that could never be completed and a symbol of a billion years of resolve.

I hadn't slept in forty-eight hours. The entire trip down to Aruba, my nerves burned with anxiety. The engine issued its throaty growl, and as I crawled into the gap, the oil of the bilge was warm and soothing. In great comfort and in oily reprieve, I finally fell asleep.

I woke to a shrill woman screaming, "Where is he? I told you to stick him in the bilge."

It was Lily, still convulsed up to eleven.

"He's inside, under the bilge," Kent drawled.

"That's great," Lily hissed back. "I don't wanna fucking see him." Her steps grew distant on the deck, and I fell back asleep, grateful for my reprieve and soothed by the comfort of the dark and the warm, pungent engine oil covering the lower half of my body.

X

Two days after spending my entire day hidden and suspended in engine oil, I graduated to worker status, cleaning planks, decks, and pipes in the unbearable heat of the engine room. They partnered me with a jittery, squirrely, but nice man named Fred, my new workmate. A public member, Fred had been on the ship for a year and a half. He had gone crazy after

210   CHILD X

doing the movement's highest rung, Level 8 on Hubbard's ladder. The days were long, and the heat so intense, that on the fifth day I collapsed. I spent a week in infirmary with heat prostration, looking out the lone porthole at the crisp blue sea beyond.

What I thought about lying in that bed was how much I felt like a baby; having someone control my mind and my physical movements. Every single one of us in the private navy—whether or not they know it—has been infantilized.

I'd been back in the engine room for five days when Kent, who was not mean and not nice, gave me more cleaning orders. Fred was nowhere to be found. I was relieved; his jitteriness made me uncomfortable. Alone in the engine room, I could scour every surface, laser-focused on eliminating every speck of grime. Every hour Kent appeared, as if from nowhere, to inspect my work. I had no sense of irony that I was being made to work on a ship in the Netherland Antilles of the Caribbean where my ancestors just as easily could have been slaves.

"Fail," Kent grunted. Then he would give me something else to clean—a plank, a pipe, a gangway—each time appearing from nowhere to grade me with a guttural "Fail." Over and over, fail. Every hour, fail. It was another of Hubbard's words, cheap and without any poetry. It was the verbal equivalent of taking a backhand to the mouth from a hand covered in tepid sweat. I had to achieve a perfect outcome in the engine room before I could ever be released to less strenuous forms of manual labor. Kent finally said to me, "Jamie, can't you see the oil that's right fuckin' there on the plank?" Even the word "oil" seemed to ooze from the big man's lips.

I wiped a pool of sweat from my brow. "No, Kent, I can't," I gasped. "I can't see what you're talking about."

Kent reared up with a strange look of consternation on his face. He was a big man, still imposing despite his years. "Jamie, do you have eyesight problems? Do you need glasses?"

"Yes," I sighed. I couldn't fully tell if this was another setup, or if beneath Kent's leathered exterior was an air of genuine concern. "I'm

THE ESCAPE

211

short-sighted. My grandmother brought me glasses a few years ago, but they were lost somewhere—I no longer have them."

That was it for my time in the engine room. Kent knew I was working myself to the bone—he could see it even if I couldn't see what was right in front of me most of the time. I was sent to "Potland," where the pots were washed in the staff galley, and I loved it.

I spent all day cleaning pots, staring out of my very own porthole at the soft blue expanse of the ocean off Curaçao. In Potland, I had no responsibility beyond the pots. There were no threats. All I had to do was clean pots and stare at the sea and think. I fantasized about reading books. I fantasized about going to the movies. I fantasized about jogging, the wind in my face and Talking Heads a constant blustering apparition in my Walkman.

From the confines of Potland, I made myself a promise that if I was ever sent back on board to the *Freewinds* again to be punished, I would leave. Escape. I promised myself that, if I continued to feel enslaved, I would leave at any cost. I would "blow"—the pseudo-navy's word for going AWOL. Every word ever invented by Hubbard has a stigma. As the words accumulate, so does your attachment and total belief in his ideas. By attaching a stigma to words, if you believe those words, it gives someone the ability to own and enslave your mind.

Eventually I was sent back to The Sandcastle, and it wasn't long before I'd made another mistake. Sandine had given me an order I didn't want to do, I told her "no" and she then commanded me that she was my superior. I did it and it resulted in a problem that caught the ear of our superiors. We'd stayed up all night.

If a person in the quasi-navy goes on an unauthorized leave, there are protocols in place all over the world to hunt them down using family, friends, and technology to bring them back.

The way out being the way through is the way the movement justifies pain. It was a phrase that Hubbard stole from Robert Frost, who said, "The only way out is through," and this is how we justify staying when we are in

212 **CHILD X**

intense emotional pain, that just on the other side of that pain will be some sort of freedom, which never comes.

At 10 the next morning, I went back to The Hacienda, the staff dormitories, to sleep. "Hacienda" is a Spanish word describing a plantation, complete with a manor, labor fields, and worker quarters. The workers weren't necessarily slaves, but on The Hacienda a worker would likely die a worker. I walked my usual route over the half mile between The Hacienda and Fort Harrison. At The Fortress, the blocky powder-blue shuttle van rounded a corner, picking up staff, taking them back to The Hacienda a few miles away. There was a distant grumble of thunder. Dark storm clouds gathered off to the south. I wondered if I would get any sleep.

X

I woke to a sharp knock on my door. In the glistening sun, I peered through the door's peephole to see my superior officer in the Hubbard navy, dressed from head to toe in scruffy navy whites. The fish-eye effect of the peephole bent his face into a comic caricature. This was the man who ran all the fundraisers, sending punters to the *Freewinds* to school in the doctrine.

"Jamie," he said through the heavy door. I sighed in response, my head still full of the previous night. "You messed up. You're going to the ship for correction." My heart bucked in my chest, like a thoroughbred horse. My nerves were shot. He was trying to be as stern as he could while innately being a nice guy. "I'll be back in one hour, with a car. A flight has been booked for you. You will be on it." Outside the wind gathered speed, swelling, from a breeze to gusts. This would be the second time I was being sent to the *Freewinds* for doing something wrong that I couldn't define. I could feel the cloying heavy engine oil mixing with seawater in the ship's bilge permeating my skin.

A year later, I would read a story by Kurt Vonnegut about fourteen-year-old Harrison Bergeron, an intelligent, athletic, and handsome teenager, who is taken away from his parents by the government and sent to

THE ESCAPE   213

prison. In Harrison's society, mediocrity is celebrated and absurd methods are employed to handicap anyone with ability. In Vonnegut's dystopian world, anyone with an ability has a physical device installed on their body to keep that ability at bay so everyone is equal to everyone else. Harrison's parents, one a scientific genius, the other an Olympic athlete, are given handicaps by the government. For Harrison's mom, it's weights and devices for immobility. For Harrison's father, it's bells that ring in ears every thirty seconds, so his complex thoughts can never gain momentum.

When the indestructible Harrison sheds every physical and mental device laid upon him, he escapes his prison and storms a TV station, declaring himself emperor and encouraging everyone in the studio to take off their handicaps. He is shot and killed. The story described a soul that truly wants to be free and can never be contained. Upon reading this story, anyone would see death as a freedom greater than a life constrained.

I'd been working at the sales division, hoarding meager commissions under my bed. That muggy Florida day I was sleeping in my navy whites. I threw everything I owned—my limited civilian clothes, a small Sony stereo, and CDs—into the middle of a bedsheet, twisted it into a bindle, threw it over my shoulder, and walked out the door. I was nineteen years old, and it was everything in this world that I owned. I made it look as if I was going to do my laundry. Somewhere in the distance, thunder cracked. A storm was sweeping in from the sea, gathering speed even though my day was still sunny. In the absurdity of my navy whites, in a town with no real connection to any sort of military, I hailed a cab.

There were always cabs around The Hacienda because people had to get back and forth between there and the Fort Harrison Hotel when the van wasn't around to take them. The cab drivers hung around, always anxious for a fare. On my way to that first cab, every time a fellow pseudo-navy member looked at me, I felt exposed, like they could see through my soul and knew what I was doing. If I was caught, I would be instantly sent to the reeducation camp where I would spend years. If I got stopped, my life was over, so I moved fast and instantly. The cabbie, a Cuban man sweating profusely in the pounding, moist Florida sun, asked me where I wanted to go.

"Tampa. Downtown," I shouted. My only plan was to create distance; the rest I could figure out later. I felt a burning spread in my neck while my palms tingled, wet with sweat. I felt a shiver down my spine. The taxi pulled away into the heat of the day. I looked over the cabbie's shoulder, through the windshield. The powder-blue van raced past us in the other lane. Crossing the desolate near-ten-mile causeway, hovering a few feet above the glistening ocean on both sides, was an eternity. I felt like there was no escape; the normally beautiful causeway felt like a place where I could be trapped.

In Tampa, my heart continued churning while I hailed another cab. I asked that cabbie to take me to a mall, got out, hailed another cab, then asked that cabbie to go to a place where there would be a lot of hotels. I knew the pseudo-navy would be looking for me. I willed my short, shallow breaths into long, deep pulls of the humid air. I walked into the hot, muggy afternoon, with my bundle of CDs and clothes, and into a Radisson—they were nice in those days. The hotel lobby was busy with people. In my mind, any one of them could have been in the movement. I looked over my shoulder through the glass doors as I walked through the rotating entrance. The taxi was gone.

A woman stood at the front desk, smiling, big hair, bubble gum, and bored to tears.

"Do I have to give you my name and ID if I pay cash up front?" I asked as I approached the desk, my heart racing and my breathing shallow.

She looked me up and down. I forgot I was still in my navy whites. Nothing could be done about that now. All I could do was own it, and hope she wasn't one to ask questions.

I could feel the eyes of hotel guests scouring me. Here I was, in a navy uniform with a laundry sack at a downtown Radisson Hotel. Someone from the movement had to be watching this, in disbelief. I feared I was going to be caught.

I think she thought I was real military. "Absolutely not," she said. "You can call yourself Mickey Mouse if you want."

"Mickey it is," I responded.

THE ESCAPE 215

I bought myself two nights in the suite up front, and, exhausted, pitched into the king-size bed. I slept for nine hours.

When I woke up, it was dusk. I had that feeling of lost time you get when you wake up in a strange, unfamiliar place.

I stepped into the hallway, checking both ends to see if anyone was around. Empty. I walked out of the suite, navy whites balled up in my hands, found a trash chute at the end of the hallway, and dropped the whites inside. I dropped in the shoes last. They were always uncomfortable: dirty-white hardened leather shoes that never stayed clean and dug in, leaving red marks on the sides of my heels. I never felt so happy than to see these shoes disappear and hear the clunk at the bottom of the chute.

I walked back to the room feeling stronger, as if I had released a necklace of Kryptonite. I called my grandmother, who had once told me that if I ever wanted to deal with my illiteracy, I could come to Westchester, New York, and stay with her. At sixteen I had turned her down, missing the familiarity of Los Angeles—its dust, crime, heat, and beautiful beaches. The movement very intentionally manipulates children through their sense of too much certainty, which every child craves, and a lust for adventure. All I could see in front of me now was a different life of manual labor; constantly being ground down for simply being there, for having the desire to exist.

My grandmother picked up. I told her where I was, hiding at a hotel near downtown Tampa.

"Does your offer still stand?" I asked.

"Yes, of course." There was no hesitation in her voice.

"Send me a ticket."

Getting to the Tampa airport without being seen by people from the movement was a major ordeal. I figured, by now they knew I was gone, and they would be watching the airport 24/7. It was the only way I could get out of Tampa. I didn't have a car. I didn't dare hitchhike across two hundred miles of swampland in ninety-degree temperatures. I thought about taking a bus to Orlando before I realized the bus station would be just as dangerous.

216   CHILD X

I waited three days at the Radisson, thinking by then the movement would assume I had already left town and wouldn't be covering the airport, then checked out before dawn. The air was already growing thick with moisture, making every breath I pulled in feel wet. Another storm had passed overnight, and I could still see a few stars glimmer in the waning darkness. I would miss the mercurial weather of Florida's central coast. The stars would soon be overtaken by a sunrise.

A taxi soon stopped at the hotel's entrance. I hauled up a cheap duffel bag I'd gotten at the hotel gift shop. I had changed into my regular street clothes; now I looked like anyone else, just a kid on his way somewhere.

The taxi merged onto the freeway toward the airport, just across the bay from Clearwater. I felt queasy heading west, back toward Clearwater and the movement's territory, nervous with the feeling they could sense the taxi bringing me back their way.

The cab pulled up to the airport terminal. "What airline?" he asked. Ahead, about twenty-five feet beyond the taxi's windshield, was the powder-blue van with FORT HARRISON printed largely on both sides. I swallowed.

"Here's fine," I mumbled and passed the cabbie some crumpled twenties. "Keep the change."

I just knew someone on that van would be a pseudo-navy member in uniform. I wanted to melt into the taxi's black leather seats. I pushed open the door and made for a cluster of people at the terminal entrance, then slipped through and into the airport. I timed my taxi to not be at airport security long. Every moment I felt like I could be caught, but I knew they weren't used to seeing me in regular clothes. I obscured myself in a corner and surveyed every approach around the gate.

I caught one of the last-ever flights of Eastern Airlines from Tampa to New York. The 747 felt like a football field; it had ten people on it. I was waiting for a movement catcher to slide onto the plane. The doors closed. I'd never noticed the sound of an airplane door lowering and clamping shut. It was loud, but it probably wasn't. My breaths were shallow as the plane raced down the runway. Feeling Tampa drop away into the blinding

THE ESCAPE

217

light, I finally relaxed and exhaled. Seated in the middle of the 747, I pushed up the armrests and lay across four seats.

Hours later, over a New York blanketed with hazy clouds, I was awakened to the telltale bump of the landing gear dropping free. "We'd ask you to fly Eastern again," said the captain, "but we won't be here." Somewhere, in the dim cabin, I heard a chuckle and smiled.

X

Robert and my grandmother picked me up at JFK. In silence I watched Robert lift my duffel bag and set it in the trunk with so much care it was as if he thought it held the *Mona Lisa*.

I've never been a fugitive, I thought, but I had just escaped a formidable paramilitary navy in Florida; a navy that had held me captive on a ship in the same Caribbean where my ancestors may have been enslaved. In the mid-1700s, "impressment" was a practice started in the British Royal Navy where poor, common Englishmen were kidnapped and trafficked into serving aboard Royal Navy warships—a hard life of danger, abuse, and disease. By 1802, with the threat of Napoleon, even more fresh bodies were needed to keep England uninvaded. I knew I would be actively pursued by the movement, trying to bring me back into the fold. I was a fresh body.

The movement keeping children illiterate and ignorant of the world is a way of impressing them. It instills dependency on the movement's constructs and doctrine. I didn't know this at the time, but I could feel it. My illiteracy limited my compatibility with the world. Education had been my family's path to freedom and power. And lack of it had been the element that kept me in a state of mental arrest. The movement had enslaved me. And even though I had just escaped, sadly I still believed in it all.

A few days later, my grandmother and I visited my mysterious grandfather Roy Jones Gilmer's grave, in Hartford, Connecticut. The drive on the Merritt Parkway in the fall is a symphony of color and golden hues. I drove her pristine brown 1987 Mercury Grand Marquis up the parkway with my grandmother riding shotgun. To this day I consider this to be one of the most beautiful drives in the world, the Merritt Parkway in the fall.

One of the first books I would read in New York was *Invisible Man*. At the end of that book, the main character, an unnamed Black man, having been exploited by communism, having fallen from grace, spends his days in a room filled with hundreds of light bulbs just to see himself. I wondered if Roy, in his desire to do good and ease his guilt for his wealth, had been exploited just like the main character in *Invisible Man* when he joined the Communist Party. I thought, *Thank god, I've never been exploited.*

My grandmother told me Roy had come back from the war with scars. I thought about him coming from slaves, his family accomplishing so much, and his life being shortened by the horror of war. I thought about how he was proud to fight for this country who had first enslaved his ancestors yet eventually gave his family so much opportunity. I thought, *Maybe I could try. Maybe I could honor Roy, this mysterious great man . . . somehow.*

That day, as I leaned over Roy's grave, I reflected on the ridiculous name Mustard. It was no more my last name than any of my ancestors who were brought here on a boat. I thought of a biblical parable I had read in a novel that someone had recently given me: "The kingdom of heaven is like a mustard seed, which a man took and planted in his field. Though it is the smallest of all seeds, yet when it grows, it is the largest of garden plants and becomes a tree, so that the birds come and perch in its branches." The parable is based on a name that is not actually mine, but I would use it to accomplish more than anyone would ever think I'm capable of.

After the grave visit, my grandmother and I went to visit an old Jewish man named Milton, a retired pharmacist in New Haven. Milton, as a young pharmacist, wanted his own pharmacy but had no capital. Twenty years before the Civil Rights movement, Roy and Milton partnered, with Roy as the financier, and opened pharmacies across Connecticut.

That day at Milton's home, he told me over and over that I looked and acted just like my grandfather. "I had never met Black men like your grandfather until I met Roy and his friends," Milton said, welling up with

THE ESCAPE 219

love. "People who have come from so much pain and accomplished so much."

As I was listening to Milton's stories, I thought, *Who is he?* Milton showed me pictures, and I stared into Roy's eyes. *Maybe I'm like him. Maybe I can fix this.*

As I drove back to New York with my grandmother in her Grand Marquis, we raced through the fall colors in our attempt to get back to Westchester before nightfall. My mind was lurching, awash with the fall colors of amber, sand, and rust. Who was my grandfather? And did the truth that he existed mean that my life ought to have been very different?

AUTUMN

3

Chapter 19

NEW YORK

My grandmother's house in Hartsdale, New York, still smelled of oranges and Robert's pungent cigars. The moisture here was no different than in Central Florida, where the damp was penetrating and all encompassing, but here the smell of wet dirt and plant life was invasive. I loved the constant smell of plants.

I lay sprawled on a bed in the upstairs corner bedroom with kids' race-car sheets and Victorian furniture, reading Alex Haley's book about Martin Luther King's antithesis. It's the story of a man with no future. His father is dead, possibly murdered. His mother is committed to an insane asylum. He is illiterate and making his living as a street criminal, until he's arrested and sent to prison. Behind bars he learns to read, breaks out of his illiteracy, and finds a philosophy—a little like the intellectual version of *The Count of Monte Cristo*, but Black.

I had been at my grandmother's about a week before my heart stopped thrashing in my chest. By now the movement knew for a fact that I was long gone. Anxiety never left my body; I knew they would be hunting me, but I did not know who and for how long.

Not long after I left the ship and came to New York, I stayed up late one night watching TV, trying to distract myself long enough to make my

224 **CHILD X**

pounding heart slow down. On MTV there was a music video for a song called "Loser" with a kid in silhouette. As I watched it, I wondered if that was the same kid who I had met hanging out on his bed with Francis. Could a kid from the movement do that? Probably not.

My grandmother and Robert always had houseguests. The first person who came to visit after the escape was Jan Branion. The daughter of my grandmother's cousin, John Branion, Jan was a buoyant, robust, light-skinned Black woman who was kind and had her life together. We sat at the kitchen table, drinking coffee sweetened with cream and honey, and for the first time I heard the story of Dr. John Marshall Branion. John's life had been like a living insane asylum. As he searched for actual asylum, I did as well.

Jan was telling me about a book about her father's story. It eventually won the Anthony and the Agatha Award for mystery and true crime in 1993. Jan talked about her childhood and the household she remembered. "There was no way my father killed my mother," she said. "It was impossible." I'm not sure if she feels that way today.

My grandmother was the most levelheaded person I knew. When she entered the conversation and explained that she aided her cousin John with money and sheltered him in her home consistently over the years, it stunned me. My conservative, college professor grandmother had aided and abetted—from the FBI—a fugitive convicted of murder. I asked her how it was possible. She looked me in the eyes and said calmly, "Jamie, it's family." And that was that.

I tried to imagine John Marshall Branion fleeing across Africa. I didn't know much about Africa. Occasionally I'd see things on the news—conflicts in countries I couldn't name, and protests in South Africa. This was 1989, and Nelson Mandela was in prison.

X

Another week of drizzly humid weather passed.

The downstairs phone rang. I heard my grandmother answer. Her voice was cold, and she spoke in clipped, short sentences.

NEW YORK

225

This happened a few times a day. These short, tense calls came from the movement. They were looking for me and kept asking her where I was. My grandmother denied that I was there.

The calls would metastasize into demands that I had to pay for every course in machine-based counseling I had taken while I was there—$90,000 worth of their doctrine. I needed to pay it off. It was a threat. I was a teenager. It would be ten years before American law covered debt bondage as a form of human trafficking.

My mouth ran dry as I listened to the movement member on the other end of the phone explaining how I was a "freeloader." What I felt in that moment, with emerging clarity, was that the whole time I was there after re-signing the billion-year contract with Francis, I didn't feel like I did much. I was their property, and I owed them the money. I didn't understand how I could possibly owe them that much money. I was illiterate, broke, and destitute if not for my grandmother, my asylum.

A week after my escape, Paco, who now lived on the East Coast selling things by the side of the road, and who had not been my stepfather for many years, knocked on the door. The movement had sent him to confirm my whereabouts. I hid upstairs in my bedroom as he and Dorothy caught up and she denied my presence. I could hear them laughing; she always liked Paco. The song "Tony the Ice Man" rolled through my head, one that Paco used to sing to me as a child, as the man downstairs, who had been sent to hunt me down, yet who I loved, talked to my grandmother.

As I listened to the muffled conversation between my grandmother and the only man that was ever truly been a father to me, I thought about "Tony the Ice Man." It was an upbeat, bouncy song about a boy named Tony who was called an "ice'n man" because he delivered delicious foods that had to be kept chilled: mozzarella, gorgonzola, capicola, sausage, pastrami, piattone, and salami. Paco would croon, with his smiling Moorish eyes, about how young Tony sees a girl and makes eye contact with her, and as they are slowly drawn to each other, they immediately begin to kiss. Tony forgets about time, the ice melts, and his food delivery goes bad. It's a beautiful song about how a young man from the neighborhood experiences love while at the same time something bad happens. Whenever we would see Paco—even if we hadn't seen him in years—we would beg him to sing it. Paco would always protest at first and eventually smile and begin to sing. Paco had a beautiful voice like Frank Sinatra, and "Tony the Ice Man" always made me and Joshua feel happy. Whenever he sang it, I felt warm.

Paco was chasing me down like a runaway slave and all I could think about is how much I loved him and wanted to run downstairs and embrace him while he kissed me as a son in a way that only a Sicilian father could—a male Italian affection Paco showered us with in a way that was confusing to us as kids who got little to no human affection, or touch. I honestly believe that if I didn't receive the physical affection and love from Paco at two-and-a-half and three years old, I would be dead. His love gave me a chance when I didn't have one.

After an hour, Paco left. When I heard him driving away, I peered out the window and saw him driving the same style of white van that he used to drive in Los Angeles. I was standing fifteen feet from where Paco had once wrested me from the tub, speeding to the emergency room. It was the last thing on my mind. I knew my ordeal was just beginning. I was terrified.

Even though Paco was still in the movement, I never forgot the warm feeling he gave me when I was little older than a baby, when he called me son. I will deeply love Paco until the day I die.

The next day the movement called again. This time I picked up and spoke to a woman who told me that if I didn't go to New York City for machine-based interrogation, I would be proclaimed "evil." In the doctrine, a "suppressive" is someone who has pure evil in their heart, their intentions, and actions, like Hitler or Jack the Ripper. If the movement were to proclaim me suppressive, I would never be able to talk to my family or my friends again. I couldn't go back to Los Angeles—another complete disregard for the human heart.

This threat made me feel owned. The woman on the other end of the phone had made the calculation that I couldn't survive outside of the movement. I had been infantilized and limited by my lack of education. I

NEW YORK

was dependent on them like a baby for mother's milk. I was their property, and they wanted it back.

The onslaught of threatening calls and letters was a constant crush of chronic stress and anxiety. Everything I did to distract myself during the days—eating, showering, reading a book—was fogged over by paranoiac numbness. Hubbard believed that the only reason someone would want to escape was because of crimes they had committed in the movement, harming the mission to save mankind. He claimed interrogations cleaned your soul. What I feel now is they make you look inward so you are weakened and can be more easily controlled.

I took the train into New York City for months. I walked into the movement's Times Square headquarters with my nerves on fire. I completed dozens of hours of brutal interrogations, searching for crimes that I must have committed within the movement. I confessed and confessed and confessed, and finally I was done.

I told the machine-based counselor that I would not be returning to the movement, and for a brief moment I thought I was free. I spoke to the woman who was my liaison in Florida, and she told me that it didn't matter. It was too late. Ken Weatherly—the brother of Kent, the big Australian on the *Freewinds*—had already ordered my excommunication due to me being an evil person. I was devastated. My entire past had just been severed from me. I wanted my friends. I wanted my family back. All was lost.

The movement targeted kids like me—those of us who were born in and raised in baby factories around the globe and who only had Hubbard's doctrine and the reality the movement chose to impose on us. It was the only world we knew. We were easier to control than an adult recruit because we didn't have an outside world to reference.

I read about the "sheeting" of Black psychiatric patients in the American South—a cruel form of therapy where a cotton bedsheet was wrapped around the patient, then saturated with water. The sheet contracted as it dried, making an uncomfortable cocoon around the patient's body, constricting air and blood flow. The movement says that the psychiatric field should be held accountable for its past. Electroconvulsive shock, lobotomies, sheeting—their past is their present, these practices are their essence. If this is true, then should the movement not also be held accountable for psychologically vivisecting us children like the Helnwein painting?

I chose to stay in New York. The threats of my eternal shunning continued. By being declared evil I would not have access to the doctrine and would be stuck in a meat body forever. I had been damned.

In 1761 the Chinese Hongmen—a triad and secret society—used a religious doctrine of salvation to recruit members from the merchant class. They were stopped by the government and their members resorted to illegal activities, forming a cartel that engaged in protection rackets and extortion across three continents. They were devoted to Lord Guan, a godlike, historic Chinese myth who embodied loyalty, patriotism, and all that is righteous. This triad is now synonymous with organized crime. The Hongmen, just like me, believed they lived utopian ideals while in reality were reaping anathemic acts upon the world.

I wandered out of the interrogations, one day, into the lobby of the Paramount Hotel—one of the first boutique hotels built in America. When I entered, I felt like I was walking into a phantasm, a sea of dark gold. The walls and ceiling were glowing with pools of amber light. The lobby was filled with people dressed in black, several with thick dark glasses engaged with one another in a caterwauling symphony of sound. It was the most exotic interior environment I had seen since The Spaceship in the oasis. I couldn't imagine who these people were, or what they did. It was a completely sensorial, overwhelming experience. I was awakening. There was a whole world out there that I didn't know.

When I went into the city to participate in these interrogations, I felt I had no choice. If I didn't cooperate, a proclamation would be issued by The Mothership on a golden piece of paper, saying that I was evil and that I was trying to stop the salvation of man. In the eyes of my friends, I would be the equivalent of Charles Manson.

I didn't know it yet, but I had been through an incredible ordeal, and part of freeing myself from that ordeal would be to one day tell my story.

NEW YORK

229

However, I had been booby-trapped. If I ever decided to tell my story, I would be given a mark of evil on a golden piece of paper. This means if I ever want to know my family or my friends, I can never tell my story. This would keep me enslaved in my mind for the rest of my life. This is how they get you. It would have been like Roy venturing out of his camp in the jungles of Burma at night to the traps, and his death—for me to ever tell my story, to my friends, would be a death. Roy would have known to stay close and stay safe by avoiding the booby traps. I would need to stay close to The Mothership, to its bosom.

X

I started to get to know Dorothy's husband, Robert. He was a Black New York State judge, quiet and intelligent. It had been many years since he'd seen me. One morning in those early days, I was coming downstairs for breakfast. Robert was sitting at the long oak dining table, watching me from the kitchen.

"Jamie," he said. "Come here a minute. Let me look at you."

He studied me for a few seconds with intensity glowing in his brown eyes. It must have been obvious to him that I had become athletic, because he suddenly told me that, as a young man, he had played football for New Rochelle High School outside of New York City. He told me his records and pictures still stood on the walls of the school. He carried his varsity team all the way to the State Championships—he was a running back. He then lamented to me, as the team captain and star player, he wasn't allowed to play in the championship game—it was an away game in the South during Jim Crow.

His voice grew heavy and staccato as he continued the story. At the end of the season his school awarded him, and the other Black player on his team that couldn't play, a gold watch as a consolation for not being able to champion the team they had built. Robert refused it in front of the entire team during the awards dinner at the end of the season. The other Black player accepted the watch. More than fifty years later, Robert was still ruminating about it daily, apoplectic that the other player had accepted the watch without hesitation. It disgusted him. I wondered if I was the kind of person who would have accepted the watch. I realized in that moment that explained things that I would have to learn. If work ethic were the monitor for success in the world, Mexican gardeners would be billionaires. I would have to have a code, I would have to learn the unwritten rules, I might have to create my own doctrine outside the doctrine I'd been learning all my life. Like the Fleetwood Mac song, a landslide had brought me down.

X

In those early days, Dorothy told me that Tunji was coming to Westchester County for a concert at a nearby university. She and I went together. Having not seen him in years, we didn't let him know we were coming.

At the end of the show, Tunji was engaged in a massive drumline, with students marching after him around the auditorium as he pounded his giant drum strapped to his body, covered in his grand Nigerian dress. I ran to the front of the drumline, leaned into his ear, and said, "I'm Ros's son."

He flashed the same big smile that he did when I arrived at his home in New York when I was four. Then he leaned into my ear and said, "Meet me in the atrium in an hour."

When he came into the atrium, he hugged my grandmother, held me by the shoulders, and looked me over. He asked me, "How is your mom?" I didn't have the heart to tell him I didn't know her and responded, "She is well."

Not long after Tunji's concert, my grandmother woke me up and told me that my cousin Harry had invited me to spend the day with him in New York City. I didn't know I had a Cousin Harry. It seemed Harry was part of a family that I never knew. He was one of the most successful Black judges in the United States, presiding over the United States Court of Appeals for the District of Columbia. He was a jurist forming American law almost at the level of the Supreme Court, one of the most famous federal judges in the country. Harry's stepmother had been Esther Gordy Edwards, Berry Gordy Jr.'s sister and a senior vice president at Motown Records. Berry Gordy Jr. was the

NEW YORK

231

visionary and businessman who, in my opinion, created the sound that has defined America. There are only three forms of music that were truly born in in our nation: the blues, jazz, and Motown—all seeded in Africa.

My grandmother and I met Harry at Tavern on the Green in Central Park with professors and administrators from Brooklyn Law School, where Harry would be giving the school's commencement address that afternoon. As we walked around the city after lunch, I was overwhelmed, exhausted, and intimidated by Harry's large entourage. Every time I fell behind, Harry would stop, his crowd would stop with him, and he would look back and say, "Jamie, catch up, catch up. Stay close." I would run to him; he would put his arm around me for a second and squeeze me, indicating that he wanted me to stay by his side as the day proceeded. The officials from Brooklyn Law School looked at him like a god. I had never seen anyone treat a Black man like that.

That afternoon at Brooklyn Law School, Harry sat me in the front row. He was introduced and received a standing ovation, as hundreds of new lawyers in black caps and gowns matching his screamed. Harry began to talk. He peered over the lectern at his audience and halfway through his oration on the importance of law, he paused.

"When I decided that I wanted to enter the law and contribute to this great nation, along with that decision I made myself only one promise, that no matter what anyone might accuse me of in this great life, one thing no one will ever accuse me of is LOW AIM!" The audience exploded to their feet. My heart shuddered with a disbelief and awe at his audacity.

That evening, I asked Harry why he wanted me included. He told me that when he was in law school living in Harlem, my grandfather Robert, now a citizen of Harlem and a working lawyer, had helped him.

X

In the mornings, before the heat of the day, I would run through Hartsdale, listening to Paul Simon's percussive Brazilian album, *Rhythm of the Saints*, on repeat. I wore the celluloid tape on my Walkman down to the

232   **CHILD X**

thread. The song I would listen to the most was "Can't Run But," with its chorus set to haunting Brazilian rhythms, that repeats about a person who isn't capable of running but can move faster. I was broken but it spoke to me. I thought, *I could move faster.*

This song aired my entire existence in three minutes and thirty-seven seconds. I was a prisoner in my own mind. I felt completely incapable of doing anything effective or useful in the outworld. I couldn't run, but I could move just a little faster. My way of walking faster, one day hoping to run, was to read books.

I read. I read until my eyes bled—ten, twelve, fifteen hours a day, six days a week. Obsessed, I sat in the upstairs corner room on Meadowview Drive in sweatpants and a T-shirt I would wear for days, burying my eyes in books. If I could have absorbed their meaning by eating the pages, I would have. I barely went outside. I barely ate. To this day, I am still paying the price for pushing myself as hard as I did to study; my body was never the same. I felt like my organs never worked the same way after this period of asceticism.

Deep into this time, one morning my grandmother walked into my bedroom.

"Jamie, put yourself together," she said. "Shave, put on a shirt with a collar, and wear a sport coat. It will change the way you study."

I felt the three days of scratchy beard that had darkened my face. My skin was white and ashy with dryness and neglect. In my obsession with making up for the knowledge I hadn't acquired, I had been neglecting myself. I shaved, showered, put on a clean shirt and a coat. She was right. It was like putting on armor. It changed me. It made me read better.

X

For the next year and a half, I attended a community college where I did remedial classes in English, math, and social studies. It was the first time in my life that I remembered doing an activity where I didn't feel like I was carrying an ape on my back. I took a basic economics class, and I was just overtaken by it. I was constantly in remedial mathematics and English

NEW YORK

233

classes at a kindergarten level that the community college offered to kids like me. I had a constant sense that I might be smarter than these kids who were teaching me, who probably thought I was born with a learning disability. At this time, I truly believed that the reason I was illiterate was because I wasn't very smart. I felt smart and stupid at the same time.

Soon I was attending a small, private liberal arts college next to a Japanese boarding school in Purchase, New York. They were looking for kids with rough economic backgrounds to help pull them up, so they were easier in the application process. I still struggled to understand commas, periods, simple paragraphs, sentences, the most basic basics of grammar, which they accepted. My understanding of English was that of a toddler. I became obsessed with reading magazines like *Vanity Fair* and *The New Yorker*, even though I had no understanding of the pop culture context. I was still struggling with this as I entered this four-year college.

A few weeks into my new school, I met a girl named Virginia. We had an intro to psychology class together. She was beautiful and bright, like an old movie star. We started dating. I was struggling with my papers and getting a D in the class—I was convinced my grade was artificially depressed. Virginia never judged me. She was an A student. I would dictate my papers to her, and she would write them with correct grammar, so I could pass my classes. Angels.

Of all the classes I took there, the one that affected me the most was Professor Lawson's American History to 1865. Lawson Bowling, a southern White conservative with sharp, kind features and a musical voice, was teaching a section on slavery in the US.

"As a conservative," he said, "I'm gonna tell you what I think and you may not like what you hear."

In this moment, my mind opened up.

"You can look at slavery as a moral evil," he continued. "It is that, but you have to understand that slaves were human beings and slave owners were human beings, and whenever you put human beings together it gets complicated—it's evil, but it's also a relationship among people. History isn't dates, it is humanity. And there's always more to it than meets the eye."

234   CHILD X

I was stunned. Lawson was someone who, despite us being from different worlds, I eventually developed a close relationship with. I learned from Lawson that agreeing on beliefs is not what you want in a friend. You want someone who, even if you disagree on every aspect of life, leads with their heart and sees what kind of person you are.

The weekend after that class, I sat at dinner with my grandmother and Robert. I asked my grandmother how she could bear to live under Jim Crow. Robert raised his eyebrows and said nothing. I asked her how she could grow up being a second-class citizen, being told she was less, and making this life for herself being a college professor with a complete possession of who she was.

Dorothy contemplated my question for a moment, then said, "We had community back then." She continued, "We were taught not to seek validation externally from the White man or anyone. We were taught that only we ourselves determined solely who we are, and that any outside opinion is irrelevant. You determine who you are." I listened and wondered if this was possible.

That first semester I was home for the weekend, I watched *Mississippi Burning*—a crime drama set during the Civil Rights movement. In the film there is documentary footage of an actual politician during the Civil Rights movement. I either saw this here or in Ken Burns's *Eyes on the Prize*, which played repeatedly on PBS, or maybe in both places. I don't remember the exact speech. The antagonist Ku Klux Klan member or politician is raging (I'm paraphrasing as the man had a deep Southern accent and was hard to understand): "They want to throw White children and Colored children into the melting plot of integration. What will be resultant is a conglomerated, mutant, *Mulatto*, mongolid society."

As I watched this scene in the film, I thought, *I am what this guy didn't want to have happen. I am this guy's worst nightmare*, and then I thought, *I'm a nice guy when you get to know me.*

I was born and taken away from my parents at birth to be conditioned as an asset. I was born without a face, born without a name, born without history, born outside of the world. I was taught to ignore my own instincts.

NEW YORK

I was ripped from my past and present, not educated, dependent on one man's whims and his doctrine. I was an asset; a child X, marked to be a producing unit in a machine for a billion years, creating a dystopia dressed up as a utopia. We thought slavery went away, but it has just been transmuted, and we call it something else.

X

I met a kid from Denmark at the liberal arts school who told me that I could apply for a year at the London School of Economics. A professor of mine offered to sponsor my application, despite my illiteracy, because I tried so hard.

I applied to both a year at the London School of Economics and a special three-month institute on economics at Georgetown in the same week. It was ridiculous. I knew I wouldn't get into either. I stayed up for two days straight finishing the applications, coming close to a nervous breakdown, because I was spending so much time and work on something I knew could never happen. My nerves were shot because I was overworking to do something that was futile, and my body knew it. What was the point? I couldn't even write my own papers. I could barely fill out the applications.

When the sprint was done and everything had been sent in—absolutely for rejection, I was sure—I left the dorm, took the bus to my old corner bedroom on Meadowview Drive with the race car sheets, and slept for two days straight. I had physically escaped the movement, but my family, my indoctrination, and my illiteracy had kept me fully chained with a collar around my neck.

I got into both schools. Angels.

Joseph Campbell—the celebrated mythologist, and the man who came up with "the Hero's Journey," a formula for storytelling that has been used in the West from Homer's *Odyssey* to *The Empire Strikes Back*—said that a breakdown is an inward journey to recover something one has lost earlier in life, like the star boy in the cave on Dagobah. I was on a quest to recover my mind. Of course, I didn't know that at the time.

X

For the first three years of my life, I had to wear leg braces because I was born with my legs crooked. Every night in the dorms, I would sleep with the heavy braces on. When I was two and a half, my mother took me to a doctor who said that I would need to wear braces until I was twenty-one and have surgeries in order to walk normally. My mother says that I exclaimed to her and the doctor that I would only need the braces until I was three.

On my third birthday, my mother came to see me in the dorms and woke me up. I don't know if this is a memory, or if she told me, but tears were streaming down her face. She had noticed that I was taller. I looked down at my legs, which were no longer deformed. I never wore the braces again. There are three times in my life my mother was proud of me: my miracle healing of my legs, my attestation to being non-reactionary, and when I first signed a contract for a billion years at five years old.

Then there were the other times.

When my mother found out that I had been accepted into the London School of Economics and Georgetown, she called me. I heard her draw off her cigarette through the phone.

"Oh, you're going to go be a wog," she said.

To her I would be joining the walking dead, those people that were allowing the planet to slowly fall into oblivion. We cling to our blood even when it's toxic. We shouldn't. Biology can kill you faster than a bullet.

As I left for Georgetown University late that winter, it wasn't a victory march. It was an insane suicide mission into the murky depths of my own mind to stare at my inadequacies, where I would surely fail. I was a glutton continuing to punish myself in the way that I'd been taught since I was a baby.

This is how I felt, but the braces had been gone for a long time, and the constraints I had been caged within were falling away each day. Education had been my family's salvation. Roy would have tried. I had to try.

All I said to myself was, "Keep moving."

Chapter 20

GEORGETOWN

I ran every morning, my legs burnt out with exertion, my face dripping with sweat. Every step upon the concrete was a staccato rhythm as I reached up to wipe my brow, adjusting my headphones so I could drown out the street.

My daily route took me from my dorm at Harbin Hall, past the steps where *The Exorcist* was shot, and east along the Potomac River, toward Foggy Bottom. Georgetown was an inland enclave of Washington, DC, straddling the lazy bend of the Potomac. It wasn't like the DC sprawl with its endless strip malls, Baroque white-stone government buildings, and a new 1990s American innovation—big-box stores. It looked like a Dutch village from the eighteenth century: red-brick cobblestone streets, canals, and row houses built in tightly knit grids and thick with old trees. It was a place built for community. When I walked those streets at dusk, after the heat of the day had subsided, I felt like I was in a different time.

My life was predictable, and I found that comforting. A few days out of the week I took the bus to DuPont Circle before taking the DC Metro—the city's subway—to work as an intern. I wore a dark gray blended cotton suit that I had bought myself at the Burlington Coat Factory on Central Avenue in Hartsdale. DC was built on a swamp. Wearing the suit in the relentless humidity of the South, as I sat at the bus stop, I felt a moisture gathering on my back, between my shoulder blades. I could feel the droplets rolling down my skin. The sensation was inescapable. At that bus stop, my sweat would always find the same place on my back to emerge, as predictable as the Metro itself. By the time I transferred, from the bus to the concrete underground of the Metro, I was relieved to be out of the sun. It reminded me of how I felt ducking out of the heat and into the parking structure off Berendo, where Miles, Johnny, and I spent our days dissecting motorcycles, and playing football on hot concrete. I thought, *What would they say if they could see me now?*

I lived at Harbin Hall—a towering apartment block of dorms looming above a Jesuit cemetery. As I was studying more and more sophisticated economics, I thought of my first economics 101 class in community college when I first saw the graphs. It was the first time I saw something and just understood it. I wonder if that was how Mozart saw music, and I thought about all the brilliant kids back in the neighborhood who could do things they were never taught to do. Poverty is humanity's greatest lost resource. If society could see that, we would help people differently, and it would turn our understanding of poverty on its head.

As I studied comparative economics and politics, I was struck by the apparent lack of humanity in my textbooks. In the movement, everything was about salvaging humanity. Here I was, at one of the most esteemed universities in the world, and my studies felt disconnected. I thought policy would make more sense if it was written from humanity. And then I thought, *What do I know?*

I was offered an internship with Denny Dennis—the chief economist at the National Federation of Independent Businesses. Despite my struggling illiteracy, he liked me and would often pull me into his office for private conversations. He would tell me about the unwritten rules of DC—to be successful in any field, you had to learn the rules you didn't see. It reminded me of the streets of Los Angeles. To survive, you had to understand what was going on below the surface.

The way I see it, children are kind of like a graphic equalizer with

GEORGETOWN

239

three sliders. Love (including human touch); education, and structure—the schedule, predictability, and safety of a child; going to bed early and getting up at the same time every day, a routine. When all three of these are turned up to the highest level, the outcome of a child is predictable. You have someone who can fare well in the world. If one of these is turned up halfway, or down, everyone in the world is raising a wildcard. This is one of the first unwritten rules I came to.

Denny consciously ignored my illiteracy, helped me with my grammar, and distributed my papers at the annual National Federation of Independent Business conference for all of its members. I told him I didn't think the papers were good enough. He had someone in the office clean them up and told me they were great. When I went to the conference dinner, included at every placement in front of each guest, arranged with dignity on the white tablecloths, was a packet of information, including my papers. Angels.

X

At the conference dinner Bill Clinton, then the president, was doing the keynote. When Denny told me that he wanted me at the dinner and that Clinton was speaking there, he said I would have to do an FBI background check. My blood ran cold. I knew they would find my affiliation with the movement and deny me access to the dinner. It never came up. I was cleared.

I walked in wearing my dark gray sport coat and a tie. I was waiting to go through a metal detector when I felt pushed from behind. I turned to see a White man with a silver beard and glasses, walking hurriedly past me toward the metal detectors. It might be the FBI.

"Excuse me," he said as he startled me, waving back apologetically.

It was Wolf Blitzer. *What am I doing here?* I thought.

I half-expected an FBI agent to come out of nowhere and tell me that because of my affiliation with the movement and the fact that I was in their raid as a child, I couldn't attend the dinner.

Bob Dole spoke to a crash of applause. The members who had made the trek to come to the annual conference were its most conservative. The federation represents small businesses in the legislature ensuring, through annual vote, that their needs are being advocated for. As I sat at the table waiting for Bill Clinton to emerge to speak, I realized I was the only person under the age of fifty in the entire hall. The men at my table grumbled, calling Clinton a monster under their breath. You could cut the tension with a knife. The entire hall was filled with hostility.

Bill Clinton walked up to the stage under a gaze of total silence. You could hear a pin drop. It was uncomfortable. I can't remember what he said, but it took him all of ninety seconds to bring a crowd of a couple of hundred hostile Republicans to their feet with a standing ovation. I was awestruck. In everything I had seen on the news, and heard in the crowd, these people hated the ground he walked on. And in ninety seconds he changed that.

As I sat mesmerized by the president, I remembered him saying a few weeks earlier in a speech that he saw intelligence as a synthesis, the ability to study old ideas, put them together, and make new ones—not the regurgitation of ideas. I had no political affiliations and had been trained my whole life to believe that politicians were fake people who only sought power at the cost of humanity. His words about ideas shook me. I thought, *I need to study and then have ideas of my own.* This idea could have come from anyone. Somehow, I knew it was true.

Bill Clinton finished his speech to another standing ovation and raving applause from the now-smiling crowd, walked straight past his Secret Service agents, and beelined for me. It must have been because I was the only young person in the audience. I was overwhelmed. I was a Mulatto kid from a Mexican slum who had just barely learned to write. Clinton stuck out his hand, grasped mine, looked me straight in the eye, and said, "How are you? What are you doing here?"

It was the only time in my life that I was completely tongue-tied. My pause was a little too long. He smiled warmly at me once again, squeezed my hand, and moved on down the line.

X

For the next several years, I analyzed in my head—how did this man change these people so quickly? I didn't care about the politics; I wanted to reverse engineer how he did it, and then finally it came to me.

There is an anatomy of charisma. No matter what you think of the man, he's charismatic. He is the single most charismatic human being I have ever been in the presence of. He was also humble. He didn't act presidential, but like a regular person that I would know on the streets of East Hollywood.

Charisma is magnetism. A magnet is created by two opposite polar energies that create an attraction. I realized Clinton's extreme intelligence, combined with his apparent humility, made him irresistible. All charisma is like that. Any power, combined with humility, is a tractor beam. Power can come in many forms—beauty, money, intelligence, and more. If you mix any kind of power with humility, kindness, and curiosity, you will draw people to you. It's a formula. Anyone can do it.

I had an intelligence that I didn't know existed yet. The violence and punishment of my life up until now had arrested me. My obsession with information and people, trying to understand my new world, simply amplified my curiosity by default. It is this curiosity, combined with any talents that I now have, that explains the "coincidences" of my life.

A beautiful person who doesn't act like they're beautiful will draw people to them. A wealthy man who doesn't act like he's wealthy will draw people to him. A brilliant woman who treats everyone as her equal will draw people to her. People do not engage in this extreme curiosity of connection because of self-protection. If you are curious, connecting with everyone you can, especially those most different from you—the ones you're not supposed to engage with because they are different from you—you *will* get hurt more. You cannot bring in good in life without bringing in some bad. However, if you live this way, are willing to experience some bad, the way of connection, the reward is an inexpressible endowment of humanity.

In my old bedroom on Meadowview Drive, I had read *King of the World*—by Pulitzer Prize–winning journalist David Remnick—a biography of Muhammad Ali. After reading this book, I watched every documentary on Ali I could find. One of Ali's favorite things was what he called "to be with the people." This inspired him and filled him up. At the height of his fame, he walked the neighborhoods of working-class Blacks in America and feeding off the way he made the people in the neighborhood feel. This was the opposite of Los Angeles, where celebrities sequester themselves and stick to their own.

I decided I would endeavor to ensure those around me never felt thrown away like I was as a child. I had been raised a child X, institutionalized, incubated in my holding pen, being grown as a vessel for labor, until I was big enough to enter a contract that would never end. This would take pieces from me that I would never get back.

But there was a lot, I was learning, that I could give.

If I just kept moving.

Chapter 21

LONDON

I awoke as the plane's wheels slammed onto the slick gray tarmac at Heathrow. The plane taxied to the gate, and I looked out through the tiny window, dripping with rain, onto a sunless sunrise, the white disc of the sun hidden behind a haze of endless gray clouds. I hadn't gotten much sleep on the flight overseas. My legs ached. My stomach felt sick with dread.

I immediately regretted coming to England. Things were different than when the movement had sent me there before, but the wet, gray, dismal, driving rain and the fog mirrored the heavy emotion I was feeling inside—stuck. I couldn't imagine the ordeal that lay ahead of me as I began the slow walk to customs.

My tired eyes were focused on the line of people in front of me, willing myself not to make eye contact with any of the hundreds of people all around me, in case any of them were members of the movement and might recognize me. The line lurched forward, the stone faces of the customs officials scrutinizing passports of every color.

Eventually it was my turn. I handed over my passport. The customs officer looked at it, then looked up at me, then looked at it again. I wanted to disappear.

244   CHILD X

"James Mustard," he said. I was convinced I was about to be arrested. It was a ridiculous name. "What's the purpose of your visit?"

"London School of Economics. Going there. Student," I stammered back.

"Right." After a moment of hesitation, the customs officer stamped my passport and handed it back to me. I had made it to England in a stupor.

I stood at baggage claim, waiting for my single piece of luggage to arrive on the carousel. I had bought a massive green trunk—the kind that you would get at an Army surplus store—that was nearly as tall as I was and weighed almost as much. I had packed everything I owned: all my clothes and shoes, stacks of books, tapes, and CDs. My trunk arrived on the carousel, and I strained, pulled with both arms to lift and drag it onto the baggage claim floor. I had almost forgotten how heavy it was. It didn't have wheels. It took me five minutes to haul it ten feet away, to a kiosk where I could rent a luggage cart. The cart gave me a reprieve as I settled down my heaving breaths.

I reached the terminal's tube entrance, and printed on the wall was a sign that read NO TROLLEYS PAST THIS POINT. My reprieve was over. I strained with both arms, dragging the trunk, fifty feet down to the train platform. It took me thirty minutes to haul it in stops and starts, scraping across the ground. I didn't know how many departing trains I'd already missed. My arms began to burn. Sweat started to cover my face, while I sucked in heavy breaths and people watched in disbelief. I finally dragged the trunk onto the crowded tube. I was making a spectacle of myself and in my discomfort, I kept noisily dragging the massive trunk.

I took the Piccadilly line from Heathrow Airport East toward Central London, dragged the trunk to another train at Hammersmith, took the Hammersmith & City Line—accidentally past Euston Station—to King's Cross & St. Pancras. I took the trunk off the train and slid it past the stairwell across the track to take the train that would take me back the other way. It made a horrible scraping sound. Then I dragged the trunk to another train that backtracked along the Hammersmith & City Line to Euston, dragged the trunk to a southbound train, and rode one stop back to Euston Square.

LONDON 245

Normally a six-minute walk, it took me over an hour to drag the trunk, inch by inch, to the entry of my new dorm. By the time I arrived at Passfield Hall, in driving rain, I was out of breath, jet-lagged, and every muscle in my body burned from hauling the massive trunk. It had taken me five hours to get there from baggage claim. I didn't have to take the tube; I could have taken a car into London—around £70, which Dorothy had offered me, but I refused to take it. I didn't want to take anything offered to me from anyone if there was a less expensive way, and I didn't know anyone in London. Even if I did, I probably wouldn't have accepted their help.

I don't know why I chose to do things the hard way, or why I was comfortable with suffering. Maybe it came from pushing my mother's oversized laundry cart two miles from our crumbling apartment to the laundromat when I was ten. In the doctrine, suffering was necessary for salvation. From birth I was told about what was "the greatest good for the greatest number"—you do things purely based on the most benefit to your life and the lives of others, regardless of how you feel.

Anyone will rationalize suffering if they think it has meaning. I didn't know it at the time, but endless atrocities and suffering had been justified this way. I'm sure I was masochistic, but being conditioned to push through, no matter how I felt, would benefit me in my new institution.

X

Passfield Hall was a gray-and-white stone building on Endsleigh Place between Gordon Square and Tavistock Square Gardens. After my five-hour baptism by trunk, when I stood across from it in the driving London drizzle, everything in front of me was gray—gray streets, gray buildings, gray sky.

What have I done? I thought. Choosing to come here was a mistake. I was deflated, and a vise-like grip that had been squeezing my head returned.

The dorm room was gray, tiny, and spartan, with sepia walls and not much natural light. I had just enough room for my trunk under some shelves, and a small plank desk that lifted up, so that I would be able to get things out of it, which quickly became the catchall station for keys, rail passes, and loose change; and, oddly, a 1930s gray-sepia porcelain sink in one corner. Luckily, my roommate hadn't arrived, so I got the first choice of bed: right under the window, where I would eventually use the ledge as my own private open-air refrigerator. The dorm room looked depressing, and I was terrified at what monstrosity of a roommate might walk through the door at any moment, but getting the window bed seemed like a small victory.

I was relieved when a tall, lean Swiss man unlocked the door and entered the room, and in a sing-songy way introduced himself as Laz and asked me my name,

"Okay, Jamie," he said. "Let's go get dinner. The Refectory doesn't open till tomorrow." We walked over a mile to Leicester Square and went to eat at a Cafe Pasta. Before heading out, Laz decided to wash his hands in the bizarre sink in our room. Suddenly, he started shouting, "Jamie, the fucking British! They can never figure out how to make hot and cold go into one tap! Wherever you go, you burn your hands. The British are idiots, right?" I sat there stone-faced, silently contemplating English plumbing.

We walked west to the bottom of Tottenham Court Road and began walking south toward Oxford Street, when my heart stopped. I looked up and saw people standing in front of a building in naval uniforms. I looked above them and saw the words "Church of Scientology London" written in a medieval Gothic font in yellow over a red background. I couldn't fucking believe my dorm room for the next year was so close to not only something I had just escaped but might be after me.

Laz would be my first friend in London. I've learned that a person can be defined by their friends, or the pack they run with. My pack was Laz, my roommate. A stuttering kid named Bastian, who was French and lived in Paris and who was also a Russian prince—he wore sport coats, white shirts, and ascots every day. Elizabeth Mateen, who was half-British, half-Afghan. Sven, a conservative kid from Sweden. Rana, a bold Indian kid from Nairobi who dressed like Jimi Hendrix. Govinda (who we called

LONDON

247

"Gov"), another Indian kid raised in London. Iggy, a slight, confident, and funny kid from Vienna. Another kid from Austria of Turkish descent named Aydin. And a strange rich American kid named Brady who looked like a tall, better-looking version of James Dean, and whose family had made tens of millions after his grandfather bought dozens of original McDonald's franchises in Florida in the 1950s. Gabriella was a bright-eyed girl raised in the Tuscan countryside from Florence. She told me once that Italians don't like leaving Italy because then they'd have to eat the food that people in other countries make. She looked at me puzzled when I laughed.

This group tethered out to all their friends, especially to Rana's group of Kenyan Indians who seemed to confidently have the run of London. Rana owned himself. He was the only Indian kid in his class at Marlborough, an aristocratic public school in England that had raised lords, dukes, and kings. Laz was softly kinetic, propelled like some heat-seeking missile of quiet excellence. He always had a wry smile and saw the joke in everything. All of these kids were confidently coming from wealthy families where they had been raised from birth to attend one of the most rarefied institutions in the world—and they knew it. LSE felt like another solar system. For the first six weeks I was there, I thought they would figure out who I was and remove me.

This was my new habitat: I would walk down Endsleigh Place and take a right into Tavistock Square, past the huge bronze statue of Mahatma Gandhi sitting cross-legged on top of a stone altar; cut back to Holborn walking up past Russell Square; and take a left into the London School of Economics just before the Strand. When leaving school, I would walk south on Houghton Street and take a right on the Strand directly across the street from the BBC's Bush House. I would walk a few blocks down where I would eventually cut into Covent Garden for lunch after passing the Royal Opera House. After lunch I would head to Soho for a coffee and then head back to Passfield Hall via the British Museum and Russell Square.

X

In my first year in London, the IRA's political arm, Sinn Fein, was looking for peace, so they were setting bombs off at three or four in the morning and warning the MI5 and London authorities about where they would be. Often, I would wake from my bunk in the dorm room hearing the distant sounds of explosions. No lives were lost. The explosions were a cinematic texture in my different life where everything was new. I grew used to the bombs just as I grew used to the bright lights and rumble of helicopters back in Los Angeles. Often, waking up at the netherhour, the occasional sound of the bombs was a strange comfort.

A short walk south from Tavistock Square took me to the corner of Malet and Keppel Streets, the T-junction where Senate House looked over the square. I recognized it as the Ministry of Truth from the film *1984*. Its Brutalist monolithic lines towered over the Malet Street Gardens, and whenever I saw it, it reminded me of The Old Industrial Hospital before the movement painted it a clownish blue. Senate House made me think how the leaders of the movement must have thought that, if they used the color of a baby blanket, people wouldn't see the harsh Brutalist architecture underneath. Lipstick on a pig.

The first novel I read in London was *Crime and Punishment*—the existentialist novel by the Russian Fyodor Dostoyevsky. Dostoyevsky's burning spear seemed to be saying to me, "You can't escape what you've done, you will be your own judge, jury, and executioner."

I wondered if I'd taken this feeling away from the book because the doctrine had taught me that I couldn't outrun my bad deeds without confessing them in their interrogations. Or was this human nature?

I felt, even though I was restoring my education, that I had done something bad. I prayed that there would not be a price to pay for trying to make myself better, if I was making myself better. I had doubts.

Across the hall in the dorm was a fascinating girl named Sarita. She once told me she had learned to fly with the Royal Air Force. One afternoon we all went to see *Bhaji* on the Beach together at the Odeon on Tottenham Court Road just a few doors down from the London Division. The movie was directed by Gurinder Chadha years before her hit

LONDON 249

film *Bend it Like Beckham*. When we were watching the movie about generational Indian disconnect in England, I realized the lead in the film was Sarita and that she was sitting next to me. I couldn't believe that she would go with us to a movie, that she knew she was the lead in, and say nothing. Years later, on a train trip back from Paris to Waterloo her body washed up on the river Thames. It was never determined if it was a murder or a suicide.

Sarita was a girl that could not study all year, then show up and get firsts on her exams. Her parents would never accept that it was a suicide. I think I heard it was because one of them was Hindu. In the Hindu cycle of karma, violence to the self could mean consequences; Sarita could reincarnate as a lower life-form, a dog or a cat. Then, her soul would be that much farther away from ascending beyond her karma. Back then, I didn't know what the word karma truly meant but it was something I deeply understood. For all I know, one of her parents wasn't Hindu. What I do know is Sarita was a sweet girl with the heart of a lion.

One day, a fax came to my mailbox at Passfield Hall. It was a "bill" from the movement saying that I still owed them $90,000 for courses and machine-based counseling and classes that I was required to do within the fold. Because I left, it was now a debt. With this fax it felt like they were everywhere. I'd worked fifteen- to twenty-hour days for almost three years, given them my childhood, and had never gone to school, but I owed them. I didn't know I had rights. You have to be taught rights to know that you have them.

After the movement got their tax exemption status back, they declared what they called an amnesty. This meant if I gave them $5,000 and confessed all my crimes, I would be allowed to return to the fold. I wanted to know my little brother. I wanted to know the mother I never knew. I didn't know what to do. None of the people I had met in London knew anything about my past. Just a half-mile away, on Tottenham Court Road, the London Division loomed like a guillotine.

X

250   CHILD X

London was a pastiche of postcolonial alchemy. It was a result of English high culture having sex with its colonial past. Elite institutions negotiating with Pakistanis, Bangladeshis, North Africans, West Africans, East Africans, Caribbeans, and Indians. They have a saying in London that when the British left India, they brought India with them. You could say that about every postcolonial country under the British Empire. The design and ecstatic art I saw was because of influences brought from all over the world into the furious, bubbling cauldron of London. The daring design and art that rose from the streets, hissed at me, and burned into me. The Los Angeles of my childhood was a sensory deprivation chamber. London felt like a Shangri-La, but maybe any vibrant city full of art, architecture, history, and immigrants like Berlin or Shanghai would have impacted me in a similar way.

Other weekends I went to the Tate, a white-stone Roman Revival building with massive columns that could have been plucked from a Jacques-Louis David painting of ancient Rome. I often bought Cadbury Fruit & Nut bars from the vending machines inside the tube, which I loved. I went to a de Kooning retrospective at the Tate five times.

The influences that rose from the streets of London into new forms of high and refined and low art, masquerading as European and English, arrested me. It was an intuitive universe of learning far beyond anything I could have imagined. Through art, I was discovering a synthesis of centuries.

In Camden Town I went to a punk show with Laz at The Electric Ballroom. I didn't know anything about punk music. These bare-bones shows happened in dark, decaying, crowded spaces, thick with the scent of warm lager and sweat. The punks had a strange and frenetic way of moving in time to the blistering, kinetic music. They were loud. They stomped and surged in mosh pits in front, near the band, starting fights and spitting.

Not long after the punk show, I was stopped by skinheads on High Holborn. They surrounded me while I was walking back to Passfield Hall with this little guy named Bobby Scarpa who was doing a year at LSE. The skins called me a "posh git" because I was wearing nice shoes and my LSE

LONDON 251

hoodie. I was scared, but I wanted to protect Bobby—he was small, with his American backpack and big white shoes. He didn't understand what was about to happen. I told Bobby "run" and to let me deal with these skinheads myself. Bobby wouldn't leave.

For some reason in that moment, I saw the faces of the two Black kids who beat me in the street in East Hollywood on Sunset Boulevard when I was ten. The skins called us "posh gits" again and started to close in. Being called privileged after everything I had just lived through was too much to handle. I became insane. I had murder in my eyes and screamed, "I'm going to kill all of you." I was no longer a person. I was living rage. Outnumbered and surely about to suffer. I lost my mind. I went mad and ran at them.

My madness and insanity scared them. Unnerved by my howling craze, they quickly tried to calm me down and then disappeared.

Ironically, what I didn't know at the time was that skinhead culture was Black. It came from the West Indies. The ska music that originated there had come from their skinheads, or as Bob Marley called them, "crazy bald-heads." These Black skinheads of Jamaica stomped and danced in wild circles, possessed by angry spirits. Working-class White English kids in the 1960s learned this culture and music from immigrant neighborhoods like Brixton that were absorbing Black immigrants from Jamaica. Ironically, the look of British skinheads has often become a symbol of racism in parts of working-class America with their Dr. Martens, rolled denim jeans, work shirts, wife beaters, suspenders, and shaved heads. This uniform has become a uniform of cultural rebellion against the middle class all over the world.

As I walked back to Passfield Hall with Bobby in the twilight, I thought about how they had targeted us not because of our race, but because of their assumption of our privilege—a privilege that I should have never attained. I thought about my studies, how I'd learned about ancient wars where wild-eyed berserkers charged into battles they could never win. What Bobby stayed for could have had a different outcome.

In the movement, before you do any machine-based counseling, you are made to do a form of counseling where you practice having someone control you for dozens if not hundreds of hours. It is called "the objectives." In this counseling, the counselor moves your body, tells you where to walk, tells you what to touch, tells you where to look, for hours upon hours upon hours. It makes one feel horrible to be controlled in sittings day in, day out. It is a brutal exercise in ignoring the body. The only way to move on to your next step on the ladder of freedom is to get to a point where you feel excellent about being controlled. We were being trained to ignore our minds and our bodies in the artifice of self-improvement. We could not return to our native state as gods unless we became one with denying our bodies and our feelings. I was not allowed to end these painful processes until I had a profound realization. My realization was that my anxiety was not my own but was my reactionary mind. What had really happened was I had become muted to my body saying "no." This is why a grown adult within the movement can see the suffering of a child and feel nothing.

X

Ever since the conversation I'd had when I was sixteen with Sophie before I left Eugene, I was afraid that I wouldn't be seen outside of race. I believed this with the same reality of belief that one has when one stares at a wall. I was too Black to be White, and too White to be Black.

Is the world going to limit me, not advancing me, stopping me, thinking I'm out of place, because of the mutancy of how I look? How much will race, or lack thereof, define my life without my agreement? I ruminated.

The doctrine had also taught me that I could bend reality to my visions based purely on my intention alone. All I needed to do was decide, and the physical world would transform to my will. Could I be so undeniable that I could reshape the understanding of race, in any human or skeptic? Could I say "fuck you" to the world and teach them that the holocaust of race cliché is an insidious disease that destroys minds and lives? Could I shame the world for ever thinking this way?

LONDON

X

Renowned historian and BBC presenter David Starkey was a stocky, energetic man who exuded intellectual power from the way he moved his bones. He paced the lecture hall, wearing a three-piece wool-tweed suit, roaring like a tiger—a one-man show of pure dramatic force, he taught European history like the world was on fire. He taught battles, wars, and politics, booming as if his own life were at stake, and I asked myself, "How did I get here?"

E. H. Hunt, a distinguished historian of economics with a mop of tamed white hair and thick white eyebrows, long enough to be combed, was assigned as my tutor, a British version of school counselor. Twice a month we discussed my progress at the school. He was a widower with twins attending college.

"My kids couldn't go here," he said to me one day while we spoke in his large office overlooking Houghton Street. He was surprised that I was attending LSE. "I don't believe you deserve to be here," he said.

Every time I saw Hunt, I would shake his hand.

"James, we don't have to shake hands every time we meet," he said with dispassionate conservativeness. His eyes revealed nothing.

I learned about the Cathars—a French cult just across the English Channel in the thirteenth century who believed that only by rejecting the physical body could one defeat evil. The Cathars gave up meat and sex. They spoke another language and owned land. They reminded me of the inner navy of the movement in their lust for money. I thought about my mother and how she would have fit right in among the Cathars.

The collision of ancient and abundant culture was just outside in the streets. My university burned with explosive devotion to ideas. Starkey and Hunt made me realize how rarefied an institution the London School of Economics was. George Bernard Shaw had helped to start it. I was in one of the top schools in the world for economics—often exceeding Yale, Cambridge, and Oxford in the subject. If I had known what it was at the time, I would never have applied.

254   CHILD X

You don't know your true abilities until you're in the largest theater in which you can act. A working-class Mexican immigrant running a $3 million tool and die shop might never know he could run a billion-dollar company—maybe make it run better than the CEO who feels it's their birthright. When we are able to use our abilities in the largest arena that we can conceive of, one we think we might drown in, only then can we find out who we really are.

One evening at Passfield Hall, Laz took me to Trafalgar Square. At one corner stood St. Martin-in-the-Fields—an ornate white-stone 1720s church built on top of a Roman burial ground. As I sat in the pews of the church's ornate yet minimalist grand hall, with a few hundred strangers gathered in the dark, I watched a string ensemble play Vivaldi's *The Four Seasons*, lit only by the glow of candlelight. I burned.

As the strings sounded, I felt as if I and everyone else listening to the music were one body. I thought of a Boy Scout trip to Lake Arrowhead when I was eleven. There was a kid in another troop named Ernest. He was small, severely mentally disabled, and could barely talk. Ernest had a harmonica. He always carried it in his shirt pocket. At nights, around the campfire when all the troops gathered, Ernest would take out his harmonica and play the theme from *Superman*.

He played it so perfectly, we would speak in whispers, and all you could hear was the forest. He would take requests for the next two hours. Whatever we asked for, he could play it by ear. Ernest couldn't read, or write, or have a conversation, but he found a way to belong. We are prehistoric-made human beings and need to belong to feel whole. We are all just the remnants of tribes. In tribes everyone has a role, and everyone belongs.

In 1187 Saladin, a great Islamic sultan, drove his men up the dunes of Hattin in a barren Syria, their curved swords hungry for blood, clean and gleaming in the desert sun. The Knights Templar, shrouded in white and iron, braced as the howling mass of Saladin's Mamluks, an assemblage of tribes, slashed into them, their poetic scimitars slicing through cartilage and spilling the blood of the Templars onto the burning sands. Then a wave of Saladin's horses came out of the dust, lances piercing armor and

LONDON

255

crushing bone. The knights became a feast for vultures. In London I became fascinated by Islam.

Violence comes from fear, and London taught me more about fear. People fear what they're told to fear. I attended LSE with a man I didn't know named Ahmed Omar Sayyid Sheikh—a radicalized man of Pakistani descent who grew up in affluent North London. On February 1, 2002, Omar would decapitate a Jewish man named Daniel Pearl in Pakistan. Daniel was raised in affluent Encino not far from where I lived in the Mexican slums; older than me, we would have been in Los Angeles at the same time.

I felt close to these two men because at some point in my life I was in physical proximity to both of them. A huge swath of the students at LSE came from Muslim countries and Muslim families, and during Ramadan, I would notice both the kids not eating and the kids violating the sacred holiday. I jokingly teased the violators and called them "Ramadan-abees," which elicited mischievous laughter. Growing up in the movement, I knew nothing about their religion. I found them to be kind and loving. Even when I returned to the States, with even the liberal media's incessant, inherent anti-Islamic undercurrents, the stigma lives in stark contrast to my human experience.

If there's one thing that I learned growing up in the movement on the poverty-stricken streets of Los Angeles, it's that fear is the primary cause of violence. Radicals from affluent homes like Omar and others will always exist as straw men. But we'll never change the reality of how poor people can be used and manipulated by religion to do horrible things. The deepest scar of poverty comes from manipulation resulting in the loss of genius. I lived my whole life manipulated to do bad while told I was doing good. This is something that manifests itself in every race, in every culture, in every country all over the world. This is something that I understand as a child X born into captivity.

X

London was full of child Xs. With its Indians, Africans, Jamaicans, and Pakistanis, it made me wrestle with the idea of race. I read more novels.

256 CHILD X

Zora Neale Hurston's *Their Eyes Were Watching God* and James Baldwin's *Sonny's Blues* transcended race. For me, they were better than Hemingway. I thought, *If Black people can write like this, years before Civil Rights, then race doesn't matter. Nothing has to matter unless I decide it matters.*

In London, for many years I lived as what Freddie Mercury darkly crooned as a great pretender.

Dr. Robert Boyce was the professor who would grade my papers for David Starkey's lectures. He gave me back my first paper with a D- and said to the class, "I think there are some people who've come from overseas that shouldn't be here."

I felt sick. At the end of the class, I asked him if we could talk, and he invited me to his office. I told myself I would never get below a B again.

I politely said to Professor Boyce, "If I get a B average in the rest of the class, I want you to forget that I ever got this grade and not see me as someone that isn't supposed to be here."

"James, it doesn't matter. You know the only grade that counts is your grade on the final exam," he said in his Anglo-Canadian accent.

"It matters to me," I said back, transfixed by his eyes.

He smiled at me as if he had a secret and said, "Okay, is that all?"

"Yes," I said. He chuckled as he looked down at his work.

In the LSE library, I was surrounded by Southeast Asian, Pakistani, and Indian kids studying. They wouldn't go the bathroom or even move. I felt like a fraud trying to study anywhere near them and expected to fail. I decided to spend five days photocopying everything I needed and took it back to my Eton Rise apartment—a red brick building with strange square windows where I rented a tiny room in the front. Getting up at 4:30 AM and working solidly until 1 PM for months, on the fold-down desk in my small cream-carpeted living room, I would write all the exams out as a ten-page answer until I had distilled it down to three pages. I cut that down to one page, then a paragraph, then down to fifty keywords, which I memorized. When I finally sat for my exam, the first thing I did was write down the fifty keywords, which brought back all ten pages. I created a cipher in an act of desperation.

LONDON

In one way, LSE was a letdown. For years I had thought education was the answer, when in fact this rarefied institution of higher learning overflowed with miserable rich kids and anxiety. I realized that even with wealth, the pain of a psychologically abusive or even distant mother or father can be more damaging than a beating every day, and in my new world the damage was all around me. I'd grown up in poverty and in illiteracy. To me poverty and illiteracy meant pain, so literacy and affluence would mean joy. I quickly learned at LSE that this is not the case and my entire motivation for driving myself to pushing past my adult literacy was not going to make me content. I thought, *If this isn't the solution, then what is?*

I had spent my life in the movement repressed, being told that sex could be evil. I quickly dropped this notion when arriving at school and joyfully became one of the lads. Women in London were aggressive. At the pubs, they would size you up from across the space, entrancing you like lionesses, and close in.

There was an Italian girl. There was a French girl. There was an Indian girl. There were two Scottish girls. For the first time in my life, I was free, and like anyone freed from his whole life in a cage, I tried to fly. I'm sure, like any young person, I remember it as far more radiant than it was. I managed to grab onto myself. I needed to work. After that I decided to focus on my studies and on serious relationships.

I would bring girls to the gay Old Compton Street Cafe where we marveled at the innovation of style. Every customer in their enigmatic dress could have stepped out of a film. Trans, eccentric, and gay customers wore theatrical bespoke suits with bright colors and pinstripes. The lighting had an ambient sepia-gold glow that washed over the white ceramic tile floor and every time I went there, I felt like I'd walked into a strange romantic play. Outside stood punks, goths, Teddy Boys, artists, and hipsters that gave Soho in London a feeling.

The 1990s were the heyday of techno. On Regent Street, there was a club called The Smashing. The best people-watching was on Tuesday or Sunday nights at four in the morning; dozens of tall men in luminous drag, drinking warm British lager. The Smashing was known as a trans hotspot during a time when it was dangerous to be trans in London. I went with Laz, Bastian, and our girlfriends. I reveled in the theater and joy of The Smashing.

My first year, I ate most of my meals and even worked as kitchen staff in LSE's bohemian Vegetarian Café. Next to the Veggie Café was The Three Tuns, our main bar on campus, with its brown tables, chairs, and deep red carpet. The Three Tuns was an institution and was filled with smoke and sweat, laughter, the occasional roar, and smelled of spilled beer. The constantly splashing lager would wet and further deepen the red of the rug. I loved it and it was subsidized by the British government, so we went there to get warm lager for 50 pence.

I would always see four old men at a table in the corner with long gray beards, tweed jackets, and baggy chinos with bicycle spats, LSE professors who rode their bikes to the pub every day. Spittle would often fly from their mouths as they engaged in lively conversation and rested their beer, never letting go of their grip around the pint. In their matching outfits and beards, they looked like a street gang of old man intellectuals. The smiling old men, with their hawk-like eyes, always engaged in deep conversation, reminded me of a film that invaded me as a child called *The Wanderers*, where all the gangs had uniforms—matching haircuts and clothes. There was the Baldies, the Wongs, the Ducky Boys, and more. The film was a kinetic poem about our tribal nature and our masculine need for love. These old men were a tribe and in their comradeship, defied their age. I would see them and think, *I hope I grow old that way.*

Rana, that bold Indian kid from Nairobi who dressed like Jimi Hendrix, gave me a mixtape early in our friendship. On the mixtape was "Loaded" by Primal Scream, who had this quote from the '60s biker film *The Wild Angels* at the beginning of the song—young teenage rebels demanding freedom before a court, saying all they want to do is be able to have a *good time*, and *party*. I wanted both. The intro to the song was meant to be a joke, but to me the ska groove was an exaltation of freedom.

The first two songs on the tape were "Could You Be Loved" by Bob Marley followed by "Night Moves" by Bob Seger. The two Bobs. It was a

LONDON

259

sign. I had never been loved. I thought Rana was trying to say, through his mixtape, that he could see it, and that I could be loved.

Somehow Rana could sense that I was emerging from a sensory deprivation and this song served as a message—"you're free now."

After "Could You Be Loved" wound down, "Night Moves" felt like an exhale of the impossible, like the scene with the drug dealers in *American Pop*.

In Passfield Hall, "Night Moves" became a prayer.

X

My first Christmas in London, I was invited to join Elizabeth Mateen at her family home in Reading, England, with all my non-American friends. Elizabeth's father, Afsaar, was an Afghan refugee, an educated man who worked across the street from the LSE at the BBC's Bush House—a grand structure of Victorian Neoclassical architecture. He read the *BBC World Service* in Pashtun to the mountains of Afghanistan. I had never met him.

A day after Elizabeth invited me, she knocked on my dorm room with wet eyes. She apologized and said I couldn't come to her house for Christmas because I was American. Her father would not have an American in his house.

I had told my grandmother I wouldn't be coming home for the holiday. I saw myself sitting in London alone without my friends. Christmas was days away, and I accepted it. Afsaar was angry that the CIA had armed their freedom fighters—the Mujahideen—against the Russians, and when the Russians finally left in this remote Cold War standoff, the Americans disappeared, leaving a power vacuum allowing the Taliban to take over the country.

Afsaar felt that America had selfishly destroyed his country to win an unwinnable war, and as it came to a close with the fall of the Berlin Wall in 1989, America had left Afsaar's people high and dry. He hated America and was apoplectic at the thought of one entering, let alone spending five days at, his home. A man of great pride, "it was impossible," he told his wife.

The day before Christmas Eve, I was lying in my bunk in Passfield

Hall reading when there was a knock at my door. It was Elizabeth with a middle-aged woman that she introduced to me as her mother, Brenda. She looked very English, like someone out of a Mike Leigh movie.

After a brief introduction, Elizabeth and her mother sat down on Laz's bed and told me they would like me to come to Christmas. Brenda's voice choked as she apologized and pleaded with me to join my friends. "No way," I told them. "There's no way I'm going into the house of someone that doesn't like me. Everyone will be having fun and I'll be sitting there unwelcome."

Brenda began to cry. I felt guilty and searched my mind and exhaled. This was supposed to be Christmas.

"There might be one way," I calmly said to Brenda. "If Mr. Mateen and I, when I arrive, can be alone before anything and talk, I'll do it."

That evening, Elizabeth called me and told me that Afsaar had agreed and that he wanted her to tell me that I was welcome. My mere presence was causing unrest in the Mateen household.

As we arrived at the middle-class home in Reading on Christmas Eve, I walked behind my friends and was the last to enter. I glared at Elizabeth. "We had an agreement," I said.

"He's upstairs." Elizabeth pointed me up a simple wood staircase. "Take a right when you get to the top of the stairs, walk all the way down, and it will take you to my father's office. He's waiting for you."

I walked the stairs and took a right down a long, dark, carpeted hallway. At the end of the hallway, I saw a door cracked open with soft light shining through a barely cracked door. When I got to the door, I knocked.

"Come in," I heard in a voice that had the command of a general. I pushed on the door and heard every squeal of the hinge invade my ears and my brain. In the conservative room was a single lamp illuminating the space. All I could see was the back of his head—a mass of black hair sitting atop a tan and brown tweed coat—as he sat at his massive desk facing the window.

He turned and faced me. Afsaar was lean with a handsome, distinguished face. He wore a crisp white collared shirt with a white-and-gold-speckled ascot. His face looked as if he had seen a thousand wars. The

LONDON   261

tension in the room was visceral, softened only by the beautiful amber lamplight. Afsaar had a jawline that could cut through the air like a knife.

"Please, sit." The dignified, aristocratic-looking man pointed to a leather and steel armchair. I was in a middle-class home with humble furnishings, and this man had the presence of someone who could have ruled a nation.

I lowered myself onto the chair quietly and said, "I am not my country's foreign policy, I'm Jamie."

Afsaar tilted his fierce head slightly. I could see the amber light stirring in his eyes, and he smiled.

A month later, Elizabeth, Afsaar, and I went to see Kissinger speak at the London School of Economics. Elizabeth and I surprised him with a ticket. Afsaar and I had become close with our lunchtime coffees, discussing politics and humanity at the Wright's Bar right next to LSE's old building on Houghton Street, just across the street from his office. Afsaar hated Kissinger. He loved hating Kissinger so much he was happy to be there with me, and he was my friend. As we listened to Kissinger's monotone in his low deep German accent, I stared at Afsaar's angular profile and thought, *They call Afghanistan "the Graveyard of Empires." No one has ever been able to conquer them.* Sitting with Afsaar that day, with his intelligence and indefatigable spirit, I knew why.

I thought that all of my best qualities I must have gotten from Stevie, the powerful uncle I always admired: Don't put on airs; don't be better than people; be curious and humble.

While writing this book, I sought out Tunji's widow who was taken to Birdland with my grandfather, Roy. She told me, "You would never know Roy was rich, a worldly doctor. You would never put that on him."

I then realized that who I am had passed from my grandfather through his son, my uncle Stevie; the powerful artistic force who taught me that humility is a quality that a man should strive for.

LSE was a place where people would go on to do remarkable things. We sat watching Kissinger in the same theater where I'd performed one of the leads as Sir Toby in *Twelfth Night* a few months earlier. The play was

262   CHILD X

directed by Nikolaus Wachsmann, a kid from Munich who has gone on to be one of the world's leading experts on the Third Reich.

Professor Boyce chased me down after the play and told me that he respected me. "An American doing proper Shakespeare," he said in his Canadian English accent. "I wish I could say I can't believe it, but I saw it, and you were great."

I got a B in his class.

X

I spent that Christmas holiday break at Laz's chalet in Gstaad, Switzerland. Even though I wasn't supposed to have a job while at LSE, I worked at the Veggie Café on campus and at Shepherd Foods, a fancy food shop on Primrose Hill. I bought a Europass with the money. It gave me unlimited train travel in Europe for cheap and then I went to meet my new friends. For a long time, I was able to keep my past a secret from them.

We had Gstaad to ourselves for a month without parents, just ninety miles away from where fugitive John Marshall Branion had been studying for his medical degree in Geneva. My uncle Stevie had been here, for boarding school, before he was kicked out for smoking ganja. On the drive up to Gstaad through the Alps, I saw the bluest lakes I've ever seen. They seemed untouchable.

At nights we drove into Gstaad and Geneva, going to jazz clubs, drinking French wine, and eating rich Swiss breads and cheeses. I'd just driven through the same mountain passes where in AD 773 the emperor of Western Europe, Charlemagne, marched his army over the Alps to war against Desiderius, his father-in-law, an Italian duke, in a senseless war.

On Christmas Eve we drove a cherry red, tiny, shitty Vauxhall through a snowstorm into Gstaad. Six of us were jammed into the car, sitting on each other's laps. "Roadhouse Blues" by The Doors blaring into the night—a song that insists in a bluesy torrent to keep your eyes focused on the road and your hands steady on the wheel. We all sang along at every chorus. As the car swerved and slid, I thought, *I'm gonna crash and die, in*

LONDON

263

a shitty car driven by rich kids. It would be a beautiful death. But I didn't care, because they were mischievous, and I never felt more alive. I was an American in a car full of anti-Americans, and I belonged.

X

My first year, I met Harold Garner. Harold had dated Gabriella, so I met him through my friends. He was refined and had been given all the opportunities. One day on Houghton Street, just outside the Old Building, Harold approached me. He made me uncomfortable. We were from different worlds. He was handsome, wore all the right clothes, was brilliant, and was born and raised in London—just at the bottom of Primrose Hill. I thought he was going to ask me to loan him a tenner when he said, "Hi, Jamie, it's St. Paddy's Day. Don't you think we should go for a pint?" I looked at him wide-eyed, and thought, *Why not?* Harold eventually brought me to Sir Richard Steele's Pub in Haverstock Hill where I drank snakebites— lager and cider—and we had conversations in the pub's library under the candlelight.

Harold has since become my most important friend from college, and just like Francis, having no knowledge of my past, he made me feel I could belong in another world. Harold showed me London as a local with good taste. I met his friend Adan, a handsome kid from Lagos, with a quiet charisma.

I went on a trip to the Lake District on the Scottish border, with Harold's friends, and stayed in a sixteenth-century cottage, walking the brushy mountainous hills during our days and cooking food at night. One of Harold's friends who lived on the River Thames bought a stereo system. We listened to Ali Farka Touré and Ry Cooder's collaborative album, *Talking Timbuktu*, over and over deep into the evening. That album, a mixture of African rhythms and American blues, electrifies me to this day.

A few weeks later, I went out to dinner at Cafe Bohéme in Soho with Laz, Bastian, Rana, and the pack. We took over a section of the entire dimly lit restaurant. It was before London banned smoking in bars, and a haze of cigarette smoke illuminated us in pockets of light. The liquor flowed. The laughter erupted. As I looked around the table at the twelve of us gathered there, I thought about Roy in Harlem, watching Charlie Parker and Duke Ellington at Birdland with my grandmother, his cousin Amy Olatunji, and his friends.

Then, all of a sudden, I heard it softly coming from the speakers in the restaurant. It washed over me and hit me like an ocean of sound. It was the opening synth and rhythm of "Once in a Lifetime." When I heard David Byrne talk-singing, with all of his intensity, my heart was burning into a cinder. My eyes felt warm, and I don't know that I have ever been more overflowing than I was in that moment.

X

A year after I met him, Harold called me and insisted I meet him at The Lamb and Flag pub in Covent Garden, and that he needed to talk to me about something important. It was a famous pub known as a watering hole of choice for Charles Dickens. It was also known for putting on bare-knuckle prizefights early in the nineteenth century, giving it the nickname "the bucket of blood." When I got there, he was already waiting for me. Harold pushed a black pint of Guinness toward me as I sat down. When I finished the pint, he hurried to the bar and grabbed me another. I had two pints very quickly, more than I normally drank, and then Harold began.

"I've got some distressing news, mate. There is a rumor traveling around our friends at the LSE that you are a member of and have given all of your money to the Church of Scientology." My entire body was overwhelmed by the shock of a cold chill. I felt an electric current surge as anxiety across my entire body. I was afraid. "Listen, Jamie, I'm your friend. I don't care about your past. I just wanted you to know."

Distressed, I said, "Harold, why did you have me drink these pints?"

"I wanted to soften the blow," he responded.

We never spoke on the subject again until twenty years later. I lost many friends that night but other friendships deepened.

LONDON   265

As I walked through Covent Garden, away from The Lamb and Flag, I thought about a conversation I'd had with my mother. I had called her and told her everything I had been through in the years at The Red Brick Building and The Fountain, and that she needed to fix it.

"I'm on a mission," she said. "When you and your brothers were born, I thought you were with me on this."

Even as babies, by just being born, she felt we had made a commitment to her cause.

It wasn't enough for the movement up until this point to take my life. They had to, for the next twenty-five years, also take my story. You can't be a human if you can't possess your own story, your own past. If I were to tell my story it would be critical of the movement, and I would be shunned. However, if one cannot master one's story, one cannot ever own their life.

As I walked down a kinetic street in Camden Town, "Institutionalized" by Suicidal Tendencies blared out of a club. The song made me think of how simple my desires were. In life's terms, I wanted nothing more than a soda pop.

I thought of Johnny and Miles, then I thought of The Red Brick Building, and I thought of Seb. He had been molested in that building. When Seb got older, he had the urge to do to children what was done to him. We reconnected at the Château Élysée in our late twenties. He was so excited to see me, but something seemed broken in him. I wondered if harm had not been done to him, whether he would have ever had the urge to harm others. Eventually I would hear that Seb took his own life in order to protect his wife, children, and any other victim from his urges. He left a note saying that he felt it was the only honorable thing to do. This may partially be the result of the animalization we experienced as children. So many made impoverished and illiterate by their service—what happened to all the kids that couldn't find asylum?

Around this time, I would go with my new girlfriend, a brilliant woman who had just finished her master's degree at Oxford, to see a ballet at a theater in Islington. She had grown up Jewish Orthodox and I shared nothing of my past with her. English ballet dancers would recreate an

American baseball game in striped uniforms in slow motion with faux baseballs under cinematic moonlight. It was beyond anything I had ever conceived possible. I realized these artists could see a baseball game differently because American baseball was not something they were familiar with. It was exotic to them. Looking at my girl in the soft light, with her red hair, I thought, *Maybe being exotic would help me see things differently, and maybe I could make my own ideas out of the unexpected.* I had not been moved like this since The Chief's monologue back in the basement of the Hollywood Inn on Hollywood Boulevard. I felt strong.

I would never look at a baseball game again the same way. You can slow the world down in art. You can see things in new ways. That's why we need artists; to show us how to see. Art is not a painting, or a book, or a play; it's a portal. It's a transportation device to help us move through an often-unfair world.

Harold's best friend from childhood was a guy named Damian. He would go on to become a famed television actor and movie star named Damian Lewis. I would go see him as Laertes opposite Ralph Fiennes's Hamlet not long after Fiennes won the Academy Award for *Schindler's List.* The Johnathan Kent production with arresting cinematic lightning design alone, as its sole set, drenched me in terms of the possibility of art.

Around this time, I went to see talks with experimental theater director Peter Brook, whose book *The Empty Space* taught me about theater; filmmaker Stephen Frears; and cultural writer Hanif Kureishi, and was awed by their art and ideas among many others.

I saw Kenneth Kaunda, the former leader of Zambia, speak in a small room at LSE, and it messed with me. He was a dictator who had stolen hundreds of millions from his country. He never opened his eyes during the entire talk. That was the incredible thing about this school: when dignitaries from around the world were in town for a day or two and they didn't want to make the trek to Oxford or Cambridge, they came by to see us.

Professor Gareth Austen taught African Economic History, where I learned about the Middle Passage as a labor shift to the New World. We examined slavery without morality, purely in economic terms. At first it shook me. Then I strove to see everything from any point of view possible, even if it bothered me.

One day, Gareth asked me to stay behind after class. He told me, if I had a professor sponsor me, I could stay an extra year or two and finish my degree. I was confused and I didn't have anyone to sponsor me.

"When I look at you in class, you look like you belong," he said, his eyes wide. I sat at the front of his class, taking furious notes like a maniac, fixated on his every word. Maybe he thought I was unusually interested. The truth is I was desperate. I always sat in front and took furious notes because of my lack of foundation and illiteracy blind spots.

"I don't have anyone to sponsor me," I told him.

"I'm offering to sponsor you under academic probation," he said. Angels.

X

A few months later, Professor Austen and I went for three days for an economic retreat with the Tawney Society—LSE's economic history society. We stayed in a dormitory on the grounds of Windsor Castle. That Sunday I was invited to church at St. George's Chapel with the Queen Mother. I was a long way from the slum dormitories of burning Los Angeles.

As I studied African Economic History, I pondered the question of how some human groups developed technology before colonialism while others didn't. Austen's lectures were catalytic, and I began to understand the causes of things. When we look at the Third World—like the heart of Africa—we're only looking at people whose skin has adapted to the endless equatorial sun and are technologically behind because they didn't have to develop technology to survive. It was partially the good and bad luck of geography that led to the evils of slavery.

In the view of the doctrine, if you were born a slave, this would have been your fault. I thought constantly about what it would be like to be a slave. A slave is the extension of the will of its owner—a tool, something

268   CHILD X

you use against nature. It is the human body reduced to an asset for production, like a threshing machine before threshing machines.

The Middle Passage was a cycle that began at ports all over the Ivory Coast. These tribes were already enslaving each other, but when they realized they could get guns, tobacco, and rum for people, a gun–slave cycle emerged, and the numbers of Blacks sold by Blacks exploded.

The great Black figure painter George Anthony Morton—an oil painter like my mother—says, "I don't use the word 'slave.'" George says that calling oneself a slave implies an identity, and this was never an identity for the people in bondage. He says the people were never slaves—they were enslaved, and it's important to tell the difference. I disagree with George, but I appreciate his perspective. I think when you've been enslaved long enough, you become the identity from the inside out.

I was trying to find meaning. I thought of all the ancestors, all the colors of all the slaves, all the movements, all the pain, all the suffering, all the death, all the unheard screams no matter the hue of all of our skins. *Nobody's pain is higher or lower*, I thought. *If I make it out of here, I will help the world to understand that everyone's pain is valid, no matter the color of their ancestors.* I thought of the choice that I made when I was sixteen not to go dark, so that dark forces would not win.

I thought back to Alex Haley asking me, "For what is the purpose that you have entered this world?" I made a vow that if I ever got out of my Hell, if I survived this challenge that was bigger than me, I would try to speak for everyone. *The only reason those of us survive is to increase our sensitivity for others,* I thought. Pain does not know a color. Our abusers are the abused. Our abused become the abusers, and only through the democratization of our pain will we ever come together. It is scientific certainty that there is no biological difference between humans beyond melanin, coarseness of hair, and broadness of noses. It is a scientific truth that when we enslave someone due to different melanin or face paint, all we've done is enslave or destroy ourselves. We don't look at a Shih Tzu and a Great Dane and say, "Look at those two races of dogs." Only humans do that. Race means everything. Race means nothing. If wealth removes

LONDON

269

pain, then why do so many of the wealthy kill themselves through drug addiction and suicide? Pain, like art, should not be compared. *Do we survive to speak for those who didn't make it?*

I became obsessed with finding the answer of my existence in the shadow of my grandfather, and then it came to me as clear as sediment falling to the bottom of a pool of water. What was completely blurred had become humanely clear:

We are all the same.

I made a vow to myself that I would never pick a side, only the human side, and I believe that decision has given me back to myself.

Pain attacks from all directions, comes in multiple forms, and spares no one. Too White to be Black, too Black to be White, I would speak for what I had learned as an *other*, as a child X, and what I am now sure is true. No one has a monopoly on suffering and pain, and the biggest lie in the human world is that, because of skin color, class, and history, one person's pain overshadows another's. Wealth protects no one and often comes at the expense of community, which destroys us. I would tell this story for the sake of my remaining humanity, to speak for *ALL THE ANCESTORS*, all the colors, all the people, all the pain.

Chapter 22

VALLAURIS

Something impossible had happened: I graduated from the London School of Economics. An infant who had been born into a baby factory on the East Side of Los Angeles, who had grown up in burned-out slums, the son of elite members of a dark movement, without education, without clean clothes, without clean bedding, without love, without any understanding of the world. I was still here. I had been gored, yet I was handed my degree by the school's director and entered a community that had produced heads of state.

The graduation took place at the Savoy Theatre in the Strand. The theater is an opulent stone monument to Victorian grandeur. It was the first public building in the world ever lit by electricity. It was the birthplace of the musical. In 1929, a spring sky was painted on the ceiling and the walls in gold. In 1990, a fire would tear through every part of the building, destroying everything but the stage where I would eventually walk and be handed my degree.

My grandmother and Robert would come to London. I could see tears welling in Dorothy's eyes as I—wearing my black graduation robes and surrounded by distinguished elder men of learning—walked across the stage that had seen more than one hundred years of human expression, shook Sir John Ashworth's hand, grasped the paper that proved my legitimacy in the outworld, and walked offstage. I belonged. Robert wore a special gold watch I had never seen him wear. I wondered if it was like the watch that he had refused to accept in high school as a pacifier for being kept out of a football game by segregation.

My mother didn't come to see me graduate. Dorothy had offered to fly her to London and pay her expenses so she could attend. She refused. The cost was not easy for my grandmother, who was conservative with money. It was unthinkable to her that my mother wouldn't say yes. There was nothing to see. I had failed her.

For three years I'd had to borrow money from Dorothy to bridge my tuition before the government grants and loans came in—$7,000 a semester, plus living expenses. For my grandmother, it was a risky business. She probably had to cash in an annuity or take out a loan on her house to pay for it. If Dorothy didn't have access to bridge the government loans, my life would have been a different story. In the back of my mind for three years was the strangling anxiety of, "What if I fail out?"

In the days leading up to graduation, I wouldn't find out if I'd passed my courses until my grandparents had already arrived in London. My nerves were blinding. I was so convinced that I had failed. When my grades finally came and I found out that I had passed respectably, it was a relief to know my grandparents hadn't crossed an ocean for nothing. E. H. Hunt sent me a letter telling me what I had accomplished was honorable and I had earned his respect. As I read his words, the streets of London swirled around me, throwing me off balance, and my eyes welled up with tears. *This was impossible*, I thought. *If I could do this, how much more is possible?*

I've always seen myself as an escape artist like Houdini; I get out of locks and chains and cages right on the brink of death. Ever since I was a small child, if I ever saw anything with Houdini, I was mesmerized and didn't know why.

After returning to New York, I didn't know what I wanted to do with my life. I saw myself wandering the smog-enveloped streets of my

VALLAURIS   273

old habitat—a city on fire. I wanted to be with my friends Johnny and Miles and the oasis football crew. That feeling returned with a vengeance. I bought a flight back into the concrete and sun.

X

The first thing I did in Los Angeles was visit the old habitat. East Hollywood was the gauntlet of my pain and my learning. The streets still baked in the sun. The neighborhoods were full of gangs, hustlers, movement kids, slum geniuses, pretty girls, and a few friends who still called it home.

I went to MacArthur Park and sat on a bench. There was a Mexican street preacher in a blue polyester suit shouting and preaching to the sky in the hot sun, dripping with sweat. *He's crazy*, I thought as I munched on my chips. I hadn't seen one of these street preachers in years.

I drove to Venice Beach with its squat red brick buildings overlooking the white beach and watched pickup basketball games and beautiful women on neon rollerblades while hippies with acoustic guitars and sunbleached hair busked in the sun, singing Oasis and Doors covers. I looked up and ran into old friends, some I was close to, some I wasn't that close to, but I'll mention Vonnie because he's famous.

I caught up with Vonnie and his new wife at a vegan bakery near Wiltshire—I think it was on Crescent Heights—while his infant daughter slept in the car next to us. He asked me what I studied. "Why population growth happens," I said as an example.

"You mean like Malthus?" he said.

"Yeah. How did you know that?"

"I was in a film where I studied it."

He probably wouldn't talk to me today. The movement makes things complicated.

One night, I drove from Downtown, north up Alvarado again, past the now-sodium-vapor-bathed MacArthur Park at dusk. I took a left turn onto Beverly Boulevard, past Original Tommy's Burgers on the corner of Rampart. All I could think, as I rolled past the Original Tommy's, was how

274   CHILD X

I missed the juice of their burgers and the soft crunch of their French fries. The horrors of The Baby Factory up the street never crossed my mind.

I got a job working for a documentary production company. They sent me all over the world to license and market their films. I went to Cannes in the South of France for work, but I didn't want to sell documentaries. One afternoon, after a conference at the Palais in Cannes, I took a cab to a place nearby called Vallauris to visit Pablo Picasso's little-known ceramics studio. Vallauris means "golden valley" in French. With its Roman architecture, date palms, and fortresses standing as a watcher on the sea, it's a Mediterranean town in coastal France. Picasso made his home here not long after World War II—around the same time my grandfather Roy returned from Burma, and he was different.

I was surprised at how Picasso could translate his signature style into the simplicity of pottery. It was ceramic sublimity. Roy would have come alive in this place—in Vallauris. "Painting was not invented to decorate houses," Picasso once said of his work. "It is a weapon of war to defend oneself from the enemy." I wondered if Roy's love of art was a weapon against all of the pain of segregation, a flaming sword he held against those who would say he was less than. "Thank you," I said quietly to Picasso for this exaltation of work. This tiny studio in Vallauris had brought me closer to the grandfather I had never known. By this time, this taking in of art had become my greatest weapon against the meanness of the world.

X

A few days later, I was walking down the streets of Cannes with my close friend Elmore, a dark-skinned businessman from the island of Bermuda who wore a three-piece cream linen suit in the beautiful autumn sun of southern France. Elmore was on a mission to make Bermudan entertainment relevant around the world, and in ways he was succeeding. He was a deeply religious man who often wanted to talk about God. On this day I didn't want to hear it, so I swore at him, knowing that, in his piousness, I

VALLAURIS 275

would annoy him. "Please, James," he said, "please respect me and not use those words."

"Not on this beautiful fucking day," I said, and decided to swear louder. Elmore smiled.

We were just a block or two off the Croisette that overlooked the Mediterranean Sea, on our way back to the Grand Hotel, when a beautiful young woman with flowing chestnut-brown hair ran up to us. I immediately regretted my "fucks."

"Monsieur! Monsieur!" this stunningly beautiful woman shouted excitedly, yelling at me in French. I was horrified. I was the American who'd come to her country to swear and had offended her.

"No compris, no compris," I said. Elmore stood watching, speechless. I began to apologize, "Excusez-moi, madame. Désolée, désolée. Je ne parle pas français. Je suis vraiment désolée."

I felt humiliated and knew better. The woman yelled on and seemed frustrated and then her face changed and lit up with the most beautiful smile.

"Oh my, I must speak English, I am so sorry," the woman said, finding words in English. Then she looked deep into my eyes and said, "I know you! I know you, Monsieur! I know you!" I studied her features for a moment. This was crazy, this beautiful woman screaming at me that she knew me. I felt a great relief that she had not heard my ugly American slurs.

I steadied myself and replied, in English, "I'm sorry, madame, but I'm just here for work, and there's no way I can know you, but thank you, and I hope you enjoy this gorgeous day."

Elmore and I began to walk away, when she grabbed my shoulder. "Monsieur, did you attend the London School of Economics?"

I froze. Elmore smiled. "I need to get back to the hotel. I'll let you two catch up," he said and walked off.

The woman and I talked at a café for an hour until we finally realized that we had sat across from each other in Latin American Economic History class. Every time our eyes met, she would always flash a smile of kindness. I don't know why we never spoke. She told me that she had to go and asked me for my phone number at the hotel.

"There's a party at my house in Monaco tomorrow. I would like to ask my mother if you could come," she said. Monaco was forty-five minutes by train. I had a couple of days left.

"Sure."

She rang that night, very excited that I was invited to the party. She quickly wanted to verify that I had something to wear. I told her I had a black suit with a white shirt and a black tie.

"Oh, that will never do, Jamie," she blurted out, adding that a tuxedo was expected. I could hear her thinking on the other end of the line. I asked her why I needed a tuxedo for a party. She quickly explained that her mother was the imperial princess of France, the direct descendant of Napoleon Bonaparte, and that musicians were coming from all over Europe to perform with her mother, the princess, a pianist who had attended Juilliard.

Then she offered a lifeline. "I will pick you up at the train station in Monte Carlo. The train arrives at 12:30. Please don't forget to get on the right train, or I won't be there. The party begins at 7:00 and we will get you a 'smoking'"—French slang for a tuxedo.

X

The next morning, I took the train to Monte Carlo. She was waiting for me. We walked to her car, a beat-up Vauxhall. I thought, *Another shitty Vauxhall. What is it with rich people in Europe and old Vauxhalls?* Excited to see me, she drove me to her house. Despite its declining exterior, the Vauxhall purred and hummed.

Monte Carlo was cradled against the turquoise of the white sea, a sumptuous mix of humanity and Eurotrash that expanded from the water, past its luxurious Bavarian-style casino, and its architectural smorgasbord of Grand Revival apartments. This was a place of immense wealth. It stood in stark contrast to the train ride through the rolling hills and arid cliffs of

VALLAURIS

southern France—a moving painting of vineyards, rivers, and occasional Roman buildings. The house was tucked away in the hills above Monte Carlo, with sandstone terraces and arbors. We arrived and I walked inside, through a symphony of chirping birds, into a grand domed foyer attached to an expansive room that held in an immense fresco.

While my friend's heels clicked away into the next room, I stood with my mouth open, taking in the majestic five-hundred-year-old fresco depicting a Dionysian harvest—golden-haired cherubs blowing flutes, while young rosy-cheeked women, with curls in every color, frolicked with half-human satyrs. One was being carried away on the back of a bull. Medieval servant girls held baskets of grapes while dogs wrestled at their feet. It was a celebration of the bounty of life. I could be remembering this fresco wrong. It could have been something I saw on a train trip to Tuscany. What I'm sure of is that it was at least forty feet.

"Jamie?" My chestnut-haired friend called me into the next room, where there were dozens of tables set with plates, dishes, and glassware, ready to host almost a hundred people. I wondered who else was coming. I wondered, *Why on earth am I here?* Staff arranged the place settings, measuring the distance between the edges of plates and the edge of the table by some archaic rule I didn't know existed. I followed my friend under the ancient wall painting and across the main hall into a massive French kitchen the size of an apartment. Rows of food sat on the wooden block island, across from a table where people were chattering to each other softly in French and had large television cameras next to their small plates. They didn't speak English. I sat and ate alone until they quickly left.

This party was actually a private concert that was to be broadcast on French TV.

After some boulé bread, cheese, and meat, my friend walked me back outside and put me in a different car with a Portuguese woman with thin lips and graying black hair, who also spoke no English. She wore a maid's outfit, and her smile made me feel warm.

"This is Angelica," my friend said. "She doesn't speak English, but she will take you to get your smoking." We drove to the center of the city to a small shop where I was fitted for a tux by an old man. He never said a word. Forty minutes later I walked out with a tailored tuxedo.

We returned to the house in the midafternoon. I was sent downstairs to where everyone lived, with all the bedrooms, to change. As I arrived in the cavernous underbelly of the house, I was among a half-dozen musicians running around, getting dressed, and tuning their instruments.

In the hallway, I started putting on my tuxedo, stripping down to my underwear, and no one thought this was unusual as they were doing the same. I slipped on the tuxedo pants and almost immediately realized they forgot to hem them. My embarrassed heart sank, and I felt the pinpricks of nerves all over my body. I was paralyzed. I didn't know how I was going to get out of this one. I couldn't imagine cuffing my tux among some of the richest people in the world, and possibly the royal family of Monaco. I stared disgustedly at the six extra inches on my un-hemmed pants.

When I looked up, I saw a beautiful older woman, who had been quietly watching my horror. She motioned for the offending pants. I took them off, folded them, and handed them over. Without a word, she ran into another room. I stood there, wearing a full tuxedo jacket with a tie and a cummerbund, black socks, and dress shoes, in my boxers.

Twenty minutes later, the beautiful woman returned, beaming with a smile, with my pants perfectly hemmed. She was wearing a beautiful ball gown of sequins and golden jewels. I thanked her, and she smiled. Everything was moving so fast. I didn't have time to think about how strange the situation was.

I went upstairs to dinner. It was dusk and the light was waning. In the massive dining hall was an array of thirty tables around a slight rise of a stage set off the ground. As I walked past the entryway, cars arrived at the valet. I saw a Rolls-Royce limousine pull away and the flash of a bright yellow Lamborghini take its place. Moments later a few Ferraris and then a Mercedes limousine arrived.

The wine was flowing as the guests took their places. As we all began to sit, my friend told me that ours was a very special table, with her, her

VALLAURIS 279

brother, her sister, and one of her best friends, who she was sitting me next to. She wanted me between her brother and her friend.

"This is Giovanni. He is an investment banker," she said as the man looked up at me. He was in his mid-thirties, with dark features and cinematic good looks, like he had just walked out of a James Bond film. He was handsome; he intimidated me. He smiled warmly, and I relaxed as we sat down.

I nibbled on raw fish and avocado as my friend's mother, the princess, walked out and began to play the most beautiful and simple sonata. I felt frozen by the music. After the interlude, the princess spoke in her superior yet kind voice with the unshakable presence and tone of an aristocrat of her nature. "I would like to introduce my good friend from Spain. She will be joining me for this next movement on this harp before we bring the other musicians."

I stared at a six-foot gleaming golden harp, offset by a warm blackened Bösendorfer grand piano with polished gold trim. A woman walked onto the stage, and I couldn't believe my eyes. It was the woman who had hemmed my pants. She looked at me, smiled, gave me a wink, and began to play. The music transported me to another world. I was floating.

The conversation was an elixir. I adored my friend's seventeen-year-old brother and nineteen-year-old sister. I spoke to them of Los Angeles and my life coming from the slums. It was like a movie to them, and they were captivated by my every word. I was from an exotic world beyond their reach, a concrete urban pastiche of movie stars and immigrants.

I asked the mysterious Frenchman, Giovanni, about his job and he told me that it would bore me to explain it. Halfway through the night he constantly smiled, laughed, and asked me if I'd ever met a movie star. "That was not my Hollywood," I explained, and his face widened, smiling with his eyes. My belly was full, and my head was in a perfect state of suspended animation from French wine.

Suddenly the Frenchman grabbed my tuxedo tie and collar with his large hand and leaned towards me. Suddenly he looked serious, and in

280   CHILD X

a deep, forceful whisper, as if he was telling me a secret, he said, "I envy you."

It went completely over my head. He redoubled his effort, this time clear and loud so others could hear. "I envy you," he said again in his deep molasses voice.

I paused, looking at his eyes, and whispered back, "Why on earth would you envy me?" I could tell he was becoming emotional. He leaned into my ear again for another secret.

"Because you possess yourself," he hushed and warmly smiled. I thanked him and nodded my head, calmed by the wine. I was happy to be with friends, and as the man put his arm upon my shoulder, we turned our attention back to the conversation at the table.

The concert ended around 11:00 PM, and my friend wanted to go to sleep. I wasn't done with the night and was invited by my friend's brother and sister out to Le Bar Américain in Downtown Monaco overlooking the marina. The three of us got bottle service at the table and talked, drinking whiskey until five in the morning. They introduced me to their friends, we laughed, and I told them more stories of East Los Angeles.

Then suddenly it was over. With the morning light, they drove me back to the train station. I left my tuxedo on the table in the dining room, praying that the maid would return it.

X

I got the first train back to Cannes at dawn that morning. I was tired, hung over, and exhausted. The beauty of the morning light and the sensorial experience of the evening were washing over me. As the sun rose, I stared at the French countryside racing past; its Roman villages nestled against towering cliffsides and its arid, brambled trees seemed like less of a mystery to me now. I had just been with its people. There were mansions and estates peppered among tiny stone houses where peasants had lived for thousands of years.

The golden valley that separated Monaco from France by thickets and

VALLAURIS   281

stone walls had seen the march of armies and empires. I lost myself in this moving painting and thought of Picasso and his studio in Vallauris after the war—a place for reinvention, the ceramics, the sculptures, and paintings he made there. A place where he took simplicity and brought it to an unimagined form. I wondered if in any of these imperial lands, or in one of these homes, sat a gift of a Burmese chest like Roy's, given to an inspiring stranger. I thought of Roy in Burma, and his love of beauty, the violin, and his adventurous honeymoon in the Tropic of Cancer in Mexico. I imagined how he looked upon cities where Aztec kings worshiped the sun. I thought of his eyes. I thought about how his curiosity passed down into my cells and instilled in me things maybe my lost father wouldn't have. I thought of the meaning of "Roy"—"king" in French; the lives of noble kings had fought for these lands.

My eyes filled with tears. In the last few years, something had changed in me.

I've often wondered, in this arc of my life, how I've met and been in proximity to so many disparate kinds of people. I think it has a lot to do with being the other. When you are made an other by the strangeness of a manufactured world based on science fiction, boats, and the accident of your birth, if it doesn't kill you, it makes you want to take in everything in the whole wide world. I know you can be left for dead and come back to live a great life.

I would not even begin to possess myself until I began to write these words over two and a half decades after the train moving through the south of France. I laughed to myself at how ridiculous the night before was and thought of the glowing brick embers, slums burning on the smoldering, silvery streets of Los Angeles. I thought of Cab Calloway, I thought of Roy watching Nat King Cole in Harlem with his libation and his friends, floating. I thought of the joy he must have felt. I thought to myself, *Roy, I love you.*

Angels.

With Appreciation

A heartfelt thank you to Glenn Yeffeth, publisher of BenBella Books, for getting me to see before a word was written. *Perpetuum gratium.*

Deep appreciation to Michael Humphrey, who has taught me never to lose faith in the power and importance of ideas to improve our lives.

Thank you to the most extraordinary editor I have ever worked with, Gregory Newton Brown, who has become a friend in our work together, Claire Schulz, Maryann Karinch, Amy "Iya" Olatunji, Dorothy Gilmer Ross, my cousin Rachel Gilmer for beautifully documenting the family history, Babatunde Olatunji, Kozza, Kwame Olatunji, Sadupe, Modupe, Col. Thomas Money, Lucy Money, Lt. Col. Paul Toolan (ret.), Col. Stuart Farris (ret.), Hilary Bevan Jones, K. B., S. F., M. T., J. J., T. B., A. L., T. W., John "Jay" Faber, MD, Libby Mitcham, Dr. Ryan Wood, Joshua Mustard, Jan Branion, Dr. John Marshall Branion, Sarah Avinger, Cassavias Tabayoyon, Lynn Randell, D. Randell, Mark Peters, Randall Reece, Chris Gilbertson, Roanne Horwich, Rowan Trollope, Beverly Mustard, Yvonne Taylor, Michael Rinder, Michael Ulwelling, Kevin Carrol, Prof. Goggin, Prof. Lawson Bowling, Dr. Garreth Austin, Harold Garner, Dr.

WITH APPRECIATION

Robert Boyce, historian David Starkey, CBE, Aref Adamali, Boris Meyer, Anna Kathrin, Tricky, Holt McCallany, Tracey McManus, Jelani Memory, Heather J. Peterson, Dr. E. H. Hunt, Manhattanville University, Westchester Community College, The London School of Economics, Virginia Ferrara, Prof. Jim Bryan, Prof. Edward W. Ryan, Holly Lörincz, George Liveris, Dr. Dwayne Edwards, Donwan Harrell, Daniel Mustard, Christopher Wojda, Mira Kaddoura, Donald Wilkes, Elmore Warren, Deborah Noyon, David Bentley, Rose Francis, Dr. Steven Nakana, Nina Bird, Nik Wachsmann, Colman McCarthy, Daniel Amen, MD, Robert Ross, Harry T. Edwards, Dr. Gabor Maté, Sunder Aaron, Adrienne Lang, Brice Watson, Leah Wilson, Alicia Kania, Jennifer Canzoneri, Rick Chillot, and the entire team at BenBella Books.

About the Author

Jamie Mustard is a conceptual artist, artistic director and writer, including work on the perception of art, imagery and ideas. Growing up in severe poverty in Los Angeles, Jamie grew up with a mélange of influences of art and ideas from unlikely places. A graduate of the London School of Economics, Jamie is the writer of *The Iconist, A Kid's Book About Resilience* and co-author of the groundbreaking book *The Invisible Machine*, on the biology of trauma.

In late fall of 2025, Jamie's first graphic novel, *HYBRED*, will be released—presenting a world written, conceived, and art-directed by Jamie, with all of the images drawn and colored in a small stone town in Southern Italy with collaborator Francesca Filomena.

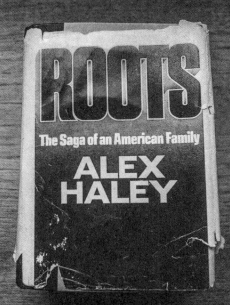

THIS IS A HIGHLY DISTRESSED 1976 (ORIGINAL) COPY OF *ROOTS* THAT ALEX HALEY SENT THROUGH MY GRANDMOTHER WHEN I WAS DEALING WITH ILLITERACY IN MY TEENS, TO INSPIRE ME TO DIG UP MY HISTORY.

VICKSBURG, MISSISSIPPI, GREAT-GRANDFATHER HOLDING YOUNG GRANDMOTHER (INDICATED) WITH EXTENDED FAMILY, 1920

ROY AND DOROTHY HONEYMOON, MEXICO, 1940
(GRANDFATHER AND GRANDMOTHER)

OY AND DOROTHY HONEYMOON,
ROPIC OF CANCER, MEXICO, 1940

NEW YORK RESTAURANT, FLIGHT SURGEON GRANDFATHER ON LEAVE WITH DOROTHY, 1944

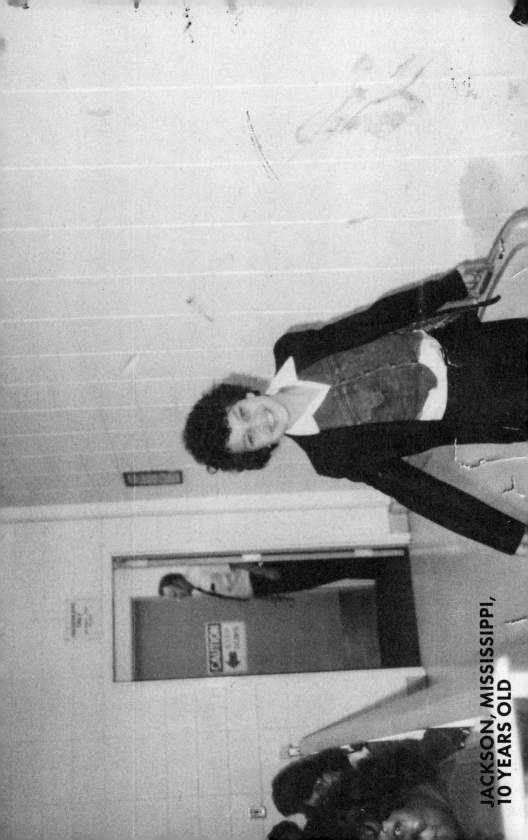

JACKSON, MISSISSIPPI, 10 YEARS OLD

CALIFORNIA, 10 YEARS OLD

ST. HILL MANOR COMPOUND, WEST SUSSEX, ENGLAND, 18 YEARS OLD

University of London Union
Membership Card 1993/4

Name ....

College ....

Course ....

Signature

Number 42580

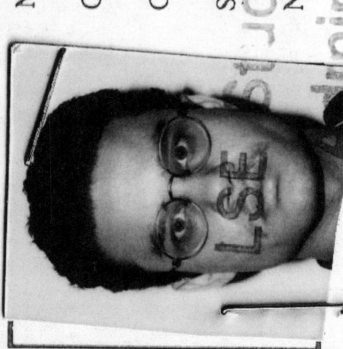

Students' Union Admin. Office

University of London Union, Malet Street, London WC1E 7HY. Tel: 071 580 9551